D1409224

NORTHAMPTON COMMUNITY
DISCARDED
COLLEGE LIBRARY

NORTHAMPTON COUNTY AREA
Bethlehem, Pa. 18017
COMMUNITY COLLEGE

Rabbi

Also by Murray Polner

No Victory Parades: The Return of the Vietnam Veteran
When Can I Come Home? A Debate on Amnesty for
  Exiles, Anti-War Prisoners and Others
The Conquest of the United States by Spain and
  Other Essays by William Graham Sumner (editor)

Murray Polner

Rabbi

The
American
Experience

Holt,
Rinehart
and Winston
New York

LIBRARY OF CONGRESS CATALOGING IN PUBLICATION DATA

Polner, Murray.
　Rabbi.

　Bibliography:　p.
　Includes index.
　1. Rabbis—United States.　2. Rabbis—Office.
3. Judaism—United States.　4. Jews in the United
States—Politics and government.　I.　Title.
BM652.P6　　296.6′1′0973　　77–23123
ISBN: 0–03–017716–2

FIRST EDITION
Printed in the United States of America
10 9 8 7 6 5 4 3 2 1

For Louise

Some say: The rabbi has as yet not succeeded in bringing
us nearer to God; our faith is still weak;
we're still not certain that God is near to
all who call upon Him and that God is good to
all and that His mercies are over all His
creatures. We're still afraid of the nothingness
of death. We're still confused about life's
meaning. Rabbi, does it have meaning?
Others say: I agree with the criticism.

—Anonymous American rabbi

Rabbis can help this generation face its problems and
uncertainties and dangers with the assurance of Joshua and
Caleb: "The Lord is with us; fear them not."

—Rabbi Philip Bernstein

The Shidlowitz rebbe, Rabbi Haim Rabinowitz, comforted
the people as they stood in the cattle cars for four days
without food or water. "Fellow Jews," he told them,
"do not fear death. To die for *Kiddush Hashem* is a great
privilege."

Contents

Preface

Some years ago a rabbi decided to leave the rabbinate, but not before he visited a rabbinical colleague in a seminary.

"I've decided not to continue," he remembers saying. "I don't believe."

"Believe?" the other answered, incredulous. "Belief? Who needs it? You can be a perfectly good rabbi without it. Besides, what do you mean by belief?" Or, for that matter, religious faith?

The answer depends on many factors. Belief in *halakha* or religious law? In something called Judaism? In the 613 commandments?

Can belief be defined as an acceptance of God? A survey of the Reform rabbinate in 1972, sponsored by their Central Conference of American Rabbis, found that 13 percent described themselves as agnostics and 1 percent as atheists; 41 percent officiated at religious intermarriages and 43 percent wanted more traditionalism in their services.

How about Jewish culture and religious practices? Diaspora Jews are abysmally ignorant about these disciplines. Not long ago the Hillel Foundation asked enter-

ing Jewish college students about Jewish holidays and
history. It found that 83 percent had no knowledge of
Hanukah, and nearly as many showed little awareness of
the prophetic tradition, despite the fact that almost 85
percent of them had attended religious school.

Attendance in synagogues and temples? Even this is no
barometer of belief, what with social pressures, literary
teas and entertainments and a myriad of other activities
substituting for religious participation. Moreover, the National Jewish Population Survey of the Council of Jewish
Federations and Welfare Funds found in 1975 that somewhat more than 50 percent of all Jewish heads of households "either attend no religious services at all, or attend
less than four times a year—these groups being split about
even." A tiny minority, about one in twelve, attends services
at least once weekly. The sociologist Charles S. Liebman,
who studied the communal aspects of Orthodox Judaism in
the United States in 1964, reported a large portion of
Orthodox synagogue goers were "non-observant, [with] no
commitment to *halakha* or even to the rituals." Looking at
Washington, D.C., Philadelphia and Providence, he found
that 25 to 60 percent of those cities' professed Orthodox
Jews did not even eat kosher meat regularly.

Or is belief expressed in the rites of passage? In spite of
innumerable compromises and, one assumes, departures
from older traditions, most Jews continue to circumcise
their sons, have a rabbi perform their marriages and chant
the necessary prayers while burying their dead. No matter
how cheapened and distorted, despite vulgarities and equiv-
ocations, in these essential celebrations of life and death
the overwhelming number of American Jews continue calling on the rabbinate for succor and strength, thereby de-
claring their association with Jewishness, no matter how
muddied and unclear it is.

Perhaps the question "who needs belief?" raised by that rabbi-administrator in the seminary was merely rhetorical. For belief and religion and even Judaism depend essentially on what one means by those ambiguous terms. Many Orthodox claim to be the sole transmitters of the Jewish tradition, and for the various and competing Orthodox groups that tradition is perceived generally in religious terms. The synagogue is the most important manifestation of their way of life. The Conservative and Reform movements, together with the Reconstructionists, think of themselves as no less the bearers of that sacred tradition, but not the only ones able to do so.

But in most instances since colonial times, the questions of Jewish belief and religion—together with a variety of other complementary and contradictory elements—have centered on the role of the rabbi. He is, I believe, the crucial element in American Jewish life. And yet he is often denigrated, by himself and by his critics.

This book then is about a number of contemporary American pulpit rabbis. It is less a portrait of a profession than it is a popular social history of a group of people functioning as religious specialists in a particular time and place. Stripped of his traditional authority, censured by his legion of critics, discarded in growing numbers by the ultra-Orthodox, ignored by millions of secular Jews, the rabbi nonetheless continues to play a central, if reduced, role in American Jewish life. But I believe he is the most significant person in that life today and for the years ahead.

I have tried to avoid rendering too many judgments about *the* rabbinate. There is, of course, no one rabbi or group of rabbis who can serve as a model for all their colleagues. What I have tried to do is view their lives in conjunction with the questions that keep pressing down upon them: rabbinical versus lay power, synagogue politics and various religious and quasi-religious issues.

As we shall see, the role of the American rabbi is filled with pleasures and frustrations, with hope but, too frequently, with despair as well. What does the rabbi do each day? What motivated him to enter the rabbinate? What pushes younger men and women in the seminaries to do likewise? What relationship do they have to their communities, their congregations, their fellow but non-Jewish Americans? What role do their families play? The rabbis' power or lack of it? Rabbinical culture and rabbinical politics? The rabbis' impact, if any, on the years ahead?

I have also focused on individual rabbis in suburbs, large cities and small towns, wherever they preach, counsel, console, pray and teach, and not necessarily in that order. Some raise money or fight with their lay members; others are viewed as father figures or with barely concealed contempt. Many labor in Jewishly barren areas, lonely and estranged from their fellow rabbis and organized Jewish life. Even so, in a striking number of instances, rabbis are still treated with genuine admiration and respect by the people they serve. It would be difficult to find other professions still considered so favorably.

Beyond this, readers can expect a definition: Who is a rabbi? Is he (and to the Reform and Reconstructionist branches, she as well) the ordained professional who belongs to an approved rabbinical group? Does he have to work for a congregation? Or can the definition be stretched to include those working outside the synagogues in Jewish organizational life or in more worldly occupations? These questions have been perennially debated—and hotly disputed. My own response echoes that of Simon Greenberg, who once argued that anyone may be considered a rabbi who is ordained and maintains an obligation to "conduct public synagogue services on the Sabbath and Holidays and to preach during those services."

All the same, I have limited this report to the pulpit

rabbis, for they have different ambitions, interests and motives than their colleagues elsewhere. My own feeling is that they are also closer than the others to the daily lives and ultimate destiny of their fellow Jews. More significantly, they serve as public exemplars—for good and, at times, even for bad—of authentic Jewish lives at a time when it has become unclear just what being a good and faithful Jew really means and whether it is really necessary to be one.

Paraphrasing Churchill, Wolfe Kelman, a onetime pulpit rabbi and for years head of the Conservative Rabbinical Assembly, concluded (I suspect with some hesitation) that "the system of rabbi-congregational relationships is the worst imaginable, but no one has yet devised a less demoralizing structure." Echoing him, Rabbi Arthur Hertzberg told a rabbinical audience in 1975, "the rabbi has only his biography, nothing else. He no longer has anti-Semitism to 'keep the Jews down on the farm.' He does not have an organized community, he has competition. With only himself and what he is, he feels terribly cold and terribly alone and he would like to say like Moses . . . 'Go send somebody else.' But here *we* are. *We* are sent. *We* cannot avoid it."

My own investigations reflect those sentiments. Part of me came away pessimistic about American Jewry's future staying power *as Jews* and doubtful about rabbinical abilities to stem the tides of religious and cultural erosion. But—and there is always a hopeful, less dogmatic "but"—Jewry has survived mass defections before. It has survived pogroms and slaughters. It may even survive freedom and success through the means of its own unique history. Nathan Glazer's twenty-year-old observation that most Jews still want to be Jews is as incisive today as it was then. "To every generation of recent times a different part of the Jewish past has become meaningful. . . . The son of the Yiddish-speaking socialist who abandons his father's movement may join the Reform temple. In this way, each generation shoulders a minimal part of the yoke." It is a hope but hardly a guarantee.

Many of the rabbis I met at work impressed me with their élan and vitality. Together with their thoroughgoing commitment to Jewish history, literature and religion, they have assumed a most crucial role today, a role I believe will do the most to determine whether future generations continue to want to remain Jewish and begin to understand again the reasons for that decision.

A brief word on style. If I have not burdened the reader with detailed studies and statistics in the text, it is not because they do not exist (they do, in superabundance; see "A Note on Sources" at the rear of the book) but because there have been very few books on the American rabbinate. My aim was to relate some of the rabbis' stories as directly as possible. And in an effort to avoid confounding the reader with too many organizational acronyms, I have tried to keep them at a minimum. They are: Hebrew Union College– Jewish Institute of Religion (HUC-JIR); Central Conference of American Rabbis (CCAR); Rabbinical Assembly (RA); Jewish Theological Seminary (JTS); Rabbinical Council of America (RCA); Rabbinical Alliance of America (RAA); and Rabbi Isaac Elchanan Theological Seminary (RIETS).

Finally, few books are the product of one mind. The resources of several libraries, most notably the American Jewish Archives in Cincinnati and the American Jewish Committee in New York City, were invaluable. I am also grateful to all the rabbis and their families, seminary students, synagogue members and many others who took the time to explore with me the world of the rabbinate, particularly those I discuss in this book. I especially wish to thank the following: Rabbis Eugene Borowitz, Balfour

Brickner, Gerald Kaplan, Wolfe Kelman, William J. Leffler, David Glicksman, Jacob Neusner, William Orentlicher, Stephen Pinsky, Emanuel Rackman, Joseph R. Radinsky, A. James Rudin, David Wolf Silverman, Malcolm Stern, Sidney Strome, Leo Turitz, Andre Ungar, Harvey Wessel and Sidney Wolf. I am especially indebted to Fred Davidow and his parents in Greenville, Mississippi. Trude Weiss-Rosmarin offered me several fascinating interpretations as well as helpful background literature. Seymour Lachman was an unerring guide into the different Orthodox groups. Rabbi Morris Sherer helped explain Agudath Israel of America to me. Alvin Schiff outlined the dimensions of rabbinical behavior and urged me to look at several unexamined areas. The comments and criticisms of Hanna F. Desser and Marlyis Harris were beyond the call of friendship. Stephen Berkowitz was a diligent and innovative researcher. And as always, my wife Louise was involved in the entire process from start to finish, the perfect critic, editor and companion. To all the above, I am deeply appreciative. Naturally, any and all flaws in the book are mine alone.

Rabbi

1. Master and Teacher

The term rabbi (or master, from the Hebrew) was used originally in Palestine in speaking of certain sages but evolved into a title for anyone able to render decisions on the law. As a rule, only those well versed in the Talmud and rabbinic literature were allowed to become rabbis, following years of intensive study. Those finally selected by their elders were examined in *yeshivot* by highly esteemed rabbis and then—and only then—judged able to administer and supervise various aspects of the community, ranging from marriage and divorce to running a yeshiva.

The rabbi of the talmudic period was quite unlike his modern counterpart. Essentially his task was to judge questions of law and instruct his fellow Jews throughout the community—and not merely in one synagogue—in the Scriptures and in oral and traditional laws. He observed carefully the vital institutions: the ritual bath, ritual slaughter and the religious court. The ancient rabbi could also have one of three roles. He might be a *nasi*, or leader of the community, its chief judge, or even an ordinary rabbi —whose credentials in learning were accepted by all—

adding up to a model of philanthropic and ethical behavior for the community and an arbiter and teacher of its laws. Whatever he was, the position was conceived as less than full-time, and payment, if at all, was only for the barest of expenses. The elder Hillel, for example, chopped wood for a living. Other rabbis of the time were builders, blacksmiths, laundrymen, wine tasters, brewers, farmers and carpenters. One typical account mentions a rabbi working at his job part of the day and spending the rest of the time in study. Farmers in particular plied their trade during the growing season and returned to their books during the winter. But whatever their vocations, they were held in some awe, not for their nonexistent roles as intermediaries between God and His people, but rather because of their extensive learning. The "elder in knowledge" was respected far more than the "elder in years" or the amasser of fortunes.

Until well into the Middle Ages, rabbis worked as well as studied and counseled. It was unheard of for a rabbi to work full-time at being a rabbi, since he was not allowed to derive income from the study of the Torah. But during the medieval years this began to change, and the rabbi was slowly transformed into the spiritual head of a community in addition to being the teacher and interpreter of the Bible and the Oral Law. With the expulsion of the Jews from Spain and Portugal in the fourteenth and fifteenth centuries and the ensuing persecutions, émigré rabbis found themselves unable to find outside sources of income, while the new exile communities desperately needed rabbis to minister to their needs.

In the fourteenth century, for the first time, a refugee rabbi received payment for his services. Simeon ben Zemah Duran had escaped anti-Jewish riots in Spain and fled to Algiers. There the local community asked him to serve as its rabbi, but Simeon balked. He said he was without funds and he had to find some paying job. In the end, a formula was fashioned whereby he received *sekhar battalah*, or compensation for the loss of time associated with duties as rabbi. If the agreement did not herald a specific offering of wages for services, it was nonetheless the legal basis in Jewish law for future payments to rabbis.

In this context then, medieval rabbis developed special roles, creating the Responsa, rabbinic literature answering questions on law and observance, which was sent to distant Jewish communities and which tied together those disparate areas. Rabbis codified law and custom; their councils established, standards concerning marriage and divorce, monogamy, inheritance and other typical concerns. In many areas they also were active in community life. Rabbinical courts were even permitted to try criminal cases where Jews were involved.

For the Jews, medieval Europe was a fearful place and time, and this led inexorably to the emergence of autocratic rabbinic authority, hierarchal power and a class structure which heightened the ability of the rabbi to command obedience and enforce conformity. Armed with the *herem*, or the right to excommunicate, the medieval rabbi had the ultimate right to turn dissenting Jews out. Few dared challenge rabbinical authority, even if they had the will to do so.

Ultimately, with the breakup of the ghettos in Western Europe and the coming of democracy, relativism, natural science and the nation-state, all of which were reflected in the birth of Reform Judaism in Germany, the rabbi—increasingly in Western Europe a graduate of a formal rabbinical seminary—became more as he is today. Certified, he was gradually transformed into a clergyman rather than a scholar, a preacher and counselor rather than an ecclesiastical sage and judge, the rabbi of an individual synagogue and not of an entire community.

"I remember," said someone who grew up in Chicago, "my grandfather, the rabbi, never sat on the *bimah* but with his congregation. No one outside the *shul* knew him, but inside he was first among equals."

This is a reasonable characterization of the twentieth-century rabbi and what he is and is not. He is not a Jewish version of a priest or minister, for he never performs priestly or sacramental roles. He leads his congregation in prayer. He is present at burials. But that presence is not necessary to consecrate the event. Public devotion may be held without him. He is not an intermediary between God and the rest of us. In fact, he is no nearer to God than anyone else, nor does he receive any "call" that inspires him to enter the rabbinate. (Several studies suggest that, in the past at least, rabbinical sons tended to enter the rabbinate more often than those whose fathers practiced medicine or sold dresses or stayed far away from synagogues.) The rabbi is, however, a teacher, and if the spirit moves him and he has the talent, a scholar as well. He can be much more to his congregation, but in any event his major purpose is, or certainly should be, to lay out the meaning and drama of Judaism for those who would continue in that faith.

And finally, an attempt at a definition. Who is and who isn't entitled to call himself a rabbi? Superficially, a rabbi is anyone who has been ordained or received *smicha*—literally, the laying on of hands. Nowadays, a diploma from any of the seminaries has supplanted smicha in Orthodox and Conservative commencement exercises, but the ancient ritual has been maintained at HUC-JIR.

"The ordaining officer," says Rabbi Herbert Brichto, dean of the Cincinnati school, "actually rests his hands on the shoulders of each man [and, increasingly, upon women too] who has fulfilled the requirements."

Still, those requirements vary somewhat.

"Conservative Judaism," says Rabbi Neil Gilman, dean of students at the Jewish Theological Seminary, "holds that Jewish law must continue to develop within changing historical conditions. We try to maintain a balance between the claims of tradition and the past and the claims of the contemporary situation."

Rabbi Louis Bernstein, a practicing pulpit rabbi and onetime president of the Orthodox Rabbinical Council of America, stresses a more rigid adherence to halakha. "The Orthodox rabbinate requires proficiency in the study of the Talmud, in the legal and ritualistic traditions and the codes of Jewish law. There is a totally different training for the Conservative and Reform rabbinates. We are trained in every aspect of *kashrut* law, the dietary observances, for example. Reform certainly doesn't require this, and the Conservatives rely on the Orthodox rabbi."

One hot, sunny morning in Philadelphia in 1788 three men, together with hundreds of other celebrants that Fourth of July, locked arms and marched in the Federal Parade to hail the new nation's ratification of its Constitution. Two of those men were Christian ministers, but the third was Rabbi Jacob R. Cohen. The ratification had marked a moment of high drama, if only in retrospect. Not since 212 c.e., when the Emperor Caracalla granted citizenship to all free males in the Roman Empire, had Jews in the dispersion been accorded such legal equality as in the document forged by the Founding Fathers in Philadelphia. Following Jefferson's Virginia Bill for Establishing Religious Freedom in 1786 and, one year later, the momentous Northwest Ordinance, Article VI of the new Constitution guaranteed that no religious tests were necessary for holding national office.

Later that day, flushed with elation and excitement, Cohen—who was really not an ordained rabbi at all—and his Mikveh Israel congregation, already fifteen years old, gathered on Cherry Lane to rejoice and to proclaim their faith in the goodness and hope of the new country and to eat salmon, crackers, raisins and almonds and dance and sing.

America, indeed, might yet be different.

It is believed that Jacob Cohen was born in the Barbary States but reared in London, where he became a *mohel* and *hazzan*. Soon after he began his wanderings, first to Quebec and then to Montreal in 1779, where he became known as Canada's first Jewish "minister," and then on to New York City. Finally he settled in Philadelphia, where he was to spend the rest of his life, dying just before Rosh Hashanah in 1811, at the age of seventy-three.

Cohen's concerns were many, but not the least were the kinds of complaints with which many of his successors could easily identify. "Sir," he wrote the *parnas*, or president, of the synagogue on March 15, 1802, "it is impossible to live any longer in the House—unless something be done with that Cistern. It is both Dangerous, Unwholesome and offensive—as to Danger the Bricks are all sinking so bad that one of our Neighbours dog fell in & was drowned—on Tuesday Morn[in]g in smell[in]g an offensive smell Betsey [his wife] look'd in the Cistern and saw the drowned dog—yours and the Congs attention thereof will oblige Sir yours."

Cohen's general duties were not unlike those who came after him, except that he had both synagogue and community responsibilities. In 1785, for example, Benjamin Moses Clava died. Clava, who was a merchant and one of the few unaffiliated Jews in the city, had also married a non-Jewish woman, and Cohen was called upon to decide if he might be buried in consecrated ground. He did have that right, ruled Cohen, though without a shroud or ritual washing. But Cohen's responsibilities went further than a mere decision, for an ancient tradition was involved, and no Americans then had the training or experience to cope with even more vexing problems. Who could offer those early rabbis and their congregations any guidance? With no religious specialists, no rabbinical sages, Mikveh Israel and the "rabbis" did what came naturally to them—they appealed to authorities elsewhere. In the Clava case they wrote for advice in Yiddish—indicating the presence of Eastern European Jews in Philadelphia even then—to the rabbis of Amsterdam and The Hague.

The difference between early and later rabbis was crucial, for the early synagogue was quite different from the contemporary model. Ordained or not, the early rabbis were the communal kind, helping to determine, as Nathan Glazer has written, "the questions of religious law, condition[s] for Jewish schools . . . [and] the baking of *matzoth* for Passover and the ritually correct slaughter of animals for meat."

Better known than Cohen, Gershom Mendes Seixas, called the "Patriot Rabbi" because of his strong support for the rebel cause, was also a hazzan, the first American-born rabbi to have a pulpit in this country. Respected, indeed admired by many non-Jews, Seixas' forceful personality seemed to strengthen the authority role of the rabbi. Local general press accounts began to call him "minister" and "Reverend," the better to censure and exhort his fellow Jews.

At the time of Seixas' death there were six Hebrew congregations in North America. In New York City there was Shearith Israel, whose "rabbi" Seixas had been Cohen's predecessor in Philadelphia. The others were in Philadelphia, Newport, Rhode Island, and southward in Richmond, Charleston and Savannah. In all, 3,000 Jews were living among a sea of Christians and thanking the Lord each Shabbat for having directed them to so lovely and so promising a land.

Like Cohen and Seixas, none of their rabbis were ordained. Actually, by 1773 there were but three ordained rabbis in the western hemisphere: in Curaçao, Surinam and Jamaica. Another Cohen (Moses) had lived for a time in Charleston before 1750 but following Sephardic custom was called *hakham* or chief sage. In fact, there would be no "official" rabbi in the United States until late in 1840, when

Abraham Joseph Rice would arrive in Baltimore from
Germany. Until then rabbis were laymen—hazzans (readers
of services), mohels (circumcisers) and *shohets* (ritual
slaughterers).

All the same, there was chaos ahead. As far back as the
mid-eighteenth century, New York City had a large and
growing number of unaffiliated Jews. Shearith Israel's
records are filled with discussions on how to lure them to
the synagogue. Meanwhile, each year brought more immigrants from Germany and Poland, so that by the 1840s
opposition had risen appreciably to the vital roles assumed
unilaterally by the hazzan. In Germany, where sweeping
changes were already under way, the word came from the
newly established seminaries: rabbis, that is, *ordained*
rabbis, were superior to mere hazzans. And further: *only*
the rabbi was permitted to preach. In 1841 a crucial question was put to the Berlin Jewish community as the subject
for a prize essay by Berlin's *Kulturverein*: "What was, what
is, and what shall the rabbi be?"

While no definitive responses came forth, it was increasingly evident after the failure of the liberal revolutions in
1848 and the concomitant resurgence of counterrevolution-
ary forces in Europe that more Jews would depart for the
New World and take their rabbis along with them. And
they would naturally try to assert their presumed rights and
prerogatives. Meanwhile, the coming of large numbers of
Polish Jews completed the transition. By the 1840s and
1850s, each group and each synagogue was choosing its
own rabbi, hazzan, *maggid* (itinerant preacher) or talmudic
authority. The community was no longer the responsibility
of the spiritual leader.

Abraham Joseph Rice was born in Gagsheim, close to
Würzburg in Bavaria, in 1802. The small villages and hamlets of southern Germany were then still immune to the

shocks of the Enlightenment and reform of all sorts, and were as yet dominated by the more traditional religious authorities. Rice studied at various yeshivot and received smicha at Rabbi Wolf Hamburger's yeshiva in Fürth (before Hamburger himself was forced out by reformers). After his ordination, Rice was urged by colleagues and teachers to go to America as the pioneer ordained rabbi to minister to the nation's growing number of émigré German Jews.

He arrived late in 1840 and discovered soon enough the absence of competent—at least as he judged them—rabbis. "In this country," he wrote afterward in disgust, "men who have studied neither Bible nor Talmud have assumed the title of 'Rabbi,' donning the rabbinical cap on their heads in the same way that Napoleon placed the crown on his head."

He was soon defeated by the powerful forces of Reform. Rice had to grant *aliyot* (a "calling up" to read the Scroll of Law in synagogues during worship) to those who had nonetheless violated the sanctity of the Sabbath. A member with influential connections died and—over Rice's strenuous objections—was buried with Masonic rites. Certain medieval religious poetry was deleted from the services by his congregation, again over his vigorous protests. In 1849 he resigned and eventually became a grocer, although for the remainder of his life he maintained a *minyan* (or quorum of at least ten adult males) that rejected the new, acculturated American ways and extolled Judaism as he knew it. "I dwell in complete darkness, without teacher or companion," he complained wearily to his revered rebbe in Fürth. And again in 1855, writing in Isaac Leeser's *The Occident*: "The heavens may vanish in smoke, and the earth wear out with old age, and still not one iota will vanish from our religion."

Soon the unlettered congregations began to import the "Germans," men of thoroughgoing secular education and all of them ordained. Simson Thorman, the first Jewish settler in Cleveland, Ohio, arrived from Unsleben in Bavaria in 1837. Two years later, a *landsmann* reached the shores of Lake Erie with a Torah scroll and at least ten fellow Jews. Before long these German and Hungarian émigrés had organized the Israelitish Society and several congregations. Even so, frontier life was rather novel to these refugees from Central Europe. Their non-Jewish peers had had to adjust too, wrote Joseph Rappaport, "but whereas the forest . . . was *not* a new experience for New England progeny, the American city was indeed a unique element in immigrant Jewish lives." The founding of the Israelitish Society, Rappaport concluded, was "more than an expression of religious faith; it also reflected a quest for balance in an unfamiliar scene."

The search tended to create a unique sort of American Jewry in Cleveland: so independent that even Reform Jews resisted for a time Isaac Mayer Wise's efforts to induce some form of conformity; self-determined, because all their institutions had to be of their own choosing and design, from scratch as it were, since none existed before; isolated, far from other Jewish pockets of settlement and without the Sephardic tradition to build on. Indeed, when Jews started drifting into the Ohio Valley in the early years of the 1800s, they were objects of curiosity. Joseph Jonas, born in Exeter, England, and an observant Orthodox Jew all his life, was the first known Jew in Ohio, arriving in 1817. He was twenty-five years old when a Quaker woman came to see him. "Art thou a Jew?" she asked. "Thou art one of God's chosen people. Wilt thou let me examine thee?" She stared at Jonas, turned him round and then, no doubt with some sense of disappointment, she said: "Well, thou art no different to other people."

Settling in Cleveland, German Jews put down roots and shared the aspirations common to many of their fellow midwesterners. The cornerstone ceremony at Anshe Chesed's Scovill Avenue synagogue in 1886 indicates the profound influence of familiar American societal patterns. Speaking in German, Rabbi Aaron Hahn of Tifereth Israel—which was founded in 1850 and would one day have as its rabbi the famous and ardently pro-Zionist Abba Hillel Silver—touched on the noble, more hopeful, if somewhat myopic, illusions of that time: "The dark days of the persecution of our race are past. . . . Judaism is flourishing under the proud banner of the stars and stripes."

One more special factor about the past of Cleveland's Jews: While its synagogues were never treated quite as reverently as the older Sephardi congregations in the East and Southeast treated theirs, there was from their very inception a tradition of loyalty to Judaism. When those Bavarian immigrants set out in 1839 to join Simon Thorman, one Lazarus Kohn, their teacher, gave to Moses Alsbacher (one of the emigrants) a letter urging them to remain Jews. "Do not throw away your holy religion for quickly lost earthly pleasures. . . . Do not tear yourself away from the laws in which your fathers and mothers searched for assurance and found it."

In that spirit, then, Tifereth Israel, the first Reform temple in Cleveland, was also one of the first to hire a full-time rabbi, Dr. Isidor Kalisch. Born in 1816 in Posen, Prussia, educated at the Universities of Berlin, Breslau and Prague, a liberal refugee from the reactionary Prussian counter-revolution after 1848, Kalisch was chosen as "rabbi, teacher, preacher, and reader" for $400 per year. Bad times forced the temple to cut his salary to $300. Soon the congregation had to cut its overhead costs even more drastically: According to the official history of Tifereth Israel, it "let Kalisch go altogether because of its financial difficulties."

Leo Merzbacher, allegedly the first ordained rabbi in New York City, was hired as a teacher and preacher in

Anshe Chesed at $6 a month "to attend meetings of the Board of Trustees to give advice in religious matters . . . to deliver a lecture every *Shabbat* after *rosh hodesh*, etc. . . . deliver a funeral sermon . . . give religious instruction several hours a week to children over 12 years of age. . . ."

Some years after, Merzbacher's duties were augmented to include settling the problems of Anshe Chesed's members. But he was too shrewd to be put upon, and demanded instead that the trustees appoint him the rabbi and pay him appropriately if they also wanted him to counsel. Merzbacher, a snob in matters of class and status, was nonetheless a realist, insisting that he be addressed as "Dr." Eventually, he made it, moving on to the more regal and remote Emanu-El on Fifth Avenue.

Morris J. Raphall is remembered for other reasons. He defended slavery as few rabbis did in the North and most did in the South. He was also the first to receive a pension of $500 yearly as a rabbi; $1,000 if disabled. Swedish-born, schooled in Copenhagen and specializing in Hebrew poetry, Raphall arrived in America in 1840, the year that Rice reached Baltimore.

Isaac Leeser, who succeeded Jacob Cohen as hazzan of Mikveh Israel and as editor of *The Occident*, was undoubtedly the most significant and influential religious leader among the Jews in the antebellum years. Like many of his peers, he was born in Germany, was very Orthodox and was exceptionally articulate. "With his coming [to Philadelphia] a new era opened for the Jews," wrote Edwin Wolf and Maxwell Whiteman, two historians. "Leeser emerged as the leading Jew, not only of the city, but of the whole country."

Indeed, the years from 1830 to 1865 could be described as "his" years, much as the years following were dominated by Isaac Mayer Wise. Leeser wrote numerous books, texts and prayer books, translated the Bible into English, published the earliest American-Jewish national magazine, urged the construction of a Hebrew college in 1843 (the proposal fell on deaf ears), formed the American Jewish Publication Society, organized the earliest Jewish national conferences, engaged in works of charity and preached regularly in Mikveh Israel against the sins of intermarriage and assimilation.

His only competitor for national attention was Isaac Mayer Wise, who broadened and expanded the influence of the Germans. Born in Bohemia in 1819, he soon became aware of the endemic anti-Semitism in Central Europe; imbued with the ideas of German Reform, he came to the United States, first to Albany in 1846, and then in 1854 to Cincinnati, at that time the nation's sixth largest city, where he would publish the German-language *Die Deborah* and the English-language *The Israelite*. He wrote bad novels and undistinguished tracts on religion, but as an organizer, administrator and inspirer of others he was a genius. He issued a call for rabbis trained in Germany to come to the new promised land. In 1873 he started the Union of American Hebrew Congregations; in 1875, Hebrew Union College; in 1889, the Central Conference of American Rabbis. The Reform movement now had its structure. It also had a following. By 1881, Reform dominated American Jewry. Of 200 synagogues in the late nineteenth century, only one dozen were still Orthodox. Even as early as 1824, some of Charleston's Jews scorned the old Sephardic Beth Elohim—which had been founded in 1749—and established their own Reformed Society of Israelites, introducing prayers in English together with abbreviated services.

Their tenet, like that of Wise and his followers, was a purely American faith on American grounds. "America is our Zion and Washington is our Jerusalem," said Wise, echoing an article of faith among his adherents. And who could argue that faith in America's redeeming qualities was misplaced? The eighteenth and nineteenth centuries were a remarkable age for many of his adherents. A stable and small minority before the mass migration of Jews from the *shtetls* of the decaying Czarist and Hapsburg empires, living in a land with little overt anti-Semitism, the well-off Sephardic and Ashkenazic elite found life as good as it was comfortable. The hatreds were directed elsewhere, toward Blacks for one, and in the Far West toward Asians. As late as 1916, the Native Sons of the Golden West, the most potent anti-Japanese organization then in San Francisco, held a rally to raise money for oppressed Russian Jews. Wise sensed this larger tolerance of Jews and he saw in the educated, ordained Reform rabbi the central means by which their values could be transmitted to the next generations. James G. Heller, a biographer, wrote that Wise considered the "Rabbi as a scholar, an authority on Jewish literature, a dedicated servant of Israel, a teacher, but above all a man of moral rectitude, of light and leading."

And in addition, a way in which the past might always be recalled. Remembering his visit in 1864 to Mikveh Israel in Philadelphia, Wise once reflected in his magazine: "I imagined myself to sit in the great synagogue of Toledo, and the gigantic forms of Ibn Esra, Gabirol, Maimonides, Halevy, Nachmonides, Abarbanel . . . and others, stood before me. . . . Then I thought of the exode [exile] of the 600,000 Jews from Spain, and their sufferings, and tears whetted [sic] my eyes. When the service closed I had lived through a number of centuries."

His movement flourished, and toward the last years of the nineteenth century it came to represent, as Nathan Glazer has aptly put it, "the religion of economically comfortable Jews who wanted to be accepted by the non-Jewish world." They denuded their temples of as many of the old ways as they dared. They evaded the subject of revelation. Often their temples did not look like "synagogues."

"We have," wrote Kaufman Kohler, a prominent Reform

rabbi and inveterate organizer, "introduced the so-called Minhag America [synagogue ritual], the prayers are considerably shortened, many have been omitted entirely. . . . There is no calling up to the Torah. . . . The congregation dropped the elementary school." In his Kansas City, Missouri, temple in 1886–1887, Rabbi Joseph Krauskopf lectured on "Evolution and Judaism." One of the first American rabbis to be ordained by Wise's HUC, Krauskopf—as Joseph L. Blau has pointed out—spoke of Orthodoxy as a hodgepodge of accumulated "borrowed heathenism" from older ancient cults. "When the mind . . . has outlived an age it will not permit itself to be lulled to sleep by the lullabies of the past." Instead, he offered American Jews another option, "the Judaism of to-day," a faith that evolved (it was after all the age of Darwin and Spencer) without peculiar "Oriental" ideas of chosenness or national homelands.

This effort to go "Protestant" as critics charged, or simply to appear as inoffensive as possible to their gentile neighbors, greatly offended Judah L. Magnes of Temple Emanu-El. Magnes, who would quit that pulpit in protest against the plush temple's reigning economic and social judgments, often clashed with his very rich members. But most aggravating to Magnes was its nondescript character.

"A prominent Christian lawyer of another city," he said in a 1910 sermon, "has told how he entered this building at the beginning of a service on Sunday morning and did not discover that he was in a synagogue until a chance remark of the preacher betrayed it."

But Reform Judaism was determined to assimilate and Americanize. "We accept as binding," declared the Central Conference of American Rabbis in Pittsburgh in 1885, "only its [Mosaic] moral laws . . . but reject all such as are not adapted to the view and habits of modern civilization. . . . We consider ourselves no longer a nation but a religious community and . . . expect neither a return to Palestine . . .

nor the restoration of . . . the Jewish state. . . . We recognize in Judaism a progressive religion, ever striving to be in accord with the postulates of reason."

In time the Reform rabbis would modify and repudiate these views, as they did in Columbus, Ohio, in 1937 when the weight of Eastern European influence had begun to dominate their ranks and the rise of Nazism compelled them to alter their hostility toward Zionism. All the same, they have continued to avoid the dead end of parochialism and have sought repeatedly to turn a sympathetic ear to larger social ills: child labor, the exploitation of working men and women, the sweatshops. In 1908 they formed the Committee on Labor and Synagogue, their "first real social committee," noted a student of that period. By 1916 they favored fair wages and collective bargaining, as well as an eight-hour day and the entire industrial fringe-benefit system now in wide use. They courageously opposed the Palmer raids against alleged radicals, excoriated the executioners of Sacco and Vanzetti, defended Negro rights in the North as well as the South long before it was fashionable to do so, concerned themselves with joblessness during the Great Depression, and attacked fascism early on while defending the Spanish Loyalists. Socially conscious, politically aware, ethically attuned, they supported political liberalism, identifying closely with the New Deal and later progressives as a source of solace for the millions of needy. In their 1976 convention the rabbis voted to support the busing of public school pupils, a move the vast majority of their fellow Jews opposed. If they were at times unable to foresee the dismal future, the abandonment of European Jews to Hitler's ovens, they were and have been caught up in the very lives of their fellow Americans and in exhausting efforts to achieve major social and ethical gains within the existing system.

Sweeping improvement and upward mobility were precisely what the vast majority of immigrant Jews desperately needed during the decades before the outbreak of World War I. Ignored by the elitism of the Reform temples (many immigrants, in turn, could not bring themselves to accept Reform as Jewish), yet scorning the Old World shuls from which they had fled, some turned toward Conservative Judaism, which sought to walk a tightrope between the two antagonists. Conservatism emphasized the group as an ethnic entity and in time organized the Jewish Center movement ("a shul with a pool," quipped Rabbi Joel Blau). The Conservatives believed they had thereby enhanced the role of their rabbis and lured more of the unaffiliated to the synagogue. Like their Reform peers, the Conservative rabbis would in time assume many roles, mainly pastoral, without which no synagogue center would be viable today.

Because Conservatism had no charismatic leader, its rabbinate became indispensable, the movement's historian, Marshall Sklare, has concluded. Casting about for an alternative to Wise's Reform seminary, which opened in 1875, two rabbis—one Sephardic, the other Hungarian-born and German-trained—called for a new rabbinical training school patterned after the famous Breslau seminary. In 1887 classes began, first in the 19th Street synagogue of Shearith Israel in Manhattan and soon after at Cooper Union and later at 736 Lexington Avenue. All the same, the leaders of the Jewish Theological Seminary knew little or no Yiddish and thus could hardly appeal to the new immigrants. They were stung as well by Orthodoxy's refusal to recognize the authenticity of its ordinations. By the turn of the century the JTS was set to close when Cyrus Adler, at the time librarian of the Smithsonian Institution, approached the rich Germans in elegant, exclusive Temple Emanu-El. Despite the Reform sympathies of the Schiffs, Guggenheims, Lewisohns, Sulzbergers and Warburgs, Adler persuaded them to come to the seminary's rescue. They sensed that the Eastern European masses needed some form of Jewish association but would not accept Reform. Conservatism—

that is, traditionalism stripped of its shtetl characteristics—
was good for the masses, or so those nabobs thought.

Reconstructionism, the brainchild of Mordecai M. Kaplan, developed during the second generation of Eastern
European Jewry. Born in Swenzian in Lithuania in 1881,
Kaplan was brought to the United States at the age of eight.
The Jewish population in this country was then 400,000. He
received the customary Orthodox training and four years
later matriculated at the JTS. Yet he also attended City
College of New York and earned his M.A. there at the age
of nineteen. It was a portent of the major theme of his
life: how to live in Jewish and non-Jewish cultures; how to
benefit from a rationalist and naturalist world as well as
from a religious faith.

Kaplan's growing doubts led him to the edge of abandon-
ing the rabbinate for an insurance career. But JTS President
Solomon Schechter persuaded him to take charge of the
seminary's Teacher's Institute. The next year and for nearly
a half century thereafter, Kaplan taught homiletics in the
rabbinical seminary. As a result, his direct influence on
subsequent generations of rabbis has been incalculable.

"They recall his sturdy stride, his large and penetrating
blue eyes, his fierce black beard (later to turn pure white),
his monumental temper which flared when he encountered
stupidity or fuzzy thinking, his benign smile when the storm
blew over, his warmth and friendliness which were not easily
apparent behind the stern exterior, and most of all his constant insistence upon honesty and clear thinking," remembered Rabbi Ira Eisenstein, his disciple and son-in-law and
the editor of *Reconstructionist*.

"Students coming from traditional homes and schools
went through traumatic experiences on first exposure to his
relentless logic. But they were ever thankful to him because
he made them think. And while they did not always come

to agree with him, they never ceased to praise him for his courage, his deep insights, his ever-youthful hospitality to new ideas."

Out of his fertile mind emerged the highly intellectual and often abstract Reconstructionism, which understood Judaism to be an evolving civilization, shaped by each generation, adapting, taking on and discarding without the inflexible guidance of halakha, or the sacrosanct notion of the Chosen People, or even the revelations to Moses on Sinai. It was also uniquely American, given the emphasis it placed on the individual, who was to decide for himself which of the folkways and rituals should be practiced. Rabbi Harold M. Schulweis of Encino, California, stated it well: "Every Conservative Synagogue has something of Reconstructionism in it." And, added Trude Weiss-Rosmarin in the pages of her *Jewish Spectator*, so does "every American Jewish congregation with an English-speaking rabbi."

"For all its shortcomings," commented Gilbert Rosenthal, "Reconstructionism has enriched the quality of Jewish life, prodded Jews to rethink old views and has pointed Jewry in new directions for tomorrow."

Meanwhile, subjected to all these hammer blows, Orthodoxy stumbled along, plagued then as now—in Marshall Sklare's acute judgment—with too many unobservant Jews. But with a new wave of immigration in the 1930s, portents of great change were in the air. The Nazi devastation brought in its wake such remarkable men and seminal thinkers as Rabbis Moshe Feinstein, Aharon Kotler and Joseph Soloveitchik (who had arrived in 1932), who would not only revolutionize Orthodoxy's flagging spirit but also reinvigorate its rudderless religious institutions.

What is found in contemporary American Judaism are varieties of the Jewish experience. From the worldly concerns of secularists to the more religious expressions of that ancient tradition; in experimental (and rabbiless) *havurot* and in *shtiebls*; in talmudic yeshivot along with the synagogues and temples—in all these Jewish life proceeds. There is no official organization that speaks for all, as does the British or South African Board of Deputies. Here everyone is on his own, competing, cooperating, challenging, duplicating, even innovating at will. Eliezer Berkovitz, professor emeritus at the Hebrew Theological College and himself Orthodox, has said: "To be a Jew does not mean 'I believe this or that.' To be a Jew means 'I am.' There are elements in Jewish identity which identify a Jew even against his will. To be a Jew means to open up a book of Jewish history and say, 'This is my history, this is me.' "

Stanley Steinhart is very happy as a rabbi. He has ample time to lecture and study, he says, and his suburban Conservative temple of 550 families in Jericho, New York, is a stable congregation. "My home, my shul and my religion are my anchors," he says. He speaks to Women's ORT (Organization for Rehabilitation Through Training), Pioneer Women, and Hadassah on prayer, the Bible and religious customs and ceremonies. And in a Long Island with 600,000 Jews (but no kosher restaurants other than delicatessens), few yeshivot and but one *mikveh*—in Great Neck) he considers that no mean feat.

His major complaint is that his fellow Jericho Jews' definition of being Jewish is not his. Daily minyans are hard to come by. There are few religiously dedicated lay people in his synagogue. At least half the town's Jews are not members of his or the neighboring Reform temple. Still, they want to remain Jews in their own way. Women and their role in Judaism are high on their list of priorities. Poor Jews in the Bronx and Brooklyn. Israeli war wounded. Compassionate goals that have tended to supplant the religious emphasis, at least in Jericho. The life of these second- and third-generation Jews in the suburbs was described by Irving Howe in this way: "not, as a rule, marked by a distinguished culture, nor . . . notable for spiritual intensities, but it had strong elements of humaneness and social decency as well as, now and again, a touching self-doubt." Which accounts for the fact that they need and want their rabbi. "He's like a father," said one teenager. Added her friend: "You can always talk to him." And her mother: "We see him as the person who knows more about being Jewish than anyone else here. Anytime we have any questions or want something done for Israel or Soviet Jewry we call on him."

Rabbi Sherwin Wine preaches Judaism without God in his Birmingham, Michigan, temple of 150 families. A graduate of Hebrew Union College, a member of the CCAR, Rabbi Wine has exorcised the name of God from the temple's prayer books; he has reinterpreted and reedited the Bible where he thought it necessary to reconcile its text with his rational and skeptical creed, which he chooses to describe as humanism. He and his congregants—there are two similar congregations in Highland Park, Illinois, and Westport, Connecticut, plus budding groups in Boston, Houston, Buffalo and Toronto, and a 250-member Society for Humanistic Judaism—nonetheless insist that it is neither Unitarianism nor Ethical Culture they are engaged in, but rather Judaism. Or more precisely, their version of it.

A Bronx rabbi, Hailu Moshe Paris, whose Falasha parents were killed during the Italo-Ethiopian War in 1935, attended yeshiva and is a practicing Jew at the all-Black Congregation Mount Horeb in that borough. But the best-known Black rabbi was Wentworth A. Matthew, who, according to one account, was ordained by Arnold Ford. Along with Matthew, Ford was the most important figure in Black American Jewish history. He once served as choirmaster in Marcus Garvey's Universal Negro Improvement Association, which stressed the "Back-to-Africa" movement. "It is certain," comments Howard Brotz in *The Black Jews of Harlem*, one of the few reliable guides on the subject, "that [Ford] studied with some immigrant teacher and was a key link in transmitting whatever approximations there are to Talmudic Judaism in the practices of these sects."

In 1923, after his rejection by Garvey, Ford organized some three dozen followers into what he called the Beth B'nai Abraham, and sketched out a program which rejected all Christianity as "white"—even his father's evangelical group in Barbados, from which he sprang. "His anti-Christianity found a partial vent in Judaism," wrote Ruth Landes in 1933. After the disintegration of the Back-to-Africa movement, Ford turned more bitterly anti-white, insisting that only Blacks were Jews. He vanished, never to be heard from again. Some say he went to Africa; others mention Detroit. There are even rumors that he became a Muslim.

In a Black Jewish population variously estimated at from 12–15,000 to 100,000, Rabbi Matthew trained most of the half-dozen active Black rabbis. In 1971, in an effort to improve communications between their congregations, the Israelite Board of Rabbis was organized, under the leadership of Rabbi William McKeithen, who has since changed his name to Levi Ben Levi.

Matthew also provided the major impetus for growth and continuity, and starting in 1930 and for more than forty years until his death in 1973, he served as the spiritual leader of the Commandment Keepers of the Congregation of the Living God, Harlem's largest synagogue. Visitors in recent years saw a synagogue hardly different from small Orthodox shuls anywhere. A map of Israel hangs on the wall, men wear yarmulkes and sit apart from the women, sing the *Shema*, read from the Torah and, at the close of the services, intone the *Kaddish* and *Adon Olam*.

Matthew was born in Lagos, West Africa, in 1892 of a Christian mother and moved to St. Kitts in the British West Indies as a child. In 1913, at the age of twenty-one, he arrived in New York City, where he soon found himself involved with Ford and the Garveyites.

Harlem was quite Jewish between the two world wars, and records indicate that ten Black congregations existed throughout the city. Immediately after World War I, Rabbi Matthew formed his own congregation and began the study of Hebrew, Yiddish and general Judaica. Within a decade he opened a synagogue and a rabbinical college. Under his leadership the group flourished for a time, inasmuch as many white Jews were increasingly sympathetic to their Black counterparts. George Gershwin, the German-Jewish poet Ernst Toller and Dr. Jacques Faitlovitch, who rediscovered the Ethiopian Falashas in the early part of this century, were among the prominent Jews who attended services in Matthew's shul. By Matthew's own account he had 550 members in 1936 and 1,000 in 1957. Says Robert Coleman, a Black convert who works for the Synagogue Council of America: "Black Jews are really holding their own kids. Many of the families are now well into their third and fourth generation as Jews. In Cincinnati, for example, with a known population of about 25, their major concern is getting their kids into yeshivas. How many white Jewish parents are that obsessed with a Jewish education for their young?"

There are also "gay" synagogues. Beth Chayim Chadashim in Los Angeles was admitted to membership in the UAHC in June 1974 after a three-year trial period. Another, Beth Simchat Torah, is in New York City. Its Rabbi, Aaron—whose Sabbath services are advertised regularly in the *New York Times*—has a Hasidic background, was ordained in an Orthodox yeshiva and is homosexual. "I feel that we, as gays, have something special to say to the Jewish community, some important message for our time," he told an interviewer. "The very fact that they reject us gives us a special significance." Turning to a congregant he asked, "What is that psalm I'm thinking of—you know, the one about the stone builders reject?"

"Psalm 118, verse 22," the man answered.

"Ah yes, here it is," Aaron said, leafing through his Bible. "The stone which the builders refused is become the head stone of the corner."

Jewish Science, founded in 1924 by Rabbi Morris Lichtenstein and directed after his death by his widow Tehilla, is a counterpart to Christian Science; there are Jewish Science synagogues in Manhattan and Old Bethpage, Long Island. Lichtenstein's approach, best evidenced in his book *The Healing of the Soul*, stresses goodness, the effectiveness of prayer and the spiritual instead of the ritual side of Judaism.

Andre Ungar has a Conservative congregation in New Jersey, but his was a long journey from his birthplace in Hungary to pulpits in South Africa, London and finally the United States. South Africa was hard for him. Apartheid meant that in exchange for a life of ease and safety one sacrificed another people.

"My two years in South Africa persist as a haunting memory," he wrote in *Present Tense*. "As rabbi, I was treated with almost feudal deference; men old enough to be my grandfather would rise when I entered a room." But he could not accept South African racism and thereby risked ostracism and exile. Once he planned a vacation with a Cape Colored friend. An officer of the congregation, also a friend, phoned him: "Rabbi, why are you doing this to us?" That and his public statements condemning apartheid were too much. He was expelled. "The last thing my congregation desired was a Utopia based on Hebraic sources. They did not need me to tell them how to live, what to do and not to do, what to prize and what to condemn. My task was to consecrate the status quo."

Arriving in America, he found this country's Jewish life different from what he had experienced elsewhere, a sort of cross between the "tribalism of South Africa and the denominationalism of Britain." The American synagogue, he found, was thriving, as were the rabbinate and the rabbi, "chief executive of a busy hive of activities by Jews—though not necessarily Jewish activities. He has a radius of influence and power."

Poignantly, with feeling, Ungar speaks of the daily tasks of the rabbi: "Trying to solace a young widower in his grief, both sharing and deflecting his rage against God. Exuberant at a wedding; caught in the cross fire of a marital squabble. Soothing Jewish feathers ruffled by imaginary anti-Semitism, . . . some petty, some crucial, some specifically 'rabbinic,' some plain Jewish responsibilities. But most of all, what the prelude to the *Shema* summarizes as 'Learning and teaching, keeping and doing . . .' constitutes the essence of my—or our—work. Few callings have greater restraints or fuller freedom, more heartbreaks or dizzier thrills. And certainly no other profession . . . has more permanent and satisfying bonds with that stiff-necked and glorious people, the Jews."

Admittedly, then, there is a great variety in public life because Judaism is more than a religion. Yet despite the absence of one approved manner of doing things, there is, I am persuaded, a consensus among most Jews that they are indeed different and somewhat special, a link in a very old chain in a very particular way not often clear to them at all. And rabbis—and this is one of my theses—more than the housewife in Omaha, the Ph.D. in Los Angeles, the poet in New York City, the garment manufacturer in Philadelphia, the retailer in Dallas and the professional Jewish communal worker anywhere, tend to know more, I believe, about Jewish venerable traditions than do most of their co-religionists. As a result, they are vitally important in any future designs to transmit the drama of Judaism than any other segment of the population.

Even so, rabbis are neither more moral nor less fallible than anyone else, neither wiser (except in matters formally Jewish) nor more incisive about how to ensure the safety of Israel or how to extract a greater measure of justice for Jews in the USSR or how to aid the growing number of Jewish poor or how to raise moral consciousness among amoral Jewish businessmen.

Nor have rabbis any more collective or individual sagacity about preventing intermarriage. Estimates vary, but between 1966 and 1972, 31.7 percent of marriages have been with a non-Jewish spouse according to the National Jewish Population Survey. Even rabbinical families are marrying out. The granddaughter of a world-famous religious philosopher married a non-Jew. One rabbi in western Pennsylvania resigned his pulpit after his daughter's marriage to a gentile. "I have failed to preserve Judaism with my own child," he told his congregation in overwhelming sadness. "How then can I presume to try to influence others to stay Jewish?"

Nor are rabbis to be found among the great wielders of political authority. Rabbis Stephen Wise and Abba Hillel Silver may have been the last "superstars." And today, despite their continual complaints at rabbinical conventions and in the Anglo-Jewish press, rabbis tend to be ignored as ineffectual and irrelevant by the more influential Jewish federations that collect and disburse funds and by the national secular agencies, all of which help shape national policies for the many different Jewish communities in America.

In one of the few systematic analyses yet made of internal Jewish politics in any large city, Rabbi Kenneth Roseman looked at Cincinnati's Jewish power structure. He quickly found that rabbis have little or no influence, and that real muscle is exercised by enormously wealthy lay leaders, men "abysmally ignorant of anything but the most elementary information about Jewish history, theology and practice or about the Bible and Hebrew." Concerned with impressing and mollifying the general non-Jewish community, they were—Roseman went on—"genteel, sophisticated and worldly . . . operating with only a minimal regard for the opinion of rabbis."

Cincinnati may not be America, but in the former stronghold of Isaac Mayer Wise, founding father of the Reform movement, where David Philipson once preached his classically Reform sermons at the exclusive and elite Rockdale Temple and where the Hebrew Union College, the major Reform seminary, still dominates, it is a striking indication of the lack of rabbinical community power. The tales of impotence are repeated endlessly at all rabbinical conventions, in their publications and privately.

"When I became a rabbi I found that I was expected to give more than a surface deference to the rich and prosperous leaders of the Jewish community," says Bernard Weinberger, an Orthodox rabbi in Brooklyn's Williamsburg section. "Usually these men had more money than learning." The Jewish establishment—unhappily an ill-defined term— was "dominated by a small aristocracy of rich, peripheral Jews and assimilated Jewishly illiterate [people] who have arrogated to themselves, by virtue of their wealth, the right to speak for the Jewish community."

But speak they do. In 1966, Rabbi Arthur Hertzberg raised the issue. In a thoroughly secular nation, he argued, where most Jews rarely, if ever, attend a synagogue service, "the rabbinate that Jews have known for two millennia ended in America within the last decade." Hertzberg went on to charge that rabbis had let themselves become subordinate to the national organizations, whose own sophistication and effectiveness convinced rabbis that complex matters were better left in their hands. If the rabbi was called on at all, it was to invoke the inevitable benediction or serve as a figurehead. The American rabbi, he concluded, to a wave of indignation, was "neither judge nor leader [but only] the agent of a remaining powerful and pervasive emotion about Jewish togetherness. The purely religious function of the rabbi has been becoming ever more vestigial. . . . He has become peripheral to the major social struggles of this age."

Richard Rubenstein, whose aptly named book *Power Struggle* detailed his own dilemmas, wrote: "Rabbinic authority is often illusory." Serving as the rabbi in Brockton, Massachusetts, he could not denounce the land-developer member who had transformed the bucolic charm of the countryside into ugly, symmetrical housing developments. Another rabbi reported that when he criticized the practices of some landlords and storekeepers in the Black Watts section of Los Angeles, he was given a private dressing down by members of his board, some of whom were slumlords and storekeepers charging inordinately high prices to Black tenants and customers. And in Memphis, Tennessee, following the murder of Martin Luther King, Jr., a storm of disapproval erupted against Rabbi James Wax after he appeared on television to excoriate the mayor and local power brokers for creating the nasty political climate leading to King's death. "My congregation is very liberal," says a Miami area rabbi. "They let me say anything about matters that make no real difference to them. But if I condemn the Mafia and hotel speculators trying to throw the poor out of South Miami some of them let me know I have no right to speak out."

"While I was growing up in Cleveland," says David Polish, now a rabbi in Evanston, Illinois, "the great synagogues or temples were identified as 'Silver's temple,' 'Brickner's temple' and 'Goldman's center.' What happened was that many Jews find synagogue life irrelevant." And, presumably, their rabbis.

Their general role has indeed been drastically altered, says Jacob Neusner, professor of religion at Brown University. Once a "judge, administrator, holy man, scholar and saint," he is now "a medicine man made obsolete by penicillin . . . a surrogate father and God."

A surprising number, perhaps even a majority, feel their roles have been emasculated and their larger influence on Jews curtailed. Serious professionals as a rule, they resent deeply the shift of power to nonreligious agencies and to the wealthy, whom the agencies tend to court.

"Will all those rabbis in this room who are content with their lot please meet me in the phone booth in the hall?" This widely cited, if apocryphal, paraphrase of a remark by a onetime president of the Conservative Rabbinical Assembly is heard often in conversations with rabbis.

"I know we are not happy or content or satisfied at all," said Rabbi Max Routtenberg to the Rabbinical Assembly back in 1960. "Underlying our mighty structure and behind the facade of our prosperity, there is a deep undercurrent, a restiveness and a sense of unfulfillment. There is a mood and a feeling among many of us that our failures center around the issues that concern us most as rabbis and as Jews."

And even more problems.

There is a growing divorce rate among rabbis. Moreover, some wives speak of other aspects of their husbands' tensions and unrelieved anxieties, of adultery and mental upsets, of stormy domestic battles, or acrimonious struggles with congregants. There are neither statistics nor studies, but the tales are there, endlessly repeated.

"When my husband tried to get an insurance policy," a young rabbinical wife said, "one that would include psychiatric therapy, the agent told him it would be terribly expensive. Rabbis, or so he told Bill, have a very high incidence of mental illness. I don't know if that's so" (the agent later told me he had no statistical evidence, only a "gut feeling" that more rabbis seek help than their peers in other jobs), "but I do know it *sounded* right." Surprisingly, other women echoed her view.

But—and it is a very significant but—this is not the

whole story. I am reminded of the words of the talmudic scholar and iconoclast Trude Weiss-Rosmarin, mocking those who bemoaned the loss of rabbinic authority: "Honor flees its pursuers." And to those who belittled the role of the rabbi she argued that the reverse was true. In most communities the rabbi is the only scholar of Judaica, the only teacher and pastor, "the principal pillar of Jewish survival strength in this country."

Above all else, the lesser-known as well as the well-known rabbis are involved with their congregations and the people they have to deal with on a daily basis. Preaching, counseling, reviewing books, publishing at times in the Jewish book houses such as Bloch, Behrman House, Feldheim, Hebrew, the Jewish Publication Society, Ktav, Jonathan David and Schocken, a few even with big commercial publishers, 3,000 rabbis are on the job, their effectiveness ranging from mediocre to excellent, the size of their congregations varying from a handful to several thousand. From a tiny shul in a small midwestern town to Temple Emanu-El in New York City, from a makeshift minyan in the Rockies to the elegant ceremonies of Beverly Hills, indeed everywhere that Jews live together there are rabbis: permanent or student or merely visiting.

Everywhere—even in the VA hospital where Herman Grossman has been stationed after eight years in a Pottstown, Pennsylvania, synagogue. "I spent deliriously happy years in Pottstown before I came to the VA in Northport [N.Y.]. My years here, however, have been most rewarding."

Does he ever get depressed with his surroundings?

"My answer is no. Perhaps each day I can help someone to find something worth living for. It isn't easy. But somehow, 'He answered me and set me free' can help a person here."

2. The Seminarians

Not far from the Jaffa Gate of Jerusalem's Old City and just down the broad avenue from the King David Hotel stands a white stone building, its marblelike facade gleaming in the sun much as a Middle Eastern royal palace. This splendiferous setting is the home away from home of the Hebrew Union College–Jewish Institute of Religion. HUC Reform seminarians now spend a mandatory first year in Israel, a dual irony indeed. Dual, because much of the Reform rabbinate rejected Zionism until news leaked out of Hitler's slaughters and because the obscurantist Orthodox rabbinate in Israel today tries very hard to make life terribly difficult for Reform and Conservative Judaism and is reluctant to accept their converts, often refusing to consider them as genuinely Jewish.

Rene is from Brazil and a graduate of the Conservative Jewish Theological Seminary. He has lived in Argentina and Brazil, and for him Israel is merely one more stop in the continuing effort of Jews to live in peace. He is pleased, he says, with the quality of HUC's faculty and thinks its curriculum excellent. At the JTS, he says, discussion of the

Mishnah at dinner was common. All the same, he is satisfied with the possibilities of being a Reform rabbi, even if he believes many of his fellow students are too self-conscious about their lack of scholarship in rabbinics. HUC will give him the knowledge he thinks he will need to become a successful congregation rabbi, something he believes the JTS did not. "I'm not here at HUC to become a talmudic hakham. I'm here to get what I couldn't get elsewhere. The practical side. I'm here so one day I can serve a Jewish community in America."

A Chicago rabbi once told him that Israel was impermanent and that rabbis, as all Jews, had to learn to deal with the larger question of what might happen to Judaism should Israel ever cease to exist. Older than most seminarians, Rene was reminded of the saintly Leo Baeck, Berlin's last rabbi, who outlived a concentration camp. "As Leo Baeck did then, we'll have to be the leaders who will preserve it in the States."

He is also impressed with what he sees as the special, even awesome, responsibilities of the rabbinate. "I was in Chile during Allende's presidency. If I were a rabbi in Santiago then, would I have dared advise Jews to leave? In Argentina, would I suggest exile today? Düsseldorf in Germany now needs a rabbi. In *that* country? Yet someone has to serve."

In speaking with the young rabbis-to-be, two impressions quickly emerge. They are naïve, untested, not yet cynical; they still have high ideals, are optimistic and ebullient, quick and bright and vigorous, a mirror of the best in Jewish life. The temptations of moral corruption have not yet been met. And having to live and wander and study in Israel they benefit enormously from their temporary exclusion from Reform's campuses in New York City, Cincinnati and Los Angeles, with their obligatory obsessions with textual criticism. In Israel the students are forced to live with their common past and to try to understand it.

"I'm alive here, I feel a full, free Jewish consciousness," says Yossi, who grew up in Los Angeles. "I have no Jewish guilt. None whatever."

He and his wife attended Brandeis Camp in California and say they always thought of themselves as Jewish, but in substance rather than in style. "At Northridge, three years ago, a rabbi told me that all study of the Talmud's tractates was unnecessary. *His* concern was fulfilling the needs of his members, whatever those needs were. And *their* concerns were 'Rabbi, what should we name the baby?' or 'Rabbi, when is the next young couples' social?' I want to be a rabbi because I want to make clear to people what is right and wrong with tradition and then help them accept a moral road. Only I'm a little scared of the responsibility that entails."

"I grew up near Los Angeles," says Janet, "where we belonged to a Conservative synagogue in Santa Cruz and lived in Tarzana. My family and their friends knew all the forms but not the content. I'm hoping people will not grow up 'Jewish' as I did. Back home I thought of myself as a modern, dedicated Jew. Here in Israel, I'm an ignoramus. I want to help bridge that tremendous gap. Something has to be done to educate American Jews in Jewishness."

"The rabbi," says Robert, also a native Californian, "does all I want to do with my life."

He explains that he had no rabbinical role model in mind when he applied for HUC, since his family could not afford to join a temple; nor, in fact, were they even observant Jews. His own wife was a Baptist convert, and his decision to consider the rabbinate seriously was a great shock to her. When they first met, he recalls, he was on the brink of entering a Christian seminary, since he considered the historical Jesus an ideal worth emulating. More important though, he suddenly, almost unexpectedly, came upon the Holocaust. He wrote a paper on the subject, and the reading he had to do was an overwhelming, life-shaking experience.

"Being in Israel as a rabbinical student can't be matched anywhere else in the world, in time or place," he says. "Where else could I visit regularly with Reb Hirsch of the Naturei Karta in the Mea Shearim? One day I got up the nerve to ask him about the Holocaust. Why? I wanted to know. He answered simply: 'It was God's punishment.' But he was wrong. My answer would be 'Jewish ignorance.' "

Alan, born in Cincinnati, attends the JTS and expects to be ordained in 1977. Reared as a Conservative, he had been active in synagogue programs, but his passions remained secular, all the more so when he entered the University of Cincinnati as a premed student. But his outlook began changing, slowly.

"I finally began the process," he says, "of discovering what I wanted for myself, rather than what others wanted for me." He switched his major from premed to psychology. He revisited his local rabbi and joined actively in the synagogue, leading adult education sessions, holding morning and evening prayer sessions with college students and giving bar mitzvah lessons. Gradually he learned the life he had thrust himself into was a good one. But not without the inevitable tensions. "Over this long period of time I was coming to view my American nature as my temporal or secondary state and my Jewishness as my fundamental or primary state." Shortly thereafter, with a bachelor's degree in psychology from the University of Cincinnati, he enrolled at the Jewish Theological Seminary.

As a Jew from the Midwest who wants to return to that region, Alan believes his responsibilities are somewhat special. It is not so easy to observe the laws of *kashrut* there. Jews also lack the feeling of being a potent minority which they have in the Northeast. When a rabbi chooses a congregation in Middle America, he often comes to serve a wide geographic area. "Your library becomes *the* Jewish library. It has to be complete and good." He gestured toward the bookshelves in his room. "Thus, it's vitally important that I know the texts to the best of my ability. I've got to be able to give my congregation what they cannot get elsewhere."

Ben and Michael are upperclassmen at the JTS. Their motives are hardly novel. The first wants to "help maintain Jewish life," the second, "the chance to transmit Torah scholarship." But they have mixed feelings about their school: respect and affection but also a certainty that the courses were too often dull; the practical aspects of being a rabbi were largely overlooked. Ben thought the exclusion of women from the rabbinate unjust, even cruel.

At Yeshiva University's Rabbi Isaac Elchanan Theological Seminary—patterned originally after European yeshivot where ordination was secondary to learning—nearly half the students declared in a mid-1960s survey that their preparation was inadequate, especially in respect to questions dealing with halakha, the Torah and the prophetic tradition. Their complaints were hardly new. The school underwent an unsuccessful upheaval as far back as 1908, when students demanded a broader cultural curriculum to supplement talmudic studies and to better prepare them to be pulpit rabbis.

So it has always gone. Rabbinical students are no more stable or sober than their peers in secular settings. Perhaps less so. Aside from the usual crises of personal growth, rabbinical students often have to pass through the turmoil of doubt about their faith, their God, their profession. Others are bothered by the endemically low esteem in which some Jews hold the rabbinate. Others are stunned by their initial experiences with the world off the campus.

Larry—a pseudonym—was sent by the JTS to a New England small town as a part-time student rabbi for the Rosh

Hashanah and Yom Kippur holidays and occasional weekends. It was a chance to get in touch with a life he had long yearned for, a good way, he thought, to get a little work experience. He was soon appalled as he discovered— bitterly, since his youthful idealism left little room for nuances or exceptions—that his congregants were narrow and bigoted in their attitudes and interests, "indifferent to religious values, hypocritical, venal." The town's eighteen Jewish families were all wealthy and politically conservative, while he was lower-middle-class and liberal, if not radical. They were blasé about Judaism while he was passionately involved in it. They praised Israel with fervor, but only that country's hard-line right-wing hawks. Yet they would never encourage their young to settle in Israel. Larry was a pacifist and a dove; he had spent nearly two years on a left-wing Mapam kibbutz and dreamed of returning to live there. *They* also rendered lip service to the cause of Soviet Jews, but not one in a community of prosperous businessmen offered to place a Russian Jewish family in a home and a job of promise. "I left, thinking that for that crowd conversions would be good for the Jews."

An excellent and systematic study on the seminarian was conducted by Norman Mirsky, himself a rabbi and sociologist on the HUC faculty in Los Angeles. Looking carefully at the students he met in the late 1960s at HUC, Mirsky found one contradiction after another: middle-class youngsters thrust into an upper-class setting; textual criticism dominating the curriculum instead of such prerequisites for the contemporary rabbinate as "skills in administration, public relations, psychological counseling, public speaking, journalism, and the social graces." The school, he went on, created "friction and tension," factors hardly conducive to producing "spiritual leaders."

The HUC faculty members, largely foreign-born, were

reared in Orthodox families and considered their students (who continually raised questions about rabbinical legitimacy, authenticity and authority) theological innocents. Halakha was not observed. The cuisine was anything but kosher. Yarmulkas and *taleysim* were shunned. Chanting while praying was considered boorish. Mirsky found the sons of four Conservative rabbis struggling "with what they feel is an attempt on the part of the school to make them into goyim." They tried to eat kosher food and set up more traditional religious ceremonies.

Mirsky developed a typology of HUC students. He separated them into the Careerist, who views his stay at school as a minor inconvenience to be suffered easily as a prerequisite for becoming a pulpit rabbi; the Scholar, who becomes infected by textual scholarship and decides to spend the remainder of his life teaching and studying Judaism; the Student of the Middle Range, "who comes to the school somewhat lost and who goes through the most changes of ideology, is most vulnerable to either the immediate gratification or the immediate rejection of experience with faculty, with administration, with congregants." Half of all students fall into this category: "It is they for whom the experience at HUC is most devastating because it is upon them that the conflicts in the school, in American Judaism and in the individual psyches of faculty members and fellow students take their toll."

Marshall was born in a large state into an upper-middle-class family. His parents were not originally Reform, but somehow his father became involved in a building campaign and thereafter joined a temple. He was not an especially good student but did excel in Sunday school, later becoming active in temple youth groups and then pursuing his interests in a private university. His goal was to be a professor of history, but his average was only 2.5. Following graduation he applied to Yale and Harvard (rejected by both), Michigan (accepted with a tuition scholarship in international relations) and HUC.

At HUC his career was considered spectacular, and he was thought of as a "Scholar." Still, he read little (*Newsweek* and *Time*) and had few outside interests; most painful for him was that he could not deliver a sermon adequately. One day he cried in an adviser's office. A sermon? Yet so serious a flaw was this considered by the academics on campus that he began to lose face and soon gave up the rabbinate.

Gregory came from a midwestern city, the only child of a stormy marriage. His mother was a schoolteacher and his father the owner of a women's specialty shop. "He hated everything about religion," said Gregory, "probably because of his father's ultra-Orthodoxy."

At first Gregory attended church Sunday school, where he was enthralled by Jesus and such Christian symbols as the crucifix and rosaries. He also loved, he said, the "illicit" appeal of those symbols. In guilt, he returned time and again to the Christian textbook *One God: The Ways We Worship Him* and its segments about Judaism. "I was," he confessed, "a real Sunday school freak."

Gregory's family moved and his mother finally joined a Reform temple, enrolling him in its school. She claimed it was better than his previous one, but Gregory had his doubts. "I suspect it had a higher social status. My mother has always been a bit of a social climber."

He was a faithful pupil and decided early on (actually, inexplicably) to enter the rabbinate. "Everybody in the family predicted I was going to be a rabbi and everybody more or less encouraged me, though I suspect now they thought it a bit odd or cute."

Eventually, after a creditable four years at a good university, Gregory entered HUC, although he refused to tell

Mirsky why he had done so. He came to HUC, commented Mirsky in an aside, "neither believing in God nor desiring to be a pulpit rabbi, though he did feel an attachment to the Jewish people and Jewish history." Unlike Marshall, he shone at chapel sermon and played the role of rabbi, wearing his robe like an actor in a stage play. But when the time came for him to accept a congregation, he backed away. He was unprepared, he felt, to accept it as a career. When Mirsky saw him last he was trying to compromise, serving as an assistant rabbi while matriculating as a graduate student in sociology.

In their final student years, seminarians undergo their initial experience as student rabbis in small-town America, where the Jewish population is often fewer than seventy-five families. There they experience a glimpse of their futures: a woman in West Virginia who wanted to convert to Judaism but was really insane; a first funeral to perform; a family to console whose child had died of leukemia; a decision to marry or not marry a Jewish young man and his Congregationalist fiancée; the sharp recognition that in small towns Jews are isolated *as Jews*.

The High Holy Days are *the* event upon which Jews depend "to reassess and reaffirm [their] position as a community. It is the time for collecting money for services, to take an informal census of who does and who does not wish to be counted among the Jews of X-ville, Texas, or Y-ville, Kentucky," according to Mirsky. For student rabbis, it can be a foretaste of an ennobling, if often frustrating, role as a full-fledged rabbi. They become the center of the stage for isolated Jews in America's tiny settlements and "the principal figure for celebration"; a means of entertaining small-town Jewish women; a freak or invalid, treated (say some student rabbis with annoyance) by men as though they were women. "They help me on and off with my coat,"

said one, "open doors for me, but especially they watch
their language in front of me."

Twenty-six Conservative rabbinical students graduated
from the JTS in 1975, granted diplomas ordaining them as
"rabbis, teachers and preachers." Across town, in Temple
Emanu-El, seventeen HUC-JIR Reform rabbis were ordained before 2,000 onlookers. Together with their peers in
the other rabbinical schools in the country, they were now
on the job market.

Each branch of Judaism maintains its own placement
bureau. The JTS placed fourteen of the graduates of its
1975 class, the remainder choosing other fields instead. The
year before the JTS had found jobs for eighty-four rabbis,
several in Canada, one in the West Indies, another in
Curaçao and the rest in the United States. Seven became
educational directors in larger congregations, three became
military chaplains, one went with the Veterans Administration and another became director of a summer camp.

The old way of placing job-hunting rabbis was personal
contact and knowing the right people. "We are dealing with
the careers of 160 men," said Louis Finklestein, then
chancellor of the JTS, in 1929; "two or three times as many
congregations, an annual salary of close to a million—that's
business that cannot be attended to in the Seminary hall-
ways between classes." Nearly fifty years later the stakes
are vastly greater.

According to Rabbi David H. Panitz of Temple Emanuel
in Paterson, New Jersey, head of the Conservatives' Placement Commission, there are "800 Conservative congregations and 870 living graduates of the JTS, among our 1,100
members. With nearly a hundred of our members now in
Israel, others occupied with full-time academic positions
and still others retired, we don't have enough Rabbinical
Assembly members to fill the requests handed to us." Thus,

Reform and Orthodox rabbis are also solicited—via their own placement commissions—to help fill Conservative synagogue vacancies.*

"We're a professional group. We have standards, rules and regulations. A rabbinical change can start in one of several ways. The congregation approaches our Placement Commission with a request. Rabbis notify us of their desire to make a change. Also, deaths and resignations present obvious placement needs.

"When a congregation seeks a new rabbi or assistant, the chairman of its placement committee gets in touch with the placement director. First, we look into the situation; if there is an incumbent rabbi, does he know that a replacement is sought for him? Does the rabbi seeking a change notify his congregation of his desire?

"Periodically, we send out lists to our member rabbis informing them of possible openings. We also send a questionnaire to the requesting congregations asking them for information that would help rabbis in deciding whether they are interested in being considered. After all, we are not a hierarchy; we do not assign rabbis to congregations, or congregations to rabbis. Basically, we try to match the proper rabbi to the proper post.

"First," he said, "there are a number of questions about the congregation, about its size, its physical facilities, its budget, its religious school, and the standards for its teachers. The religious school is very important to our Jewish way of life, and the rabbi is deeply concerned about it. Does the school have an educational director or a full-time principal? Are teachers paid or are they volunteers?

---

* According to Wolfe Kelman, executive director of the Rabbinical Assembly, the post–World War II expansion caught the JTS short; by 1976, however, attrition and the growth of Conservatism meant that even hard-to-fill pulpits were able to choose among young rabbis.

How many hours of study a week are required for students, and so forth.

"Then," Rabbi Panitz went on, "there are a number of questions about the service. How traditional is it? Is there a cantor, a choir? Is an organ used at services? What is the average attendance . . . for Friday evening services . . . for the Sabbath service? Is there a daily minyan, and when is it held, mornings, evenings, or both? Does the congregation have a Sisterhood, a Men's Club, and how large are they? What is the youth program? Is it affiliated with the United Synagogue Youth? After all, a rabbi can only be happy, and keep his congregants happy, if there is a basic meeting of the minds.

"There are also a number of questions of personal concern to the rabbi and his family. Some rabbis won't accept a post in a community where there isn't a day school for his own children to attend. Others are interested in the universities and colleges in or near the community. What are the housing arrangements for the rabbi, and if housing is provided, how far is it from the synagogue? And finally, of course, there are questions about the proposed salary, fringe benefits and the like."

Then the Placement Commission begins its real job: matching the rabbi to the position. The commission sends a list of prospective applicants with whom the congregation can set up appointments.

"Of course," Rabbi Panitz said, "there are personal checkups by both the congregation and the rabbis. Does the congregation change its rabbi every few years? Similarly, is the rabbi overly restless? Congregational committee members may sometimes visit the applying rabbi's current congregation. Rabbis may be invited to deliver a sermon. From all this give-and-take, a *shiddach* [literally, betrothal] is made. And it's remarkable how successful the process is. For aside from the normal movements of the young rabbi from the very small congregation on to the larger one, as he gets more experience, or from an assistantship to a senior rabbinical post, turnover is comparatively small."

Rabbi Malcolm Stern, Reform's counterpart in placement, says one of his biggest headaches is that more congregations today are stressing youth rather than experience, thereby shrinking the openings for men who have spent many years in the pulpit. But he has other problems, such as too many Reform rabbis and too few jobs available.

In fact, Reform Judaism *seems* to be growing in the United States, at least in terms of its synagogue membership, up 2 percent in 1975 as compared to 1973. The NJPS reported in 1972 that while Conservative Judaism had the most adherents in this country (40.5 percent of heads of households), Reform followed with 30 percent and the Orthodox with only 12.2 percent. Still, there are problems. Rabbi Alexander Schindler, president of the Union of American Hebrew Congregations, the parent Reform organization, recently predicted that Reform would see fifty new temples by 1980. He drew upon the national population study, in which 1.6 million Jews described themselves as Reform (Schindler noted that only 1.1 million were officially temple members). But a UAHC report issued in June 1975 was more pessimistic, at least in the short run. It cited curtailed temple budgets, personnel cuts and restricted programs. Other Reform officials, such as Rabbi Stern, have wondered whether the rabbinate isn't "close to saturation." The population is at a standstill, and rabbis are not retiring in numbers large enough to maintain job openings for Reform's 700 temples. Younger rabbis as well as those in the seminary are worried. Says Stern: "Unless and until the economy improves we are going to be facing a declining job market."

No doubt the entry of females into the rabbinate will also increase the competition. Stern must also contend with the feeling that screening of candidates is resented deeply by rabbis who believe they have been bypassed for choice locations. His answer is that the process of selection tends to mitigate against that sort of inequity. In any typical instance, he says, more than ten applicants, selected on the basis of seniority, are sent to congregations looking for a rabbi. "They make the choice; we do not sit in moral judgment on others."

Obviously the system of finding jobs is not without its traps. "Those kingmakers in New York have screwed me out of my life's work and hurt my family," charged a southern rabbi. "Organization men," sneered Arthur Hertzberg in 1966, "seem to get the best assignments."

The charges were denounced as "unbalanced, bitter and destructive" by Rabbi Max Routtenberg, then president of the Conservative rabbinical group. And editor and talmudist Trude Weiss-Rosmarin, American Jewry's gadfly, praised the Conservatives for "bringing order, dignity and decency to the placement of rabbis."

But a Conservative-appointed study group found criticism widespread among its rabbinate: "lack of interest . . . impersonality . . . no support of colleagues . . . placement haphazard, unimaginative, frozen . . . a haunting sense of personal insecurity blights the rabbi's life."

"They really control our lives, censuring the troublemakers and rewarding the ass-kissers," says one Reform rabbi who has had a medium-sized pulpit for nearly a decade in a mid-western state. "It wouldn't be above the brass in Cincinnati and New York to try to hurt me in some way if they knew I said this about them. I suppose they really do mean well, but the system is corrupt and it can reflect on those who make the decisions."

There are four categories of placement in Reform: A, for newly ordained rabbis, congregations under 125 families; B, at least three years' experience, 250 families; C, the same three years' experience, but with congregations greater than 600 families; and D, more than ten years' service, with no limit to member families. Obviously, the higher the category the more money, fringe benefits and lifetime tenure contracts.

Recent Reform placement newsletters listed both Reform and Conservative openings in Anchorage, Alaska (40 families), Asheville, North Carolina (120 families), Waterloo, Iowa (120 families), and Barranquilla, Colombia (150 families), together with want ads from Düsseldorf, Cape Town, Johannesburg, São Paulo, Chicago and St. Paul.

Orthodox seminaries have their own placement centers and share virtually identical complaints and praises. For every critical rabbi-to-be there seems to be someone who is overjoyed with his newfound congregation.

In view of the tightening job market for rabbis, why don't most try to find positions on their own? "You simply can't free-lance in job hunting," says another rabbi. "The penalty would be getting dumped from the CCAR, loss of rights, pensions and the like. [Rabbi Michael Sternfield of San Diego was expelled from the CCAR in 1976 for disobeying a Placement Commission rule stipulating that Reform rabbis must have been ordained for so many years before accepting a major pulpit.] The CCAR is a trade association for rabbis. So the price would be too high to pay. Besides, I think Placement does a damned good job in matching the right temple with the right rabbi."

Jobs can be sought in other ways. Each issue of the *National Jewish Post* and *Jewish Press* carries want ads. When a congregation in Midland, Michigan, failed to renew its rabbi's contract, a *Post* ad drew twelve applicants the first week. By the second week the number had doubled. And there are free-lancers, those who eschew permanent pulpits and instead concentrate on performing weddings, funerals and dedicating cemetery monuments. Some perform circumcisions. Few if any display any communal responsibility. "I am," said one, "in business for myself."

But for the young especially, the first pulpit is an exhilarating experience. "I'm deriving more satisfaction from my pulpit work than I ever believed was possible," said a new rabbi in Upper Nyack, New York. "This is a pretty good job for a Jewish boy."

3. Suburban Activist

On a cold December evening Temple Beth-El in Great Neck, New York, invited 1,300 townspeople to its lavishly appointed reception hall, where bar and bat mitzvahs, weddings and a myriad of other affairs were normally held. Hundreds of residents had to be turned away that night. Effusively, emotionally, a town weekly—there are two—described the event as the "largest sit-down dinner ever held on the peninsula, the quintessence of togetherness; an uplifting moment in an otherwise despairing and disheartening episode; a triumph of commitment and determination over logistical odds; a bridging of generations . . . the happiest Bar Mitzvah you ever attended . . . a Great Neck version of the Woodstock version." The diners paid $12.50 each as a declaration of support for the school superintendent who was the subject of an effort by the local school board majority to fire him.

In any event, it was not the extravagance of the affair, nor the reasons for its setting, that explained Rabbi Jerome K. Davidson's pleasure as he sat with the rector of a local Episcopalian church. Davidson had turned his temple over to the impassioned volunteers for "Mort" (Morton Abramowitz, the superintendent), those who wanted to take sides in an acrimonious dispute that was becoming ugly, even for Great Neck. Davidson had always been an "activist" rabbi anyway, against the war in Southeast Asia, supportive of the community's Blacks, interested above all in the humane possibilities of human beings and their institutions.

"It's the way I feel, the way I believe," he explained one afternoon as he maneuvered his automobile through the back streets of the borough of Queens en route to a meeting at the Central Conference of American Rabbis. "I have never believed that a temple's concerns are limited solely by its special interests. What happens elsewhere," he said, as his auto finally reached the end of the 59th Street Bridge and entered Manhattan, "also affects Jewish life in this town and in this country. No doubt about that."

The next month, as on many previous occasions, Rabbi Davidson was out in the rain speaking in the Grace Avenue Park (a parcel of green not far from the town's shopping district), where 1,000 youngsters from the four secondary schools had marched to protest what they understood to be the harassment of the school superintendent.

"Who's Next?" "Shame on Nina" (a reference to the then board president, anti-Abramowitz Nina Taft), "Save Our Schools" signs dotted the crowd of students. Guitar-strummers played "We Shall Overcome," and students with clenched fists and bullhorns roared approval at Davidson's affirmation of support for the superintendent.

There was an element of irony in this school conflict. For years Great Neck, while home to wealthy Jews, had followed a deliberate pattern of discrimination against Jews. Virtually no Jewish schoolteachers were employed until the postwar boom brought in large numbers of Jews from New York City. There were no Jewish principals or administrators, let alone board members. "And yet," remarked Harold

Applebaum, then Long Island area director for the American Jewish Committee and a close observer of developments within the town, "the first time they ever got a school superintendent who was Jewish, three board members—like Abramowitz every one a Jew—tried their best to have him disgraced and fired." Said another observer who had watched a similar occurrence in a suburb halfway between Boston and Providence: "Naturally, Jews in the suburbs who have come to dominate with their presence seem to spend their time struggling with each other over a million concerns, few of them specifically Jewish but camouflaged, really, as in the 'Jewish interest,' whatever that means. Their relations with non-Jews, who tried their darndest to keep them out, are cool and distant, if superficially warm. Formal too. No gentile in a Jewish suburb would ever dream of attacking Jews. Nor for that matter would a Jew take them on. So each fight their own, with all the anger and contempt they once reserved for outsiders."

According to a locally produced history, a "prosperous" farming community called Great Neck—founded in 1696—was initially settled by Indians and afterward by the Dutch in the early eighteenth century. Walter P. Chrysler lived there and bequeathed his magnificent estate to the United States Merchant Marine Academy in King's Point (one of the many incorporated villages within Great Neck, its median income in 1975 was $40,791 annually). The extraordinarily wealthy Phipps family gave its lands in Great Neck to the public schools. The Ring Lardners lived on East Shore Road, and F. Scott and Zelda Fitzgerald on Gateway Drive (Fitzgerald's Egg Harbor in *The Great Gatsby* was, of course, Great Neck). Eddie Cantor lived there, as did Ernest Truex, Groucho Marx, George M. Cohan, Ed Wynn, Fredric March, Leslie Howard, Martha Raye, Lillian Russell, Maurice Chevalier, Herbert Bayard Swope, Oscar

Hammerstein II, P. G. Wodehouse, Will Durant and the unflappable W. C. Fields, who delighted in taunting his neighbors by practicing golf on his front lawn.

The United Nations was first housed in the town's Sperry Building at Lake Success (also an incorporated village) from 1945 until 1950, bringing in its wake the earliest political demonstrations and the only attempted aerial bombing.

The Metropolitan Opera's great tenor, Richard Tucker, who belonged to an Orthodox synagogue, was a resident until his sudden death in 1975. Today the comedian Alan King lives there, as do former Yankee left-hander Whitey Ford, composers Peter Nero and Morton Gould, Sol Chaikin and Gus Tyler of the International Ladies Garment Workers Union, folksinger Oscar Brand, Herbert Mitgang of the *New York Times*, the industrialist Saul Steinberg, Federal Judge Jack Weinstein, Arthur Krim of United Artists and 44,000 others—manufacturers, television producers, editors, salesmen, professors, college presidents, lawyers, stockbrokers, publishers, retailers, teachers, social workers, and a superabundance of doctors, dentists, therapists and analysts. Nearly 59 percent of the heads of households are college graduates. They are also predominantly Jewish, perhaps as many as 65 percent of the total population.

Great Neck is not really a town but a cluster of self-governing villages and unincorporated neighborhoods that borders eastern Queens and follows along the neck of a peninsula to Manhasset Bay, an arm of Long Island Sound. It is more properly a park district (dedicated to recreation and leisure) and school district (certainly among the finest in the nation, despite the endemic civil strife) and library district (amply stocked, extensively used, so well-supported financially that the townspeople have never rejected its budget). It is also politically liberal, having supported Eugene McCarthy in 1968 and George McGovern in 1972.

And in 1976, in spite of hawkish Henry Jackson's "Jewish" campaign in the Democratic presidential primary, Great Neck Democrats voted for dovish Morris Udall in the primary, and Jimmy Carter in the general election.

Great Neck has, moreover, a Long Island Railroad depot, two post offices, four bookstores, a symphony orchestra, at least four theater groups, easy arterial access to midtown Manhattan (15.7 miles away), two kinds of Blacks (very rich and very poor), one Catholic church, one Baptist, one Christian Science, three Episcopalian, one interdenominational, one Mormon (actually, just over the city line), two Methodist (one, a Black church), one Presbyterian, two Lutheran, one Unitarian—and seven synagogues, with three more within walking distance, just across the city line. Of the seven synagogues in Great Neck proper, two are Orthodox, two Conservative and three Reform.

Why so many synagogues when most of the Jews belong to none? Status is important, as are age, family tradition, aspirations, and the degree of acculturation. The personality of the rabbi may also be a factor. Groups have broken away from synagogues because of a variety of differences. Fees may be too high for some. The quality of the Hebrew schools is a factor, along with social activism or the lack of it. For whatever reason, membership in a Reform temple in Little Neck, in New York City, does not seem to be as prestigious as membership in Davidson's Beth-El. "At least in Great Neck," said a father who had just seen his son confirmed in Temple Beth-El and who himself had passed through the same ritual in the same temple thirty years earlier, "we sort of inherited and grew up with our temples. Not like the newer, postwar suburbs which had to struggle."

Beth-El was established in 1928 and properly financed by its affluent members almost from the start. Jews in other communities, possibly less than a thirty-minute drive away, were less rich and less supportive. In Herbert J.

Gans' pioneering *The Levittowners* we have a compelling portrait by a trained sociologist (as well as a participant-observer) of those early struggles.

"Clearly the Jews—Reform and Conservative alike—sought a subcommunity rather than a religious congregation. They wanted to be Jews (and to be with Jews) and they wanted their children to learn Jewish culture patterns which parents themselves were neither willing nor able to teach them at home, but they did not want to attend services, except at the 'High Holidays.' "

And their rabbis?

They were somehow, in some way, to prevent the young from marrying non-Jews and to uphold Jewishness—always fuzzily, badly defined—among the settlers. A Conservative layman told Gans, "I work on Saturdays, and I eat ham, but I want my rabbi to walk to the synagogue and keep kosher. My children are growing up here, and I want a traditional environment for them so that when they are about 17, they can choose for themselves."

The search for the Levittowners' first rabbi produced conflict. The "scholar" they hired could not bring in new members or donations. His replacement, a "go-getter," did. But he also allowed nonkosher food at synagogue social affairs because it was less expensive and was not "dismayed" at "poor attendance at Friday night services." More privately, he satisfied his own religious needs by meeting for daily services with a few Orthodox Jews.

Two Great Neck residents read the Gans passages and one said quickly that it reflected the town's population and rabbis "to a tee." The other, just as definitively, shook his head and disagreed. "We're different," he said.

Beth-El, a Reform temple, the oldest synagogue in town, stands like a fortress on Great Neck's Middle Neck and Old Mill roads, its windowless stone walls dominating the immediate neighborhood, resembling more the seventeenth-century Polish shul which was designed to repel potential pogromists than the contemporary architecture favored by most temples. But if the exterior is forbidding, even frigid, the opposite is true inside the building. One morning in early winter a Hanukah show for preschoolers had just ended, and the halls were filled with their high voices and excited chatter. An adolescent stood next to Stephen Pinsky (who later became a senior rabbi in New Jersey), Davidson's assistant rabbi, talking quietly but intensely to him. ("He's a living doll," one of the secretaries cooed about Pinsky. "You should see how he gets along with the kids.") Not far away some women, chic in dungarees or slacks, were laughing aloud. They were planning a cantata for a Sunday evening.

In the coming months Beth-El would schedule a plethora of activities: guest speakers such as Shulamit Aloni, head of Israel's Civil Rights Party, member of the Knesset and an articulate critic of Israel's ruling Labor Party; Rabbi Gunther Plaut of Toronto's Holy Blossom Temple, who spoke on "ambiguities in Reform"; Father Edward Flannery, a Catholic specialist on Christian anti-Semitism. There were other activities: brotherhood breakfasts on Sunday morning which drew hundreds to Davidson's talks on biblical history; a Purim Megillah service featuring a symposium on "Our Violent Society," bar and bat mitzvahs, couples nights, singles nights, adult and adolescent classes, the regular Hebrew school, and fourth- and fifth-grade religious services.

And on Shavuot (or the Feast of Weeks, marking the giving of the Ten Commandments), a warm and sunny day in May, 83 tenth-graders, generally sixteen-year-olds, almost equally divided into 42 boys and 41 girls (8 of whose parents had been confirmed themselves in Beth-El some thirty years before), were confirmed according to the Reform tradition. The 900-seat sanctuary was filled to capacity, and latecomers were required to wait in the outer lobby. As the youngsters made ready to file into the hall where their families sat, both rabbis urged them—there was an air of tension and excitement in their tones—to think about the meaning of the service to follow and about the sentiments of a cantata the students had written collectively, not merely the words. Pinsky added, less relevantly if reverently, "Don't put your prayer book on the floor *ever*. It's a matter of respect."

Inside the sanctuary, Davidson's voice was strong in the flat nasality he had inherited from his native Kansas City. And the eighty-three sang and spoke their "Alone and Together," a presentation that began with Abraham venturing out from Beersheba, moved on to "Try to Remember," a popular song from the show *The Fantasticks*, to quotations from Robert Frost, Bob Dylan, Rabbi Abba Hillel Silver and the Hebrew poet Saul Chernichovsky, to condemnation of American actions in Cambodia and Vietnam, to Ellis Island, to Bergen-Belsen and to Ma'alot, where Israeli students died in a shoot-out between Palestinian terrorists and government troops in a high school in 1974.

"What has all of this to do with Abraham and Moses, with the Jewish people's past?" they asked, in unison. And the reply: "Our people's history has given us strength. . . . How can we recall the dark years of persecution, crusades, the Inquisition, pogroms, and not pledge ourselves to the dignity and sanctity of human life?" They repeated the poet Abraham Shlonsky's words, "I have taken an oath: To remember it all, to remember, not once to forget."

Like virtually all Reform rabbis today, Jerome K. Davidson is a graduate of the Hebrew Union College–Jewish Institute of Religion, a seminary established in Cincinnati by Isaac Mayer Wise and merged after World War I with Stephen Wise's JIR in New York City. Davidson, who attended the Ohio campus, is in his early forties, quite good-looking, medium in build, dark-haired, a tennis buff, father of two small children. His wife Gail is working for a doctorate in art history at Harvard University, a distinct departure from the stereotype of the *rebbitzin* or rabbi's wife.

Davidson, who has been in Great Neck since 1961, is exceptionally well liked by his congregants, at ease especially with the duality of social concern and material satisfactions he and they evidently share, young enough and "American" enough to advance Reform's uniqueness and sufficiently eloquent and respectable to represent his congregants to the non-Jewish world. He has earned their overwhelming and continuing favor in spite of his frequent forays into issues outside his synagogue.

Beth-El has 1,300 families on its membership rolls who pay average annual dues of $450 and who are, more often than not, highly educated, ambitious for themselves and their young, and supportive of Reform. Speaking with many of his congregants reveals how highly they think of him. A few—indeed, very, very few—find his actions somewhat troubling. "Why" asked one, "does he always get into issues that have nothing to do with Jews?" Still, most of the others disagree. A lawyer who is employed by a publisher of scientific texts said she would always remember Davidson's Rosh Hashanah sermon on the implications of God and personal belief. "I'm not at all sure I understood him or even came away believing in a personal God. But *nobody* had ever raised the subject before in my hearing, and *nobody* had ever talked that honestly to me about something I think crucial." Afterward, thinking about the sermon and its ramifications, Davidson mused, "I thought I laid a bomb. But people are searching for faith, for renewing their search for faith. I was very much afraid to talk about God, but it elicited a great response. For weeks after my phone rang."

He is, as a rabbi, far more than a preacher and organizer of programs in the temple. He is always on call, for weddings and funerals (funerals are very hard for him he says), unveilings (of cemetery memorial stones, usually one year after death) and counseling, and for those who simply need to talk to someone with some knowledge and some appearance of authority. One Sunday in April he conducted two funerals, one unveiling, one joint ceremony with the local monsignor at a Head Start storefront and, at the close of the day, a marriage ceremony.

All this has to be accomplished on time, since mourners or celebrants tend to brook no inexplicable delays. He also has to prepare for weekly Friday evening and holiday sermons, all of which he takes quite seriously. His subjects are legion, but they are linked by a common theme—ethical behavior in the Jewish prophetic tradition. Thus, in any given period, he will speak about—and condemn unequivocally—the "new" sexual morality, open marriages and, in particular, the planned opening of a topless bar in town as dangerous to the Jewish family and therefore to its survival. He has also preached on "Doing Good," acts of morality and charity that in his frame of reference included bitter antagonism to the U.S. embroilment in Southeast Asia. His sermons are a grab bag, interwoven with tales of sages in the shtetls of Eastern Europe and ancient Palestine, biblical aphorisms and morality plays, quotations from Tolstoy and the popular philosophers Harry and Bonaro Overstreet and sprinkled with comments about Watergate and Israel. He has reviewed Susan Fromberg Schaeffer's splendid novel *Anya*, about a girl in Nazi-occupied Poland; *Widow*, Lynn Caine's moving account of how a wife and mother managed after her husband's death; *Agunah*, the Yiddish writer Chaim Grade's tender fictionalization of the dead world of shtetl Jewry; and the Kalb brothers' *Kissinger*.

His temple bulletin, well-designed, clearly written and

printed on good if not expensive stock, is sent to all temple members and features his first-page editorial. During one winter, Davidson wrote urging members to buy temple cemetery plots and praised Christians who backed Israel during the 1973 Yom Kippur War. He also wrote feelingly about the daughter of two Austrian converts from Judaism —Viennese refugees from the Nazis—who met and married a Great Neck boy and then herself converted to Judaism under his tutelage. "Her Christian parents will be there [at the marriage ceremony]," he wrote, "but her Jewish grandparents, long dead, will also be present, I'm sure of that. 'I almost believe'—he quotes the bride-to-be—'it is God's doing.' "

"I'm not complaining, mind you," says Davidson, "because I love my work. But still, I'm—in fact, any congregational rabbi who does his job well—I'm overburdened with work. I've no time for my family, for reading anything I want to read, for the theater, for travel, for rest, even for regular tennis. We've got youth groups, three of them, to work with here, singles, single parents, young couples, a 45-plus club, a sisterhood and a brotherhood. Plus everything else. We have to work and serve each of them."

He sat back in his comfortable, street-level temple office, surrounded by books, virtually all on Jewish subjects, and by Jewish art hanging on his walls. On the desk were a few letters. One, to an adult study group that met monthly in members' homes, was signed "Jerry." Another was a memorandum from someone reminding him to visit a couple who had just had their first child. Another, a briefer handwritten note, asked him to see a member who had suffered a heart attack.

"I'm driven to speak well, to enunciate everything oh, so meticulously, to develop a commanding style. Would I ever leave the rabbinate, leave this temple? Well, there is this occasional exhaustion I have, but what else is there? Now the time might come someday, but on the other hand, no other job interests me. I'm lucky that Beth-El doesn't have those terrible and bitter political fights. The action is where I am right now. Here in this temple. In all the temples and synagogues in America. That's where Jewish life is taking shape."

For a moment he paused, as if in thought. His eyes narrowed. He shook his head, slightly.

"But I do often ask myself, though, who am I touching?"

Jewish comics love to tell about the Reform temples that are closed for the holidays. The joke invariably brings howls from the audience, but it makes Davidson angry. He says he has heard variations on that theme all his life. "Rabbi, I'm not religious, I'm Reform." Or, "That was a wonderful service, Rabbi, but if my father knew I'd joined a temple, he'd turn over in his grave."

It is evident he believes fervently in Reform's authenticity and in Reform as a way of life. At one service, on a Saturday, he offered a sermon on the "truth" about Reform Judaism. His two closest friends are both Reform rabbis, his years at HUC among his happiest recollections. His grandparents were founders of a Kansas City Reform temple, and he remembers with gratitude and pleasure his teenage experiences in the youth group, the National Federation of Temple Youth.

Presumably, many Jews feel they carry the burden of their people's fate, but not all in the way Jerry Davidson does. In Kansas City, where he was reared, he saw the rabbi as a central, even a crucial figure, alone in a desert of Jewish life. But in a community such as Great Neck, there is a wide assortment of Jewish organizations in addition to the synagogues, all concerned as much as he is with keeping Jews within the fold, passing on the history and culture and religious rituals of the group, maintaining the safety of the State of Israel, and exposing and fighting any intimations of anti-Semitism anywhere. Yet, despite what he describes as the many varieties of Jewish communal life in the town, there is no doubt in his mind that the synagogue is at the heart of efforts to maintain Jewish continuity and that the rabbi—again, any rabbi—is the center of his synagogue.

"People want certain things from me, from any one of us in the rabbinate," he explained one day. "Rites of passage, milestone events, sure, these are naturally very important to them. Even nonmembers approach me all the time. Marry their kids, bury their dead, answer their questions. 'Rabbi, my nephew goes with a non-Jew. What shall I tell him?' Or, 'Jerry, I don't believe in God.' My own feeling is that these people and all the rest who search me out need a Jewish experience, they want to learn about their past, their tradition and yes, their religion."

He and Beth-El certainly do their best to fulfill those needs. One Sunday morning his Bible lecture drew 275 people. More than 100 are enrolled in five home-study groups. He is, he says, trying to teach them, trying to pay attention to individuals in so large a congregation.

He also hustles for money.

"I'm a poor fund raiser, but the president and I go to members for building-fund pledges. I am also asked to cocktail parties for donors. My pitch rarely varies, namely that the synagogue is vital in our community. I don't feel guilty at all when I say to them, 'Look, you give to Israel. But you can't give to Israel at the sacrifice of the American Jewish community and its synagogues.' The point being that if those atrophy and die then who will be loyal to Judaism in the next generations? Jewish loyalty—and of this I'm absolutely persuaded—Jewish loyalty is produced and developed in synagogues. If not for it, you wouldn't have had all those kids on the streets during the Yom Kippur War asking for money to help Israel. Who told the young about the '48 and '67 wars? Who kept after them about the Holocaust? All of this was taught and retaught in our synagogue classes, not in the public schools. We asked a couple in our town—members—two people who had survived Auschwitz, to speak to our eighth-graders recently. I tell you, they brought tears to the eyes of those kids, relating what they had to pass through as well as the Jewish experience in all centuries. More important, though, the kids were hearing all this in a Jewish setting."

He maintains close contact with the graduates, particularly those in college. Since a typical graduating class from the town's two high schools sent, in 1975, 92 percent of its seniors to college, all but a small fraction away from home, Beth-El'ers are sent a regular newsletter edited by one of their peers. One issue featured articles on the philosopher Franz Rosenzweig, on conscientious objection and on the Jewish Chautauqua Society. There was also a review of a French film on the Holocaust, along with announcements of study and work opportunities in Israel. On the last page of the issue was a reminder by the student editor of the extensive homecoming activities scheduled at the temple. Further, 500 graduates received in the mail a personal letter from Davidson accompanied by a menorah for Hanukah. At other times, they have been sent the enormously popular *Jewish Catalog*—its contents ranging from making challah to a guide to Jewish communes—and a Haggadah for the Passover seder. Steve Pinsky, when he was assistant rabbi, was dispatched to such cities as Boston and Washington to meet and hold informal discussions with college students.

To be sure, the fear of intermarriage is in part the rationale for most of these efforts. "Rabbi, what's the point of remaining Jewish so long as one behaves ethically?" is a question he frequently hears from the young. It is a question, he says, that he tries to answer throughout the year he spends preparing pupils for confirmation. To this end, he thinks the question and the implications and doubts it raises can be separated into three components: What does it mean to be Jewish? How are Jews defined in the world? What are the commitments to Judaism that Jews, together and by themselves, must make?

Davidson believes the start of the answer is not to say "You were born a Jew and you have no choice" but to work from the concept that Judaism's values grew out of a historical experience and that one cannot simply sever the values from that experience. It would be, he says, as if there were two roses in a vase on a table and someone suddenly entered the room and asked, "But who needs the rose bushes?"

More to the point, he finds meaning in the Passover seder, in which every Jew is supposed to participate vicariously in the travail of those early, wandering Hebrews. "It's not just reading the right passages in the Haggadah. It's the yearly experience that's vital. It reminds us again and again why we believe in freedom. We know what slavery meant, we are saying, we lived through it. Being a Jew is the living experience of the ideals we are supposed to espouse, and there's no cheap way of getting by that. It includes—and we teach that explicitly—a democratic spirit, a unique and extraordinarily ethical outlook, a view of morality where life is primary, in which a sensitivity to human needs places the individual in a significant spot, and the importance of the family, as against today's trends which are tearing the family apart, subtly yet corrosively.

"Incidentally, we're no different in this temple with our divorces and separations, especially among those married one or two years and those who've been married for twenty years or more. So, the synagogue is important here, and we do family things at Beth-El. We've got, of course, the inevitable tensions between women, say thirty to fifty years old, who believe Women's Lib has raised their sights, and their husbands, who feel challenged. In Beth-El we're getting more single-parent families. We provide Jewish education for the kids and their parents. I *urge* the parent, for example, to set up stable experiences so as to give their children a point of reference.

"But all this has to do with continuity and survival as Jews. With trying to answer over a long period of time the question many kids keep asking. In this free society now we have a choice. No one insists on anyone staying Jewish. So, I work hard at their question 'Why be Jewish?' in other ways, ways that I think essential and that guide my own life. Remember, I have two children, too.

"For a long time, for example, I wanted to give that sermon on God but kept putting it off. I'm not sure I can even spell out my theology in a systematic way. But still, I wanted to confront it, for my congregation and the kids and for myself. And publicly, before the people I know and trust. And do it as best I could. My talk was devoted to why we avoid talking about God. And about faith. After I finished I thought it had been a mistake. Nobody said much. But then, as you know, for weeks after people kept calling me, wanting to see me and talk about it."

Again, it was the hunger for more knowledge and the wish to believe that astounded Davidson. His listeners were Jewish, but what they wanted desperately to know, he thought, was "Why and toward what end?" The very same question posed by their children.

Another method he uses in tackling the question is to try to get his members to identify closely with Reform, to try to have them understand why it developed in nineteenth-century Germany and the United States and why it is an authentic voice of Jews. Many Jews still delight in taunting Reform and in asking the unanswerable: If you are not Orthodox, why bother at all? Or, which of the 613 commandments does one adhere to and which reject? And by what authority?

For Davidson, raised in a Reform family, educated in its temples and schools and camps, graduate of its seminary, such taunts are both inane and peripheral. He sees his task as locating the families of Beth-El squarely within the Reform tradition, and in this way helping secure many of their children for Jewishness.

"It's an old argument, and I explain that Reform is a justifiable portion of Jewish life, that change is a part of our tradition and that while we've abandoned halakha we still keep certain observances. It's ridiculous," and here his voice rises, in exasperation, for he has obviously heard these challenges many times, "*ridiculous* to *still* have to explain to some that we are observant and learned Jews, hardly marginal at all. We make choices. Unlike the Conservatives we don't try to bend everything to stay within the letter of the law. Rather, we try to keep the spirit of the law even though we've discarded the letter of the law. My grandparents were members of a Reform temple before I was born, and I'm not at all interested in doing as the Conservatives do, try to appease the traditionalists. I'm not against developing guidelines that will lead to greater observance because I think that might help hold onto more families. But I am against tradition in Beth-El for the sake of tradition. When our cantor tries to get too traditional because he thinks he's evoking his Lower East Side memories, I rebel. I don't like it. I don't mind singing a lot of songs in Hebrew, but I don't want to do it for its own sake. We've got to evolve something that has meaning."

Outside the temple, Davidson continues to lend his active support to causes he deems worthwhile. He does not endorse political candidates except where he believes there is an "overriding moral issue," such as in the school controversy. He preached against support of Nixon in the 1972 presidential campaign; but while he obviously voted for McGovern, he asked that his name be removed from McGovern-for-President letterheads.

In support of his activities he quotes God's injunctions to Abraham: "I will bless you" *and* "In you all the nations of the world will be blessed." And so, he continues doing as he pleases, following his conscience, backing, in addition to the Jewish "causes," Cesar Chavez's United Farm Workers, fair housing legislation, day-care centers. Indeed, on certain political issues he is often thought of as one of the more important people to espouse a position. Occasionally, he is asked by local politicians, school board members and others to call together representative townspeople to think through vexing problems, as in the Abramowitz affair or even during the invasion and bombing of Cambodia.

But a Davidson critic asked afterward: "Is it the role of a rabbi to become implicated in such outside issues? Shouldn't he stick closer to *Jewish* issues, to Israel, to his temple's requirements?" A peeved temple member added: "Why doesn't he raise money for Israel, or the Jewish poor, not Abramowitz?"

A non sequitur perhaps, but the complaint is heard. But it is also quite clear that not only do most Great Neck Jews accept many of the positions he has taken, but that his 1,300 families do, too. If many rabbis have to be careful lest they offend someone's sensibilities or economic station on his temple board, Davidson has virtually none of these concerns, supported as he is by that board and its president. In the end, his humane commitments are methods he uses, sincerely and deeply, to keep the interest and allegiance of many of the Beth-El young. During one Rosh Hashanah, with many of the young in attendance—a fact he views with vast pride—he alluded to his involvement outside the temple walls. Later, he remembers receiving two nasty letters and a "storm of approval."

Looking back on his years at Beth-El and in Greak Neck, Davidson nonetheless chides himself for not being involved enough in "social action," a pet phrase of the Reform rabbinate. He recalls with respect his Kansas City rabbi who helped fight the corrupt Pendergast machine.

"That taught me a valuable lesson. That Judaism and politics should mix. Stephen Wise once said, politics is the arena in which action takes place, in which the ideals are brought to fruition. If a religious man stays out of it, then he is not fulfilling religion's mandate."

Davidson's critics are motivated, it seems, less by the positions he takes than by their own fear of their standing as Jews and what the gentiles will think. For one thing, Great Neck's Jews know next to nothing about what the formerly dominant non-Jews think about them and their public life. The feeling is submerged, barely uttered aloud except in the privacy of their living rooms. Are the town's Jews too far out front, too exposed despite their new majority and the lack of overt hostility?

This nagging anxiety was heard, really whispered by most, after the remarks by the chairman of the Joint Chiefs of Staff, General George S. Brown, at Duke University about Jewish "control" of banks and foreign policy; after the OPEC oil blockade ("Will *they* blame us if things go wrong?"); after Kissinger's efforts to censure Israel for the breakdown of peace talks in March 1975 with the Egyptians; and after Spiro Agnew's televised expressions of anti-Semitism. But locally, some Jews even worry whether anti-Semitism is still prevalent in Great Neck.

"Sure there's anti-Semitism among some kids," said a cynical South Senior High School senior. "But most of them are Jewish, those who can't stand their parents." On another, more significant level, there is puzzlement concerning non-Jews: What are they *thinking* about? Under what circumstances might we see a repeat of "trouble"? And the more Jews nationally and internationally feel such apprehension, the more it will affect thinking in Great Neck.

Said a housewife about the Vietnamese refugees: "After they let them in I thought back to this country's generosity towards the Hungarians and the Cubans. But history tells me no one was that thoughtful to Jewish children running from Hitler's ovens." And another: "If Israel goes down, who will care? Non-Jews have a blind spot when we're in trouble."

Of course, there is no "trouble" in Great Neck, although a nearby suburb, Herricks—where 50 percent of the population is Jewish—experienced a wave of rumors which led the Anti-Defamation League man on the spot to claim that "Jews of Herricks were living at a fever pitch of anxiety." Myron Fenster, a Conservative rabbi, asserted that his sixteen-year-old son had been beaten inside his Shelter Rock Jewish Center. Other incidents were reported, although unverified. Harassment at school, a dunking, fights at bowling alleys and pizza parlors, anti-Jewish graffiti. The non-Jewish school superintendent rendered his judgment. "I'm not sure if all this is anti-Semitic at all," he told a *Newsday* reporter. "Anytime there's a little flare-up of tempers, everyone wants to assume it's anti-Semitic." Many Jews agreed with his assessment. But others, who asked the reporter for anonymity, did not. One Long Island rabbi, not Fenster, said, "Things are worse than you imagine. There were far more incidents than you have reported. But if you quote me, I will deny it and never speak to you again." Concluded Melvin Cooperman, Long Island director of the ADL: "The level [of anti-Semitism] seems almost constant, not just in Herricks but all across Long Island. In fact, I've heard of far more minor incidents in the two years I've been on Long Island than in thirteen years I spent in the Midwest."

Steve Pinsky thinks there are really two Great Necks and that some tension between the two is inevitable. The Vigilant (volunteer) Fire Company, for instance, has a Jewish chaplain, but its unofficial quota had long included no more than a token number of his co-religionists. Memorial Day parades down Middle Neck Road bring back painful memories of hatreds, acrimony, fistfights during the Vietnam War years, many—but by no means exclusively—between Jewish doves and non-Jewish hawks. Moreover, there is economic resentment, although most of the non-Jews are as materially well-off as their Jewish neighbors. All the same, Davidson and Pinsky think that imperceptible aggravations do exist and that there is a strain of opposition to Jews as Jews.

"There is a curious interrelationship between Jews and non-Jews here in Great Neck," explains Davidson. "We used to have a women's interfaith study group—Catholic, two Protestant groups and us—but it broke up. It was stopped by a local priest. It took me three months to get him to tell me why, and at last he said, 'We've been marrying some of *our* best kids to Jews and we have to reevaluate our whole relationship.' We're still on a first name basis, and although he thinks highly of my predecessor he considers me a bit of an agitator. Yet he was one of the few clergymen I had no trouble in getting to support Mort Abramowitz. He said he wasn't going to stand by while a small group tried to destroy the superintendent. So, I've got to admire him.

"But in general the other Christian ministers are resentful of the attrition of their membership. They're friendly, but some of their resentment, I guess, is because Jewish power now runs Great Neck. I'm sure, too, that a lot of other people in town—not clergy—don't like that either. It's a gut feeling I have, but I am not imagining it. Three weeks ago I was going out to play tennis and, getting out of my car, a car passed me and someone yelled out 'Dirty Jew bastard.' Now, they couldn't have known who I was, but they figured I must have been a Jew. We've found 'Fuck the Jews' notes about the temple. I think we're going to have a little more of those kinds of things in the future. We have to keep our eyes open."

Sometime ago two dozen men and women met in a large living room to talk about the rabbinate. Inevitably, the talk turned to their own rabbi. What, they were asked, were the characteristics of a perfect rabbi? Warmth, feeling, a good teacher, a religious person, a scholar, one who lent meaning to their lives, someone who held things together for them. "Someone," said a red-haired woman while her husband nodded in approval, "I hope to measure up to."

The suggestion was not lost on the others.

"Jerry *is* the perfect rabbi," said another and everyone applauded, spontaneously. "The rabbis I knew while growing up were rebbes for the shtetl. Jerry is our rabbi for today."

Before leaving, another woman asked her peers and fellow temple members to consider the impact Davidson had on her and her family. "Every time we go for Friday night service we're refreshed. When Jerry opens the Torah I know then the Shabbos has begun. And for us, it's like being reborn."

4. Mississippi

Sundays are uncommonly quiet in small-town Mississippi. On one such Sunday in October 1962—it happened to be Rosh Hashanah—a student rabbi from Hebrew Union College in Cincinnati sat in a Columbus living room watching John F. Kennedy plead on television for moderation and nonviolence. Farther north, in Oxford, James Meredith was trying to enter Ole Miss.

After the telecast, Robert Alan Seigel left Columbus, a small city of 25,000 in Lowndes County, close by the Alabama state line, and drove home to Starkville, where Ole Miss' traditional rival, Mississippi State University, was located. Seigel noticed that thousands of students had gathered on the campus and with the help of the state highway patrol had hung the Confederate flag from the main flagpole. Nearby, from the limbs of two massive oak trees, Kennedy and Meredith hung together in effigy. "I saw hate, destruction and the will to kill," said Seigel, still stunned. His part-time congregation, "moderates," were badly frightened.

Fifteen years later Mississippi's 4,000 Jews could look

back at those cruel days and relax, the crisis having passed and peace once again having been restored to campus and state. Kennedy was dead, ex-Governor Ross Barnett lived in seclusion and Meredith was a lawyer in Jackson, living in a largely white neighborhood.

When Mississippi entered the Union in 1817 there were already one hundred Jews in the state, primarily German immigrants who had drifted southward from Cincinnati and Louisville, west from Montgomery or north upriver from New Orleans, all of them drawn by high cotton prices, cheap bottom land, the heavy river traffic and the limitless number of available slaves. By the eve of the Civil War, they were mainly peddling and running "Jew stores" not only in the state's few towns but also in the tiniest of crossroad villages: Summit, where a Jewish congregation misspelled "Chaveay Scholem" existed until the 1890s, when its synagogue was leveled by a Gulf tornado and its members scattered; and Clinton, West Point, Brookhaven, Woodville, Lexington, Ruleville, Alligator, Hollandale and Belzoni. After the southern defeat, many of them cooperated with the carpet-baggers and Black Reconstruction government, and thereby prospered. They moved in some numbers into the Delta region, that exceptionally fertile cotton plantation country between the Mississippi and Yazoo rivers, where there also lived tens of thousands of impoverished freedmen.

One of the few local Jews to become a professional writer was David L. Cohn, who grew up in Greenville. In 1935 he observed: "The [Delta] Jews, by legend both intellectual and shrewd, seem in this soft climate to have lost both these qualities. They are distinguished neither by learning nor by riches. The national frenzy for uniformity is at work here."

Today, whatever one may say about these characteristics, Jews in and outside the Delta fare well, and some are very wealthy. Yet Viola Weiss of the Jewish Children's Family

Service in New Orleans, whose area of professional concern covers several Deep South states, says she has evidence of a growing, if still small, number of poor Jews in Mississippi. But that, like so much in the state, is a paradox. For one thing the rabbis, poorly paid in the past, are now better rewarded; the result is no dearth of candidates for vacant pulpits. Indeed, many Mississippi rabbis lasted for more than a quarter of a century in Greenville, Jackson, Meridian, Vicksburg, Natchez and Cleveland. And everyone belongs to a temple. Virtually all are Reform, but some are a blend of this and that. There is one Orthodox minyan, Ahavath Hayim in Greenwood, founded in 1893, which today has thirty families.

Membership in a congregation, but not necessarily attendance, is as widespread among Jews as it is among the state's Christians, for Mississippi is Bible Belt country. Roadside signs saying, "Are You Ready for Jesus?" and the like abound everywhere. Evangelists tour the state, and Jews no less than anyone else are ready targets for "salvation." The Delta *Democrat-Times* in Greenville blandly listed in its "religion briefs" section in February 1976 this item: "Mr. and Mrs. Gary Zimmerman of the International Board of Jewish Missions will present work that is being done among the Jews of the United States. Zimmerman seeks to promote goodwill and understanding among Jews and Christians. He demonstrates the services of a Jewish synagogue and Passover feast. Interested Jews of the Greenville area are invited to attend."

Hard-shell Baptism and other fundamentalist creeds represent a thriving business in the state, as politically potent as it is religiously significant. Such aggressive, unquestioning and orthodox practices are anomalous in secular America. And given the apostolic basis upon which these practices are grounded, a foundation which science and rationalism have ridiculed but not undermined, local mores demand a degree of conformity. Therefore, much Jewish membership in the "Jewish Church," as it is often called, can be traced to the expectations of the white Christian community.

Mississippi Jews also take pride in the general absence of anti-Semitism. Talking with many of them leads to the conclusion that they are admired if not always respected. Throughout the troubles of the 1950s and 1960s their stores were generally left alone (although two temples in Jackson and Meridian were bombed in 1967 and 1968). Their families are often—but not always—admitted into the country clubs, for many southern Jews the most telling barometer of social acceptability. At times their daughters are even permitted into the Junior League, an organization conferring an equal amount of status to many local Jews as membership in a country club. Their wealth grants them certain prerogatives, such as access to key politicians. Their camp for children and adults at Utica, a center of Klan sympathies, has been accepted by local residents. "Those Jews in Utica are *re*-ligious Jews," said a Utica filling station attendant, "They're *our* Jews," said a storekeeper. Meaning, of course, that they are acceptable in the same way the late and unmourned Senator Theodore Bilbo, mean-spirited and bigoted, was accepted. "A pert little monster, glib and shameless," Greenville writer William Alexander Percy called him. "An SOB, but at least he's our SOB." Bilbo often resorted to the worst sort of anti-Semitism in his public remarks, but privately, behind doors—or so say Vicksburg and Port Gibson Jews who knew him—away from press and cameras and rural rednecks, Bilbo was a gracious friend of "his" Jews.

But was there truly an absence of anti-Semitism? The non-Jew W. J. Cash wrote in *Mind of the South* that Jews were held to be "aliens even when their fathers had fought in the Confederate armies," a "butt and a scapegoat as old as Christianity," tending to initiate a complex set of fears and hates. Many Southerners, he wrote in 1941, still believed Jews crucified Christ and still saw the Jew as an "eternal Alien."

"Jewish life is pleasant and easy" in Mississippi, said Rabbi Charles Mantinband of Hattiesburg years later. But then came Martin Luther King, Jr., James Meredith and the Freedom Riders.

"A few hours ago our synagogue was bombed. I have given up trying to get to sleep, or to read. It is nightmarish, this reaction to what for years I have accepted as inevitable. How can a Rabbi sleep, when the forces of evil attack his cherished House? I sit here now and wait for the daylight's 'I told you so's,' 'I warned you that the Temple would be bombed.' And I wonder! Not afraid! Wonder! How will the majority of my membership react now? Long ago I have been helplessly reconciled to those who reject my concepts of Judaism and the role of the synagogue in Jackson. I have been unable to stop their pursuit of the multitudes for that evil which has afflicted this lovely city and state."

It was September 1967 when Perry E. Nussbaum, rabbi of Beth Israel Congregation on tree-lined and placid Old Canton Road in Jackson, made that entry in his diary. Founded in 1861, the temple's new structure dedicated only five months before had presumably been bombed by the Klan, leaving the walls of one section collapsing and fourteen windows shattered. Some classrooms, offices, the library and the rabbi's study were all ruined.

During the next two months the bombers struck again. The home of Robert B. Kochtitsky, a white Methodist lay leader, was hit. With Nussbaum he had helped form the Committee of Concern, a statewide interreligious group that raised $250,000 to rebuild fifty Black churches that had been bombed in 1964 and 1965.

The night bombers struck as well at nearby Tougaloo College, a predominantly Black school, and later at the home of Reverend Allen L. Johnson in Laurel. On November 22 a bomb was set off in the front yard of the Nussbaum home, virtually destroying the entire structure.

Following this attack, Nussbaum, who for years had been involved in civil rights activities, but always secretly, went public. Speaking bitterly, with an acid tongue, the rabbi became a public figure, a "controversial minister" said a non-Jewish Mississippian years later. The great fear could no longer be avoided. The bomb could have been detonated during school hours. Jewish and non-Jewish homes invaded. Their rabbi assaulted. So private guards were hired to protect religious and personal property. Despite those members who wanted to say nothing, at least openly, and in spite of their endemic fear of the goyim, the majority of the congregation held on and backed their rabbi (but privately he was urged to move elsewhere).

It's easy to forget the state's repressiveness in the 1960s. Mississippi was then under the control of the most lawless elements. A police state, one rabbi confided privately to another. Phones were tapped. Mail opened. Faculty fired. Clergy warned. A "closed society" said James Silver, an Ole Miss historian. One recalls with reverence the sacrifices of Mitchell Schwerner, Andrew Goodman, James Chaney and others who were killed, as well as those jailed, humiliated and insulted in hate-filled newspapers and on local television stations.

But in Nussbaum's case there was more. His decision to fight in the open was personally vexing because of his wife's growing anxiety about his job and safety. Born in El Paso, Arene Talpis Nussbaum was as insecure about her husband's tenure in Jackson as were undoubtedly hundreds of other rabbinical wives in small pulpits everywhere. Their married life had been a peripatetic one, for his career had been a string of anonymous and unheralded pulpits: Amarillo, Wichita, Pittsfield, Pueblo and Long Beach in Nassau County, near New York City, hardly the flagships of Reform Jewish life. Then too, she pointed with undisguised alarm at the widespread reluctance of white Mississippi ministers to upset the status quo on racial matters. Why should her husband jeopardize his career at this late stage of his professional life? Who would protect him physically from toughs only too ready to resort to violence? Why should they receive vicious telephone calls at night? Or see eggs splattered on their front door on Good Friday? And the one hundred fifty vulnerable Jackson Jewish families in a sea of true believers? Why were they to be made martyrs for a cause they barely understood or most likely did not even sympathize with? Yet from the beginning she stood alongside Nussbaum, attending interracial meetings, volunteering to work in Black causes, accepting his principles and sharing his burdens.

Nussbaum went on publicly to castigate the KKK and white segregationist groups. He called the state leader of the Citizens Council a fascist. He threatened Governor-elect John Bell Williams with unfavorable national publicity unless he denounced the bombers. He quit the Rotary Club after telling the members that from their respectable ranks the "Klan, the Citizens Councils and others of that ilk had received money and encouragement." When the most prominent Baptist minister in Jackson—and Baptists have extensive power everywhere in the state—reluctantly visited him after the bombing, offering his condolences, Nussbaum told him in effect to "go to hell," suggesting that he preach the next Sunday to his front pews, "where all the segregationists regularly gathered." (Charles Evers and Robert Smith, Sr., two pioneer Black leaders, did drive to Nussbaum's house to express their regrets, but decided to remain in their car lest Nussbaum be embarrassed by their presence in his shattered home. When the rabbi saw them he left a group of whites to shake their hands.)

"We're changed now," said one of Beth Israel's trustees. "But I'll never forget those days."

Musing over their common experience, a group of the temple's members sat and reminisced late one afternoon in 1976, nine years later.

"We met at the Sun and Sands Motel just after the first bombing. Ninety percent of us were very upset and wanted to go public. The others were still afraid, and we let them carry the day, to see once more if their way worked. They had argued we ought to wait for the respectable whites to come forward and offer their support. Well, we waited two weeks. A few came forth, but none spontaneously. The only way we got them to back us in the newspaper ad we ran—upholding our rabbi and calling the act sacrilegious— was to get on the phone and plead with them. One Catholic priest offered to open his school to our kids, but the Protestant ministers said nothing.

"But after the Nussbaum home was blown up we acted as a group. We went to the Chamber of Commerce and cursed them. We told them we weren't 'their' Jews and we didn't appreciate the kind of Jackson anti-Semitism that kept us out of country clubs such as Petroleum and Capital City. No Jewish girl had ever been selected as a Junior League debutante. And do you know what their answer was? We were, they said, too sensitive and too cliquish. So we told them that in the future we'd help ourselves."

Perry Nussbaum was born in Toronto in 1908 and was the first Canadian to graduate HUC. He took a job as a social worker, served as an army chaplain and became a colonel in the reserves. He was also a prison chaplain in Pueblo, Colorado, before World War II, where he remembers accompanying a Jewish boy, no more than nineteen or twenty, to the gas chamber in the state penitentiary in

Canon City. "I have never forgotten that awful experience of the gas chamber, and particularly the crowd of sheriffs, deputies and lawmen who avidly peered through the glass watching him in the last throes, as well as hearing one of them say, 'Take that, you damn Jew.' I may be forgiven if I thought that if the boy had not been a Jew without any political support the governor might have shown him some kind of clemency."

But Nussbaum was like many of his peers during the Great Depression who had no connections with the Reform rabbinical establishment (the Placement Commission was not formed until 1945). Wandering from one obscure synagogue to another, suffering real and imagined affronts, he grew increasingly bitter and resentful.

Early on, following his ordination in 1933, he accepted a post in a new "Liberal"—really, Reform—congregation in Melbourne, Australia. The result was a dismal failure because, Nussbaum mused years later, he had been too young, too idealistic, too much the inexperienced rabbi. "My only experience had been two Rosh Hashanah–Yom Kippur stints in makeshift minyans in this country. My first, in a little town in Arkansas, had me preaching to an over-sized mural of the crucifixion—on the wall behind the congregation but there staring me in the face every time I overcame my nerves to look up. I had no religious school teaching experience, or biweekly pulpits."

After Australia, he passed through small towns in Texas, Colorado, Kansas, Massachusetts and Long Island. With the coming of World War II he enlisted as an army chaplain.

Twenty years of nomadic life. Twenty years of hoping to settle down. Twenty years of the strains of organizing or trying to revitalize small congregations. Twenty years of bafflement and then indignation at being passed by, ignored, and the agonizing recognition that the rabbinate had for him been the wrong profession.

But in 1954, when he was forty-six years old, Nussbaum's

life changed. "Worn out, nerves shot," he went to the CCAR's annual meeting and complained to a rabbi on the Placement Commission. Why couldn't they find him something worthwhile? What had all the past two decades been worth if there was no meaningful way to end up a life of service?

"Perry," the official asked, "how would you like to go to Jackson, Mississippi?" The rabbi there had just retired.

Nussbaum remembers that conversation.

"Perry, it's a wonderful congregation. There they'll appreciate you. The South is known for its *derech eretz*— respect—for its rabbinical leaders. You can do as little or as much as you want to. Jackson is beautiful—wide streets, clean, a wonderful southern city. Perry, you'll like it. Take Arene and your daughter down there—and drink mint juleps the rest of your life."

Four weeks after the Supreme Court's momentous ruling in *Brown* vs. *Board of Education* against public school segregation, Nussbaum flew to Jackson. At the airfield (later named for a former Jackson mayor and political boss whom Nussbaum grew to loathe for his alleged racism and anti-Semitism) he was met by a small delegation of local Jews. It was, he remembered, very hot and very humid.

After a few moments of amiable greetings but while they were still standing by the plane, one member of the delegation asked him their crucial question. "Doctor, what is your position about school desegregation?"* Everyone paused politely for his reply. Nussbaum was taken aback. In 1946

---

* Nussbaum has no doctorate, yet another source of personal regret, since like so many other rabbis he loves to teach. HUC had rejected him in 1933 as a doctoral candidate in history because of his alleged shortcomings in Hebrew. Still, he was in the final stages of a doctorate in modern history at a northern university when he moved to Mississippi. In Jackson, he says, he had neither the time nor the money to resume his studies.

he had been offered a rabbinate in another Mississippi town and refused because "the war had spoiled me for living in areas of racial prejudice."

Unprepared, worried lest he lose his last opportunity, yet trying to remain true to his principles, he stumbled over a deliberately ambiguous reply. He says he responded by noting he had always thought himself liberal. But at the same time he had always taken care not to cause trouble for his congregants. Nussbaum knew he was not their first choice nor even their second. But by the time he arrived on that sweltering day, the Jackson congregation was desperate. Soon after, he was hired.

Jackson's only congregation was then ninety-three years old. But by the time he arrived in 1954, it had—in Nussbaum's words—"nothing." Other than a religious school, which he sarcastically dubbed "a pretense at religious education," and a small group of women, the sisterhood, "this was the whole program of the congregation, including of course Friday night services, which had settled down to hard-core attendance." In 1976 a group of members who had known his predecessor as well as Nussbaum added this about him: "Before 1954 there was no Jewish commitment at all. Nussbaum was loved and hated, but he made the Jew in Jackson Jewish-conscious. Israel and Zionism were no longer stigmas." Nor would he have much to do with the assimilationists. He condemned Christmas trees in their homes. He introduced bar mitzvahs, once taboo. "Perry," said a physician's wife (she is South Carolina–born, and her husband is from Canton), "left a Jewish heritage to us."

But in 1954, Jackson's 150 families and 400 Jews wanted a rabbi who would hold his tongue. Fear of the whites was the key. They needed, indeed yearned for, acceptance by the white community. Not more than five of Nussbaum's member families dared sympathize openly with the struggle for Black equality. "Third-generation Jews are no different from Christians," said Nussbaum. But the greatest objects of his contempt were those in his congregation who believed they had to be "200 percent Southerners" to prove their worth to non-Jews.

Still, he also recognized the delicate position of most Mississippi Jews. In spite of their increasing presence in Atlanta, Memphis, Birmingham, Dallas and Houston, they still play a small role throughout the Old Confederacy, certainly when compared to their influence in other parts of the country. Judaism may rank higher in the moral order of Bible Belt fundamentalist circles than, say, Black Christianity or Roman Catholicism, but it remains nonetheless a less-than-equal sect, an extraneous and foreign religion in an area of xenophobes.

"The power structure of Mississippi has never accepted Judaism as one of the three great American historical religions," says Nussbaum. "There's never been the acceptance of rabbinical leaders in Mississippi. There's never been an automatic inclusion of the synagogue.

"I would have church people come to visit the Jewish 'church.' They would walk in, and by their indoctrination, they expected there might be some kind of magical devices hidden away in this altar of mine. I had a Baptist group visit, and one of the women wanted to know if the closet at the bottom of my Ark—just a storage closet—was where we held the paraphernalia for the sacrifices. Ten years ago people thought that Jews were still offering animal sacrifices. But Christians down here, as a rule, can't help themselves, and they've got to try to pin me down about why I do not accept Jesus as the Christ even though I may have spent an hour explaining that this is what makes us Jews and not Christians."

Jews were also susceptible to economic reprisal. Many were in retail businesses, and despite the greater diversification of Jewish occupational patterns since then, storekeeping remains important. In Brookhaven, for instance, where 54 Jews live among 10,700 gentiles, with only the services of a part-time student rabbi and, on occasion, the Natchez rabbi, most Jews are in retail business: Abram's Mercantile, Deb 'n' Heir, Herman's Jewelry, Samuel's Appliances, Shirley's Slipper Shop. In Anguilla, with 600 people, the Kline family runs a general store. The pattern is repeated throughout the state. The threat of boycott from Blacks and whites was genuine.

Before the bombings, Nussbaum tried hard to see both sides. "I laid down an axiom: I know what the problems of being a Jew are in Jackson, and I know what the problems of being a Jew are if you're a Jewish merchant. On the other hand, I do not believe that we Jews need to join the Citizens Councils because I think we have enough here so that we don't have to be picked off one by one the way they *were* picked off—in their isolated conditions in the Delta, where you had one or two Jewish families in a town and the whole town went Citizens Council. I am not going to advise the Jew in the Delta about belonging or not belonging to the Citizens Council. He will have to make up his own mind because the alternatives are going to be rough." And they were in some Delta towns: boycotts, loan requests denied by banks, social ostracism, isolated acts of terrorism.

Trying to satisfy the fears of his congregation and the demands of the prophetic tradition, as well as his own humane interpretation of the American past, was painful. To Ardis Whitman in New Britain, Connecticut, he wrote on May 7, 1965—Mississippi Jews were like everyone else. "We have our segregationists and integrationists. A closed society is a product of history. Not even the Prophets of Israel assumed history can be reshaped overnight."

Writing, always writing, for he was both an inveterate correspondent and memoirist, he wrote earlier, on October 6, 1964, to Rabbi Samuel S. Soskin in Brooklyn, New York:

"I have never shut my door or rebuffed my colleagues. . . .
But some things are hard to take—like the young man who
was here for a total of 48 hours, told me how thrilled he
was over his insights, and how thrilled he was for me that I
am helping to make history. *A mazel oif Columbus*! I told
him to make history in his own backlashed community."

In 1964 an article appeared in a northern Jewish publication portraying Jackson's Jews as "Mississippi Marranos."
Nussbaum's response bordered on rage: "Do you understand what went on in this capital city of the Deep South,
you in the North who from the security of your own
kehillahs were quick to advise and consent about our leadership?"

"We were always a hair's breadth away from an 'in-
cident,'" he wrote in one of his letters to a rabbi. "The
daughter of Rabbi X showed up for Kol Nidre (never saw
her until then) and loudly proclaimed that the service was
terrible. I had not dealt sufficiently with civil rights that
night! What this girl didn't know was that for six Friday
nights [before] that's all I had been talking about, and
against my own intentions I wound up devoting both Rosh
Hashanah sermons to the same subject.

"Or, the young lawyer who had been here all summer
and also showed up for Kol Nidre, spent his time clipping
his finger nails, and then tried to provoke an argument with
some of my people about the rebuff of Jewish civil rights
workers. I had organized a list of several families prepared
to help them break the fast in their homes without saying
anything about the numbers we fed and entertained all
summer. Our rule was: If you came to Temple, some of us
were prepared to give you personal attention."

In Georgia the situation was the same. A group of nine
northern rabbis had come to Albany, Georgia, in 1962 in
support of Black freedom. The New Haven (Connecticut)
Journal-Courier of August 31, 1962, quoted Rabbi Robert

E. Goldburg of Hamden about "Cruelty in Albany, Ga., Jail." Goldburg accused the local jail guards of being anti-Jewish and of having "ordered" drunken Negro prisoners "to commit degenerate acts." Alvin Koplin of Macon, Georgia, wrote to Rabbi Richard Israel of Yale University Hillel on the same day: "When a rabbi from New Haven, Connecticut, takes part in such demonstrations, you have no idea the position Jewry in our state is placed." And Lee Sterne of the Sterne Company–Food Brokers of Albany wrote to Rabbi Israel: "You have now been to Albany, Georgia. You have prayed on the steps in front of City Hall, you have gone to jail, you have put up bond and you have returned to the place from whence you came. . . . Last night, for the first time in nearly forty years, the KKK had a rally here, with more than 4,000 in attendance . . . you and your colleagues can take full credit."

Albany is in southwestern Georgia, an area densely populated with Blacks and white fundamentalists. It was once a trading center for slave plantations within a one-hundred-mile radius. "Here," said W. E. B. Du Bois, "the cornerstone of the Cotton Kingdom was laid."

The Albany rabbi got in touch with Nussbaum. "It is incomprehensible to me how many of our colleagues are sitting in judgment over situations that do not even remotely affect them . . . we, who have to bear the brunt . . . are left isolated and remote. We must still continue to serve our people, for if we alienate them what chance is there? [Some of our colleagues] are quite willing to fight to the last Southern Rabbi." The tension between taking sides or saying nothing was genuine, for letters also reached Nussbaum from rabbis in other southern areas. "Hope that UAHC's invitation to Martin Luther King does not make the Jackson papers via AP," wrote a Beaumont rabbi, "but his press agent will make sure it does." "I am like a voice crying in the wilderness," complained a Montgomery rabbi. "I am the only white minister who belongs to the Human Relations Council," wrote the Columbus, Georgia, rabbi. "[Yet] I am appalled at those who make a simple black and white picture of our dilemmas."

Even so, after Rabbi David Ben-Ami was fired for his civil rights activities in Hattiesburg in 1965 (as his defenders charged), Rabbi Randall Falk in Nashville criticized Nussbaum's and other southern rabbis' ambiguities. Born and reared in Little Rock, Falk was deeply sensitive to the dilemma of the Jew in the small southern town. But, he cautioned Nussbaum, "I feel that Jewish history cannot survive chameleon-like, taking on the coloration of our environment for survival's sake. Either we stand by our moral principles as Jews in a difficult and often untenable environment, or we must leave that environment before it destroys us, either physically or spiritually."

By the early 1960s the Freedom Riders began to fill the local jails. "I should hope that the local rabbi, if not his community, would have the courage to *visit* the jail," wrote Henry Schwarzschild to Nussbaum in 1961. Schwarzschild, who had fled Nazi Germany with his family and years later would lead a national drive for amnesty for anti-Vietnam War exiles, was arrested in Jackson for his role in the civil rights movement. But he didn't know when he wrote his letter that Nussbaum was away at a rabbinical convention. In Greenville, Rabbi Allan Schwartzman allowed the Freedom Riders to shower in his congregation-owned home, immediately adjacent to the Hebrew Union Temple in that placid riverfront town. But further north, in the Delta town of Cleveland, Rabbi Moses Landau reminded Nussbaum that it was his right to be a martyr, but could he say the same of the 1,000 families in the state?

As the Hinds County (Jackson) jail became overpopulated, the major body of the new inmates were sent northward to Parchman Penitentiary, eighty miles from the state capital. With the UAHC urging him to do something, fearful lest his congregation find out and explode angrily, Nussbaum nevertheless drove to the county jailhouse and insisted on his right as a clergyman to visit with the Jewish prisoners. "Perry," asked the county sheriff in astonishment, "how can you want to have anything to do with those nuts?" But they both belonged to the Masons and the Rotary Club, so the sheriff let Nussbaum in. The UAHC sent him some money for the purpose—for toilet articles, cigarettes and the like—but cautioned him not to mention the way he was spending the money.

Later, with the transfer of the prisoners to the state penitentiary, Nussbaum set aside Thursdays for the long trip over poor roads. Since no books or magazines were permitted any prisoners, he brought the Bible and prayer books. Each time he visited he held a general worship service and then conducted individual counseling with anyone who wished it. He also told them he would gladly write their relatives and friends, but not their organizations. He received afterward scores of letters of gratitude from Jews and non-Jews, thanking him for telling them about their loved ones. One former Freedom Rider from Detroit wrote in 1964 that she never failed to mention Rabbi Nussbaum "who so bravely came eighty miles [to Parchman] to see us every Thursday. . . . Those of us behind bars were very grateful. . . ." He still treasures a Star of David one Freedom Rider made for him out of prison wall mortar.

Allan Schwartzman, then in Greenville and nearer to Parchman, had once been Jewish prison chaplain at McNeil Island Federal Penitentiary in Washington, but for the moment he was reluctant to pay official visits to Parchman unless invited by the state authorities. "I am wondering whether we as local rabbis would not be harming our people," he wrote Nussbaum on August 2, 1961, "our positions as rabbis in our communities, and the good work we are doing in the racial problems of Mississippi, by 'going to bat' for these temporary inmates." Still, Schwartzman was moved by their plight. "If requested," he said, he would be on call. He went through channels, and one week later he too became chaplain to the young men and women who had gone south to assist the Blacks.

In spite of his doubts and his unshakable belief in the necessity of protecting his fellow Jews, Nussbaum—like Rabbi Charles Mantinband in Hattiesburg, who faced the same dilemma—chose to side as much as he dared with human liberty and Judaic tenets, as he interpreted them. At times he was too subtle even for his own members to recognize his continued opposition to racial discrimination; other times he tended to resort to Aesopian language. At Ole Miss he lectured on "Amos and Social Justice." His text, like the Soviet dissidents' *samizdat* publications of the 1970s, had to be mimeographed and distributed secretly by the university chaplain. He criticized a Mississippi Southern University exhibit describing Father Charles Coughlin as "one of America's great philosophers." After the publication of "A Jewish View of Segregation," a Citizens Council pamphlet written anonymously by a Delta Jew, Nussbaum expressed his shame to a Delta B'nai B'rith lodge that a Jew would dare write such trash, and was never asked back again. He began speaking to Black college groups. He was an instigator of the Committee of Concern, to aid in the reconstruction of razed Black churches. He was a board member of the Mississippi Council on Human Relations, opening his home to interracial meetings at a time when few southern moderates were prepared to run the risk. He told his congregation time and again that he could not in good conscience abet "racial Judaism, which didn't put me in good odor with my natives whose incomes in considerable measure were derived from rentals of ramshackle huts to

Blacks." He loudly denounced the incredibly reactionary Jackson *Clarion-Ledger* and its columnist Tom Ethridge. He protested the anti-Semitism of a Gulfport editor and publisher. He condemned a popular Rotary speaker for his portrait of Jews. On October 13, 1958, after the bombing of an Atlanta synagogue, he wrote in his *Bulletin* citing Atlanta Rabbi Jacob Rothschild and the Hebrew Benevolent Congregation as additional *Kiddush Hashem*.

And his congregants? They gave their reluctant approval, he says; so long as he didn't get himself or them into the public eye, it was all right. But watch out if you do. "Even such an ethical cause as rebuilding the [Black] churches and my appeals all over the country for Jewish contributions didn't sit well with some of my leaders. For years, there wasn't a Board of Trustees meeting which didn't provoke an argument and bad feelings because I would not let them resign from the UAHC."

In his fourteenth year of service in Jackson, Nussbaum, exhausted under the weight of events and smarting from the pressures within the temple, began to scout about for another post. Congregations in Philadelphia, Cleveland, Baltimore and St. Thomas in the Virgin Islands turned him down. He remembers calling a highly placed executive in New York City from a Jackson pay phone—he couldn't be sure his own phone wasn't being tapped—weeping and begging for help. Spurned, he set his sights lower and asked if he might be an assistant rabbi, but again he could not find a position. In the end, he and Arene decided to leave in 1968. Nussbaum was sixty. His $9,000 salary was augmented by a $2,500 annual pension from the CCAR, the Army Reserve and, later, by social security and a special annuity granted him by the temple.

They moved to San Diego and quickly discovered there was little a retired rabbi might do in the face of Jewish organizational infighting. He now visits the local naval

hospital as a volunteer chaplain, has learned to play golf
and sits on several boards, including the San Diego Regional
Criminal Justice Planning Board. His forty years in the
active rabbinate are over. "I was the teacher," he once said.
"I regarded myself as the custodian of [my congregation's]
spiritual and moral values as they are taught in Judaism."

Charles Mantinband grew up in Virginia and served
as a small-town southern rabbi in Florence, Sheffield and
Huntsville, Alabama, from 1946 until 1951, and then in
Hattiesburg, Mississippi, from 1951 to 1963, when he was
fired because of his civil rights activities. After that, to
retirement in Longview, Texas, where he died in 1974,
blind, almost eighty years old, forgotten.

Much like Nussbaum's public expressions, here now is
vintage Mantinband: "From the very beginning I had to
make up my mind what I would do. I vowed that I would
never sit in the presence of bigotry and hear it uttered. And
when they would say to me 'God is a segregationist because
the Bible is full of it,' I always ripped out a Bible and I'd
open it to where the opposite is stated and say, 'Do you mean
here? Or do you mean there? Or do you mean some other
place?' "

Even more than Jackson, Hattiesburg in the 1950s and
1960s was Klan and Citizens Council country. One hundred seventy-five Jews lived there, their families having
come at the turn of the century. From peddler-storekeeper
fathers to upper-middle-class and wealthy merchant-prince
sons in one or two generations—hardly a novel tale but
true in Hattiesburg. As their rabbi, Mantinband knew this
of course, but also knew of their dependence on the goodwill
of others for continued security. He understood their silent
fear of angry and rampaging whites. Despite their 9 to 5
business friendships with Hattiesburg's power brokers, he
believed theirs was a not unusual predicament in Mississippi.

If pressured to join the Citizens Council, it took much courage to say no. The national Jewish press, he said, "blew things up and complicated things for us." He went on to say that "we who live in the South and who are struggling daily with the situation know how to proceed." But having said that, Charles Mantinband was nevertheless a different breed: outspoken, unafraid, a man of profound ethical standards, one who could never be comfortable with the kind of bigotry that comes so easily to many. More than any other rabbi during the tumultuous southern years at mid-century, even more so than Nussbaum, Charles Mantinband publicly took the side of the oppressed Negroes, and of those who ventured south to stand with them. Schwerner, Goodman and Chaney were "very innocent martyrs"; Claude Kennard, who preceded James Meredith in his efforts to gain admittance into Ole Miss and was imprisoned and brought to his knees by the whites, was defended openly by the rabbi. Mantinband spoke of "my good friend Medgar Evers." He regularly invited Blacks to his congregation-owned home on a social basis. At one board meeting he was threatened, as he was on many occasions, by hostile members. "You must remember, rabbi, it is our property." Mantinband shot back, "Yes, it is *your* house but it is *my* home. If you want the house back I'll give it to you, but you can't tell me how to live my personal life." Then, a second challenge: "But why do they come to see you?" He answered, "We have things in common."

One day he met the head of the local Citizens Council, a former Hattiesburg mayor he knew on a first-name basis. It was soon after the 1958 bombing of the Atlanta synagogue. "I told my boys at the last Citizens Council meeting," the man began slowly, "how foolish it was to bomb a synagogue—a house of God. I hope they won't do that in our city." It was a cat-and-mouse game, and Mantinband was up to it.

The ex-mayor, an active Presbyterian and banker, continued. "The real mischief maker, I told my boys, was Rabbi Mantinband. I know his habits, where he lives. If you want to get him . . . ," and here he paused.

Mantinband couldn't believe his ears. The man, he thought, was deadly earnest. He took out a pen and sheet of paper, jotted down the time, place and nature of the threat conveyed.

"What are you doing?" asked the man.

The rabbi replied, "I won't ask you to sign it as a statement, but I intend to take it to the FBI. Also, to the first five white Christians I meet in Hattiesburg and say that you just threatened me. If anything happens to me in the next ten years I'm going to call for your arrest for creating the climate."

"That fellow never looked me in the face again because I had called his hand," Mantinband later recalled.

And *other* southern rabbis?

Nearly all the rabbinical sentiment in favor of desegregation came from the Reform rabbinate. A handful of Conservatives in Montgomery and Memphis spoke out as well. Orthodox rabbis were silent. Generally, where Jews congregated in a community with a liberal tradition—New Orleans, Norfolk, Atlanta and Nashville, for example—the rabbis found it easier to serve as a cutting edge and urge support for the unanimous ruling of the Supreme Court. The position of the overwhelming majority of southern Jews —or so it seems from a variety of judgments since recorded —was that southern Jewry was "in the middle," as the sociologist Theodore Lowi wrote, "somewhat ambivalent about the whole issue, but tending toward *thoughts* sympathetic to the Negro." Lowi went on to note that the liberals came from the ranks of the "New Jews," those who were first or second generation in the South; the more fearful or conservative Jews were the "Old Jews," families who had lived in the Deep South for generations.

In any event, most rabbis reflected their people's views rather than led them. Allen Krause, then a young Reform rabbi researching the subject, concluded: "Though the Conservative and Orthodox rabbis in the South did little or nothing, their Reform colleagues, on the whole, played a respectable if not overly important role. . . . There is probably not a single community where the Reform rabbis played a *key* role in battling segregation (although Hattiesburg might be an exception), but there are a number of communities in which [Reform] rabbis played valuable secondary or supportive roles."

Mantinband's judgment was harsher. Except for a saving remnant in Jackson, Atlanta, Dallas, Baton Rouge and a half dozen other places, said Mantinband, "rabbis played it safe." "I wish," he said toward the end of his life, "the record had been better."

In February 1963, after Mantinband's dismissal, Rabbi Leo Bergman of New Orleans' Touro Synagogue was sent by the Conference of Christians and Jews to speak at a final dinner in his honor. The president of Mississippi Southern University was there, as were Hattiesburg's Christian clergy, businessmen and press. Most Jews were not. "Later," commented Rabbi Bergman in a sermon in Touro, "I was told they [the Jews] feared Rabbi Mantinband's religious honesty endangered their business interests."

Today Jackson is Mississippi's only urban center. The results of federal intervention are easily seen everywhere. Blacks have been merged into the work force, as clerks; as supporters of Governor Cliff Finch, the rural semipopulist who sits in the state capitol building in downtown Jackson; as members of Mayor Russell Davis' administration. There is even a Black director of WLBT, the NBC–TV affiliate.

Black and white poverty is still endemic throughout the state, but the once uncontrollable racism of the two local Jackson newspapers has been stilled.

Jackson is growing, say its local boosters, and the attitudes of corporate executives, the rising number of newer middle-income respectables (however Tory they may be in their political opinions), and the new forces that have been galvanized among the state's Blacks and their white allies have pleased many of Jackson's Jews greatly in the years since Rabbi Nussbaum departed for San Diego. The city now has a new medical center, an arm of the University of Mississippi. It has a unique Research and Development Center, which encourages the flow of industry to Mississippi. It also has a VA hospital. And all this has led to an increase in Jackson's Jewish population, the only Mississippi community that has been growing. There were 190 families and 110 children in 1976; 250 families is the best guess for 1979.

Jackson's first synagogue was destroyed during the Civil War, and its current building sits, low-slung and functional, on green, attractive Old Canton Road, two miles from the interstate highway that runs north to Memphis and south to New Orleans. The present rabbi is Richard J. Birnholz, born in Dallas, a University of Texas and JIR graduate, a former assistant rabbi in Memphis who once held a student pulpit in Burlington, Vermont.

Richard Birnholz was hired as the rabbi because of his "youth"—he was born in 1945. He could "relate to the kids," and also was a Southerner, said several trustees of the synagogue. Short, articulate, quick-speaking, still teeming with passion and spirit, Birnholz has brought to Beth Israel a maddening pace. Like many rabbis, he has become a source of solace and an entertainer, social worker and emissary to the outer world. Here, for example, is a "typical" Tuesday, taken from his calendar:

8:30 A.M.	Arrived at Temple, read and answered mail.
9–10:15 A.M.	Spoke to fourth and fifth and sixth graders at public school. Topic: "Not Following the Crowd; Thinking for Yourself."
10:30–11:45 A.M.	Personal counseling at Temple for child and parent; planned Interfaith meeting together with Sisterhood.
12–1	Rotary luncheon.
AFTERNOON	Taught a course, "The Prophets," at Millsaps College.
4–4:45 P.M.	Tutored a child with special problems.
5–5:45 P.M.	Met with a couple considering Temple membership. Husband but not the wife was Jewish. The problem: how to interpret the ambiguous Temple constitution governing membership requirements.
7 P.M.	Prepared for Hebrew-language adult education course at Temple.
7:30–8:30 P.M.	Conversational Hebrew course with ten students.
8:30–9:30 P.M.	Study group with Temple youth on "Jewish Assertiveness Training."
10:30 P.M.	Drove home. Worked until midnight preparing Millsaps course.
12–12:30 A.M.	Worked on a bicentennial sermon dealing with two late nineteenth century Jews, Michael Wurmser and John Hay.

There are no services on Saturday, and the rabbi generally receives two or three days off each month. Recently, however, he has officiated at once-monthly Sabbath services for those members with Conservative or Orthodox leanings.

Things are quite different these days from the circumstances and events of the 1950s and 1960s. Jackson's Jews are still silent, but only in political matters, and even that diffidence is fading swiftly. Birnholz's current concerns are less racial than religious. He struggles regularly against proselytizing raids by fundamentalists. Recently, they distributed comic books and literature to teenagers, including the children of Beth Israel families. He too has been invited to the customary "interfaith" prayer meetings where the publicity speaks of all faiths "coming together in Christ." The Jews for Jesus, in reality a largely Evangelical group of apostates, have also attempted to capture his kids.

Birnholz's response is a healthy one, and is supported in every way by his congregation: he is fighting back. His "Jewish Assertiveness Training" program is just that, an effort to develop and then steel the roots and loyalties of his youngsters. JAT stresses all things Jewish. The camp at Utica—for the young during the summer months—has been a boon for implanting and reinforcing their Jewishness. He also encourages protest against the behavior of the converters, writes letters to and holds personal meetings with Christian ministers expressing his displeasure, and talks with Millsaps students and faculty.

Birnholz is new, having been hired in 1973, and he thinks he has had some success, although admittedly it is too early to know whether the persistent fundamentalist quest for Jewish souls can be beaten back in Mississippi. Yet Mississippi Jews have withstood pressures brought against them for more than a century. Stan Hart, for example. Born in 1924, he was reared in tiny Aberdeen, lived with his mercantile and restaurant-owning family in Columbus and Starkville, then married a fourth-generation Jacksonian. Hart was president of Beth Israel.

"I *never* felt any anti-Semitism in Aberdeen. *Never*. That's why the bombing of our temple and Meridian's was so shocking, and why it united us," he says.

In Hart's view the real change is the loss of rabbinic authority and influence. There are now eight full-time Mississippi rabbis, and five arrived after the civil rights decade.

"Nussbaum and Mantinband," he believes, "got over-exposed. They took the prophetic approach and went along, without their congregations." But without those two charismatic rabbis, and with younger, more malleable rabbis today, laymen like Hart believe that they have filled the vacuum, and reflect more accurately the views of their congregations. "We speak for the Jewish community better than the rabbis can," he claims.

Far from monolithic, that "community" is still southern, by virtue of birth or sympathies. Jackson Jews have in common the extraordinary efforts they had to make in order to stay Jewish.

One member grew up in Hazlehurst, the only Jewish child of the only Jewish family in town. Another came from Whitmore, South Carolina, where she and her brother were the only Jewish young. Her brother was sent to relatives in Augusta, Georgia, for bar mitzvah preparation, her parents kept a kosher home despite the inconveniences it entailed and she was told time and again to have a good time—she dated non-Jews, of course, for there was no one else—but "Remember, you're Jewish." Others recall childhoods where Sundays were spent on the road, their father and mother driving for as many as one hundred miles for Sunday school classes. Al Binder, a prominent Jackson lawyer, a legal counselor to Governor Finch and one of the temple's trustees and past presidents, grew up in Clarksdale, was raised in Benoit and later in Greenville. Then as now Mississippi had 4,000 Jews, and now as then Binder attends temple believing that because of the scarcity of co-religionists, Jews who want to stay Jewish instinctively and culturally seek out their kind, for social Judaism yes, but for other satisfactions as well.

It is these ingredients—sacrifice, privation, obstacles, isolation, being different, great distances, communal aloneness in an alien culture—that form for these Jews the basis of their bittersweet resilience and explain in large measure their fealty to rabbi and synagogue.

"Until 1948 we were a bunch of nothings," said one member. What transformed their lives and altered their outlooks dramatically was much the same as with all their fellow Jews—Hitler's ravages and the birth of Israel. But in Mississippi at least there was this curious twist: non-Jews, the mighty white goyim, for the first time openly praised Jews, or at least they hailed Israel. The fundamentalists saw it as a fulfillment of biblical prophecies. After 1967, for example, another Mississippian told a Beth Israel member, "We wish to hell we had a one-eyed Jewish general in Vietnam to smash the gooks." Even rednecks were pleased, identifying with the six-day triumph of the Israelis if only because they understood the nature of violence better than most Jews. And praise, from whatever quarter, was welcomed after the Nussbaum-Mantinband era.

Yet since then, the fulsome praise has been muted. The state is as abysmally poor as ever, still dominated by absentee corporate barons and their venal local allies. Joblessness remains rampant among whites and Blacks. When ex-Governor Waller, a "moderate,"* visited the Arab oil sheikhdoms to plead for investment of their billions in Mississippi industry and lands, Binder and a few of his fellow Jews were annoyed. Waller had been their candidate; they exacted a pledge from him that he would visit Israel too the next time he went to the Middle East, but that promise had not been fulfilled. They wrote letters, arranged for an interview on John Chancellor's NBC News telecast and fretted.

It was not only Israel that concerned Mississippi's Jews;

---

* As governor, Waller had affected a populist style and was favored by Jews. He had his Jewish "colonels" and regularly received their visitations. Some Jews did have money and received the attention accorded people who do.

they were afraid that Arab-dominated banks in the state might cut off their credit. Birnholz backed Binder in this issue, and he and four other rabbis tried without success to persuade Waller to hear their side. Clearly Arab money— in fact, any money—is deemed by the mass of Mississippians to be a potential blessing. More than $2 billion of Arab money has reportedly been invested in the state's economy. And in 1976, Senator John C. Stennis proudly announced that Mississippi construction workers would be recruited by the Fuller Construction Company to fill 700 jobs for projects in Saudi Arabia. "State businessmen," said Stennis, "will have the opportunity to sell millions of dollars worth of goods and materials for use in the project." Editorials throughout the state applauded the news, and protesting Jews retreated to sullen silence, unable to move the right people or push the proper buttons.

The fact is that there is no Jewish power in Mississippi— only a small group in competition, at rare intervals, with potent interest blocs. Although Yazoo City and Rolling Forks had Jewish mayors for years and three of the five founders of Jackson's cotton exchange were Jewish, they were the exception. Recently, however, a few Jews have dared to enter public affairs. In 1976, Rabbi Allan Schwartzman of Vicksburg and Jay Stein, a Greenville discount stationer, ran and won as Jimmy Carter delegates in the Democratic Party county delegate races. A few young Jews are now in journalism and more in law. Even so, they are too few to even create the illusion of an interest group except as *shtatlan*, or behind-the-scenes Jews, standing with their clergy—again, a necessary and expected ingredient of life in the Deep South—to nurture certain white allies with strategically placed contributions.

And the lesson of the years since 1954?

"It brought us together as Jews," said a trustee. Nussbaum, said others with hindsight, denounced the bombers and their respectable supporters "with the blessings of our congregation."

"No matter how good it looks here to outsiders, we got to keep on our guard," said Joe, a contractor who was reared in New Orleans. "They're out to get us."

A woman member disagreed. "I'm very optimistic about Jewish life here." Said a lawyer: "Joe's emotional, but there's some truth in what he says. Since the bombings we've had a steady stream of crises."

Joe, from New Orleans, elaborated.

"They try to convert our kids, so I'm glad we've got Rabbi Birnholz here. But we've got to be cautious every minute, we've got to be ready to act the minute something doesn't smell kosher. We don't want our temple bombed. We don't want Jews for Jesus or anyone else proselytizing our children. Rabbi Birnholz is showing them how to confront those people. He's teaching our kids to understand what it means to be a Jew and to talk back when they're taunted. Years ago we thought that whenever the anti-Semites started to get nasty down here you could do nothing. This is what it has to be, we told ourselves. No more. Today, all of us together raise hell."

After Mantinband was forced out, Hattiesburg took on another rabbi and quickly fired him, too—for incompetence, say some; for his ardent civil rights activities, say others. Not until 1974 were they able to hire another rabbi. Norman Lipson has since transformed B'nai Israel, by then sixty years old, into a far more traditional, if still Reform, congregation. B'nai Israel, which looks like a Methodist church, now features such Lipson innovations as Sephardic Hebrew, the optional use of the skullcap and a professional but non-Jewish cantor.

Lipson's father was a Conservative cantor in Miami, where Norman was born and raised. Ordained at HUC in

1972, Rabbi Lipson once worked for the Anti-Defamation League. Like those of Birnholz in Jackson, his problems today are less Hattiesburg's racial politics (in 1972 they gave Nixon 87 percent of its vote; four years earlier, 70 percent went for Wallace, 16 percent for Nixon and 14 percent for Humphrey) than Jewish problems. He is regularly confronted by widespread apathy among his seventy families. There are no Saturday morning services, for business and sports take precedence. Only five families, including his own, observe kashrut. There is no other synagogue in town, and the consequent lack of any Jewish leadership puts the burden on his rather young shoulders. And as everywhere else in Mississippi, the Evangelicals are ubiquitous, feverishly out after everyone they can save. "They come to the public schools, knock on our doors, appear on radio and TV. They're everywhere down here," he explains.

Social pressures weigh heavily, too. The annual Christmas school pageantry clearly violates a U.S. Supreme Court ruling, but it is a ritual that must go unchallenged. Social friendships with gentiles are generally limited to business hours. For some Hattiesburg Jews, he muses, there is irony but little justice in these facts of life. "If the Christians would not be so emphatic," one of them told Lipson not long ago, "I for one would not be active in the temple." He also hears another remark: "It's *their* pressure that keeps me Jewish. Nothing else."

Lipson senses an uneasiness among a few of his members. "They're always denying any anti-Semitism exists here, but still they're always looking over their shoulders. They consider me the 'Jewish rabbi,' who works in a 'Jewish synagogue.' As long as conditions here remain economically stable and race relations stay on [an] even keel . . . Jews will do well in Hattiesburg. But Jews are right behind Blacks as potential scapegoats."

A surprising remark, hard to substantiate. For one thing, Jews are no longer exclusively merchants, and therefore are somewhat less vulnerable to economic boycott. There are more among them who are lawyers now, more doctors, too, and some who teach at local Mississippi Southern University. Yet there is always that anxiety, and Lipson found Hattiesburg, with its special sense of the past—on which so many in the state pride themselves—so vastly different from his previous experience that he now exhibits a deep-seated pessimism.

"We had a seminar on Israel geared to the Hattiesburg clergy. Nothing unusual for me, since I try hard to stress Israel in many ways. 'We have to stand up and be counted, too,' I tell my people, and not just tiptoe around here. So I've tried to get them close to Israel and also to raise support among local Christians for Israel. The Jewish Chautauqua Society once sent down a film on Yom Kippur which we placed on TV. The Ministerial Association has asked me to speak to them. I've addressed church and civic meetings. And always, always the identical reaction: 'My, rabbi, you certainly are adamant.'

"They were flabbergasted because I don't feel we're an accursed people. Or I always meet amazement when I say we are proud to be Jewish, we will not convert, our emphasis is not on heaven and hell and we do not believe in the imminent return of a messiah."

But more central to his pessimism is his frustration over Hattiesburg's Jews.

"Unless they get more Jews it'll be the same old story," he predicts.

They are afraid lest the white beast be aroused, much as their progenitors in the Czarist empire—from which the original settlers mainly came—feared the muzhik and the Cossack. "They are deadened as well to the problems of the big cities. They are indifferent to the troubles of poor Jews, even to Israel. Almost no one subscribes to any Jewish publication," he complains, matter-of-factly. "I try to sensitize them," he explains, but the old saw, "It's hard to be a Jew," is compounded among Hattiesburg's 175 families by indifference or assimilation or whatever it is that moves many of his congregation.

"I took an informal survey recently among some Hattiesburg gentiles. Their judgment was that because of Jewish prominence in business—shops on the main street and the mall, TV and radio commercials—two to five thousand Jews lived in town." (The population of Hattiesburg in 1970 was 38,277.) Incredulous, he mused about the findings: for so small a city the Jews must really be a potent power. Did his Jews of Silence truly need to be so afraid?

"The Jews of southern communities," Harry Golden once wrote, "live in deadly fear of a disturber. The fear has nothing whatever to do with current political tensions. The studied attempt to avoid all debate, except on purely Jewish matters, has been in force so long that it would be hard to find six Jews below the Mason-Dixon line who hold sufficiently strong convictions to be accused of anything." Mark Pinsky, a young transplanted New Jerseyite who settled in North Carolina during the 1960s, also wondered: "Was Leo Frank taken from his jail cell and lynched because the Jews of Atlanta insisted on working 'behind the scenes' rather than closing their stores and marching down Peachtree Street?"*

"The Mississippi Delta begins in the lobby of the Peabody Hotel in Memphis and ends in Catfish Row in Vicksburg," observed David L. Cohn in *God Shakes Creation* about the land in which he was born and reared. Cohn died in 1960, and sweeping changes have since overtaken Memphis and

* Born in Brooklyn, Leo Frank was lynched in 1915 in Georgia for allegedly murdering a fourteen-year-old girl. Frank was innocent but victimized by racists and anti-Semites, who demanded the execution of "the filthy, perverted Jew of New York."

Vicksburg and all the incredibly lush, still bucolic, and one-time prime plantation country between. Still, the visitor to Vicksburg, on the southern rim of the Delta, senses immediately—in ways that have little to do with federal voting regulations or even with the economic changes that have slowly begun to alter the depressed economy of the region—that this pleasant Mississippi River town of 25,478 (in 1970) has remained much the same since the Siege of 1863, when it surrendered to a Union army under Ulysses S. Grant and thereby changed the course of the Civil War.

The first Jewish arrivals came forty years earlier, during the 1820s, largely from Germany. By 1841 nearly thirty families formally established the "Hebrew Benevolent Congregation of the Men of Mercy."

Philip Sartorius, one of whose descendants still lives in town, kept a journal of his years in Vicksburg. Sartorius was the first Confederate trooper wounded by Union forces as they moved down the western shore of the Mississippi River to begin their siege. "When I came to Vicksburg [in 1845] the Jews all lived kosher, had a *Chasan* and *Shochet*, but had services Rosh Hashana two days and Yom Kippur."

When the Civil War finally ended, they went shopping for a rabbi. Henry B. Gotthelf was German-born, in his forties, an ex-chaplain in the northern army. He was also a tough negotiator. From Louisville, where he was serving as rabbi, Gotthelf wrote unashamedly: "I might be the proper man for [your] young and energetic congregation [and] I might perhaps be destined to lead it." With conditions, though. "I would under no circumstances apply formally for said office, nor subject myself for a personal visit for a trial, but"—he concluded—"I would accept a call."

And call they did. Gotthelf was hired in 1866 or 1867—the records aren't clear—and moved with his wife and eight children to Vicksburg (his grandson lives today in town) for $40 monthly.

Some one hundred years after Sartorius, another Jewish witness of Vicksburg recorded his life. From 1937 until 1948, eleven crucial years in the history of the Jewish people, Rabbi Stanley Brav was "hidden away," he wrote, in this distant river town. Wars and revolutions came and went. The Holocaust. Israel. But in Vicksburg life passed lazily, without overt passion or commitment. From 1870 until 1970 Temple Anshe Chesed stood on a hilltop on Cherry Street overlooking the river and Catfish Row, not far from the Washington Street business district. The red-brick synagogue, three stories high, with a tall belfry adorning its eastern portion, was then, as now, undistinguished in style or design. (The lower floor's main rooms have now been rented to the Mormons; the upper floors have been abandoned to pigeons.)

In Brav's time there were as many as 200 member families, most from Vicksburg but others from nearby Port Gibson and Cary and across the river in Tallulah and Lake Providence, Louisiana. In 1937, the year of his arrival, Brav found no synagogue charitable groups in existence save an ineffective Ladies Benevolent Society. Hebrew was virtually unknown, and the odious Senator Bilbo was passively accepted. When Brav tried to fight the bigoted senator he was told by his members to stop.

The serenity and passivity of Vicksburg's Jewry is even more evident today. Richard Marcus, graduate of Washington and Lee University, former naval officer, real estate dealer, part-owner of a bank, member of the Vicksburg Port Commission and owner of a Washington Street furniture store, is a native Vicksburger and past president of Anshe Chesed. In 1976 he prepared a memorandum for his fellow synagogue officers. Of 113 member families, 100 were "active," but of those only 27 families had anyone under the age of twenty-one. His conclusions: there were no new sources of members; only ten youngsters were in the religious school (in 1966, fifty had been enrolled); three children were being confirmed, but no new student was entering the school; only four women in the entire congregation were of childbearing age. And of the 100 "active family memberships," 87 percent, he said, consisted of couples without young children, and 46 of those 100 were single—bachelors, spinsters, widows, widowers and the divorced.

"My community is dying," says the present rabbi, Allan Schwartzman. "Since I've been here we've had no more than five births."

Adjoining his lovely new temple on Grove Street is the cemetery, situated within the splendidly maintained and preserved national military park, Vicksburg's major tourist attraction. "The people are dying faster than they're being born," he said one day. "Soon there will be too few of us here to make any difference."

Schwartzman was appointed rabbi in 1966 after a nomadic career in Newport News (four years), Greenville (four years), and Flint, Michigan (two years). He also serves as rabbi in Lexington, 110 miles north, where thirteen families live. Born in 1925 in Baltimore, then still very much a southern city, he was schooled in the classical Reform tradition. *His* family rabbi had been Morris Lazaron, one of the founders of the ardently anti-Zionist, anti-Israel American Council for Judaism. All the same, his parents insisted he undergo the bar mitzvah and confirmation rituals. At the start of World War II, Schwartzman, not yet a rabbi, entered the U.S. Air Force and, unlike almost every one of his peers, saw extensive combat for four years as a B-24 flight engineer and gunner with the 13th Air Force in the South Pacific. Discharged in 1946, he enrolled at William and Mary and soon after at HUC. Why the rabbinate? He was, he believes, influenced by two other rabbis: Samuel Silver (now serving in Stamford, Connecticut), whom he met in the Philippines; and his elder brother Sylvan, who had been a rabbi in Augusta, Georgia, and Nashville and was until recently on the HUC faculty in Cincinnati.

With fifteen years of Mississippi Jewish life behind him now, Allan Schwartzman is disillusioned and quite candid about the reasons for his disappointments. Knowledge of Jewishness throughout the state is peripheral, he says. Jews are overly concerned about gentiles. They are still too touchy on race issues. But then, so is Schwartzman, who lived through the stormy years of the civil rights movement.

When a Boston rabbi expressed disappointment during the 1960s at Schwartzman's plea that no more crusading Jewish youth visit Mississippi, Schwartzman smarted for years. He still remembers those days.

"I was Parchman chaplain then. The Freedom Riders had been placed in maximum security. In the summer! It was hot and dirty." The Boston rabbi, he says, accused him of bigotry. Last year, amid the continued rioting there over the state of the public schools, he wrote the rabbi: "How are things in South Boston?"

Nevertheless, he was a moderate on racial and political questions, less outspoken than Mantinband—"one of my heroes, a close friend"—but far more than most other southern rabbis. His part-time Rolling Forks congregation, a handful of families in a small temple one and a half hours south of Greenville, pleaded with him in the 1960s not to speak publicly on race. Yet when the Vicksburg Rotary asked him to introduce Rabbi Benjamin Schultz of Clarksdale he refused, in part, he says, because Schultz had allegedly described Stephen Wise and Abba Hillel Silver, two of the most significant American Reform rabbis, as Communists. His board was stunned. "You want me to quit?" he says he asked them. No one did.

Vicksburg's Jews resemble Hattiesburg's more than they do Jackson's. Less cosmopolitan than their cousins in the state capital, with whom they have very little official contact, they are also more inbred—indeed, Vicksburg has no rail-

road depot or commercial airport. Like the Jews of Hattiesburg, Vicksburg Jews even find it difficult to warm to
Israel's predicament and glory, even though many white
Christians expect it of them as a matter of course. There is
in Vicksburg a substantial Syrian-Lebanese community, and
that may account partly for the Jews' reluctance to stress
their Jewish lives. But Vicksburg's Jews have always been
welcomed and accepted. A Vicksburg Jewish woman was
the mother of the state's present Roman Catholic Bishop. It
is as if Isaac Mayer Wise were still alive, still preaching as if
the messiah had come in the form of America. "We are
Americans who happen to be Jews," said one congregant,
"and not the other way around." And another: "The New
York Yids have to march. We don't." Following the Yom
Kippur War, the entire community, Christians as well as
Jews, raised only $12,000 for the United Jewish Appeal.
(In contrast, Jackson's larger and wealthier population gave
$250,000.) Israel Bond drives have never even dared try
Vicksburg.

"Jewishly, I've moved the congregation from a virulently
anti-Zionist position to a much more sympathetic understanding of Israel," Schwartzman explains. "I've pushed
them into the national organizations as best I could. They're
now working hard on the Utica camp."

Mixed marriages? Rabbi Malcolm Stern of Reform's
Placement Commission asserts that one-third of southern
congregations now seek rabbis who will perform such weddings. Schwartzman does perform them, but only if the
couple agree to raise their future children as Jews. "They
need the rabbi for these marriages," he explains. "But also
for the other rites they think crucial. They can't escape
being Jews, however vitiated it may seem to outsiders, and
we provide the means for the wish."

At fifty, with his son studying pre-law at Vanderbilt University and his wife a public school teacher, Schwartzman
earned $17,000 in 1976 ("Southern congregations are nice

to rabbis," he says, "we're in the Bible Belt"), plus an additional $1,000 for moonlighting in Lexington. He and his wife live in the home provided for them by the temple—the "rabbinage," a rather grotesque description heard in small towns—in a ranch house development on the outer portion of Vicksburg. But that edge of disillusion, that pervasive cynicism which at times he cannot mask from visitors emerges in his exasperated response as to why he, like a number of his peers, has never visited (let alone studied) in Israel. He has to pay for the journey and hotels himself, and—here the edge enters his voice—the temple has never once offered to send him there, "like other rabbis have been."

Unsurprisingly, his attentions are often centered elsewhere. He was elected to the Mississippi state Democratic convention in Hazlehurst as a Jimmy Carter delegate but lost the chance to go to the national convention when a Black civil rights lawyer received more votes than he did. He was, nonetheless, the only Jew present. And he was the only rabbi ever to have come that far in Mississippi politics, even if, as he says, he merely wanted to understand and watch firsthand the operations of the system.

But if he had to do it all over again, would he choose the rabbinate? As with other rabbis elsewhere, the answer is far from unequivocal. There were too many humiliations and rebuffs, too many hurts. His exile to distant communities has bruised him. Then there is the notion that at fifty he is still vital, intelligent, energetic and ambitious but that, to his enormous dismay, he seems doomed to have to pass the rest of his days presiding over a decaying community, offering up priestly incantations as in a death watch.

He is, I think, closer to what many Mississippi Jews wanted in a rabbi than were the activists in Jackson and Hattiesburg. He did allow himself certain modest privileges of conscience, such as welcoming Freedom Riders to Greenville and allowing them to shower in his home, no inconsiderable feat in those times. But living not far from strictly segregationist Sunflower and Yazoo counties, rabbis such as Schwartzman sympathized with the isolated Jewish store-keepers at crossroad hamlets who had thrown at them, among the gentler queries, "Abe, would you want your daughter to marry one?" Mississippi rabbis—indeed, many southern rabbis like Allan Schwartzman—were torn by their moral code, born of the prophetic tradition, and by reality, as seen by their fellow Jews. These rabbis were the central figures, wrote the southern scholar Alfred O. Hero, Jr.: respected, held dear by the Jews in solitude, representing for many of them, however mute they might be in larger matters, something higher than the mundane qualities of their lives. No doubt they pressured their rabbis to remain quiet on non-Jewish matters, but few who did not experi-ence Mississippi during those years in the 1960s have the right to condemn them harshly. If evil is banal, then so is fear for oneself and one's way of life.

In the end, it was an emotional tightrope, but more often than not, Schwartzman managed to survive, proudly. In 1962 the Jewish Chautauqua Society invited him to address the students and faculty at Alcorn A&M, a Black school in Claiborne County, a Citizens Council stronghold. Years later, someone who was present said Schwartzman was told that local traditions would not allow him to eat with the Blacks. In silent protest, he proceeded to fast rather than dine elsewhere. Afterward when he rose to speak, the Black audience gave him a standing ovation.

Farther north in Cleveland, Mississippi, Rabbi Moses M. Landau stood fast with his congregants and forsook even such demonstrations of sympathy with Black people. In a letter to Nussbaum in 1965 he explained that many of his members were scattered about in small towns, a handful of families in each community. Most were native-born Mis-sissippians, and many had extensive real estate holdings.

Yes, if he spoke out his members might resign. And yes, it would make those who remained very nervous. Landau, who was also a professor of German at Delta State University, was less concerned with his own position, though, than with the well-being of his congregation. Wasn't it essential to try to keep the congregation together?

Given these ethical dilemmas and harsh realities did Schwartzman think it worthwhile? Would he become a rabbi again? He pauses. Probably not, he answers. He repeats himself. No, and now he sounds less sure. For the third time, though, stronger: "No, but. . . ."

He recently received credits leading to a professional certificate in accounting from the University of Wisconsin's correspondence course division and believes he would do well as a business executive. If offered something attractive, he says he would leave Vicksburg. Or perhaps not. If, he says—now more slowly—if he could work full-time yet serve a congregation simultaneously, *that* would be the sort of arrangement that would keep him in the rabbinate.

"The Reform rabbinate has overcrowded the field since the Vietnam War," he says, warming to the subject. "There are no more pulpits. Even Mississippi, Arkansas and Louisiana small towns are taken. So I believe in rabbis serving on a partial basis and allowed to lead other lives at the same time."

Outside Anshe Chesed, in the clear and sparkling sunshine of a February day, a stroller passes the grave of Vicksburg's first Reform rabbi, a blessed man say those who still remember him with love. He committed suicide in 1936 for unknown reasons. "Mark the perfect man and behold the upright," says the epithet on his simple gravestone. "For the end of that man is peace."

Farther northward into the Delta, a traveler passes through villages where an occasional Jewish family resides.

Anguilla, for example, has dusty streets and 600 people and Kline's General Store. The original Kline came from Czarist Russia in the 1890s and then sent for his brothers. Abe, the senior brother, still presides over the store; his brother Charles, who arrived in 1920, once served as Democratic Party chairman of Sharkey County. Their customers are basically Black, and during the 1960s they were boycotted for a time both by Blacks demanding jobs and by the KKK. Said Abe: "I demanded respect." Both sets of pressures were short-lived, since the Klines had long since impressed upon the Blacks that their money was as good as anyone else's and the prices charged were the same as whites paid.

Everywhere there are Blacks here in the Delta, and especially Black impoverishment. Jerry-built wooden shanties and foul drainage ditches dot the landscape amid tens of thousands of acres of cotton and soybeans, the owners of which are not antebellum families but instead the nouveaux riche. They have enriched themselves through cheap Black labor, anti-trade-union laws, generous federal subsidies, sophisticated agricultural machinery and chemical herbicides, all of which helped create extensive Black joblessness and consequent migration via the Illinois Central to Chicago and other northern cities. The Delta's largest landowner by far is the Delta and Pine Land Company, British-controlled, one of the world's biggest cottonseed-breeding firms. It once planted 16,000 acres of cotton utilizing 5,000 Black workers, including 1,000 tenant families. By the early 1970s it was cultivating 25,000 acres, but only 10,000 were in cotton. The company had diversified into soybeans, rice and cattle, and fewer laborers than ever were needed. Those who remained are desperately, almost unbelievably poor, physically as well as economically. One recent analysis of a Delta plantation community concluded: "The community is ridden with sickness, disease and chronic illness. . . .

Barely a household is free of a case of high blood pressure. . . . Diabetes is a common disease. . . . Many women in Louise eat [clay] when they are pregnant."

Greenville, where Schwartzman served, is different from most of the state, more tolerant to "moderation" during the 1960s and blessed with Hodding Carter's *Delta Democrat-Times*, a first-class newspaper whose major advertisers—particularly the Jewish merchants—refused to cancel their ads when the paper was censured bitterly by racist whites. Hodding Carter III now edits his late father's paper and has expressed his gratitude publicly to Jews for such steadfastness.

Clarksdale is also different, at least insofar as its Jewish community is concerned. There Rabbi Benjamin Schultz presides over the town's only synagogue. In the early 1950s, Schultz was a devoted admirer of Senator Joe McCarthy, who once reciprocated by calling the rabbi "an indispensable man in the fight against Communism." Other right-wing Jews applauded him. Writing in *American Mercury*, Victor Lasky dubbed him "The Rabbi the Reds Hate Most," and Alfred Kohlberg, the father of the China Lobby, became the main financial supporter of Schultz's American Jewish League Against Communism, an organization of 300 to 400 Jews who felt the Republic was menaced by an assortment of liberals like Senator Herbert Lehman, Admiral Chester Nimitz and General George Marshall, as well as other rabbis, Jewish organizations and, as Schultz once said, "spiritually diseased intellectuals [who believe] the world Communist movement is declining because there is a supposed cleavage between various Communist parties." In 1957 the rabbi asked: "If you were given just one choice, shall your child be [Dr. J. Robert] Oppenheimer or a patriot like Joe McCarthy?" His answer: "Can there be any doubt?"

Benjamin Schultz was born in Brooklyn in 1906 and raised in Passaic and Rochester, where his father, a hard-working immigrant from Poland, experienced his share of poverty. Those who knew the young Schultz described him as a brilliant student, exceptionally articulate. His early goal—or so it was then reported—was writing, but according to his brother, Schultz deferred to his mother's wishes that he emulate her family with its long line of rabbis.

From 1935 until 1947 he served in Yonkers but then began to be ostracized because of his views. In 1960, following years of publicity (very favorable from many on the right and quite the opposite from his critics in the center and on the left), he was hired in Brunswick, Georgia. Two years later he was named to the post in Clarksdale.

Established by Yiddish-speaking Eastern Europeans, Beth Israel was founded in 1894 as an Orthodox shul; it turned Conservative in the 1940s, Conservative-Reform in the 1950s (with two simultaneous services on the High Holy Days) and then joined the UAHC in 1957, wholly Reform. Today it has veered again toward Conservatism, which Schultz encourages.

"Its eighty-seven families are very Jewish," he says, often expressing himself in the third person. "Zionism, Israel Bonds, Hadassah, UJA are strong. Many congregants have been to Israel.

"The rabbi is popular and the Congregation is basking in his having been elected District Governor of Rotary, a unique situation in the world. He has been president of the [Coahoma County] Ministerial Association. The rabbi was elected 'permanantly' in 1966, by the Congregation.

"The group does not mix in politics. They strongly support my patriotic activities."

Following Meredith's efforts to get into Ole Miss, Schultz was praised by the Citizens Councils for saying, "What America needs is more Mississippis, not less." During the 1960s six young Jews in Clarksdale working in Freedom Schools and Black voter registration reported that Schultz ignored them during Friday night services. They added that his sermon that night asserted there was no freer or happier place than Mississippi.

In Jackson, Perry Nussbaum was shocked, particularly as Schultz's "patriotic activities" included calls for inter-faith attacks on "Communism," denunciations of allegedly pro-Communist college faculty and a strong defense of states' rights. Nussbaum wrote angrily to Sidney L. Regner at the CCAR: "His Congregation thinks he is wonderful. The rabbis of Mississippi think contrariwise." Schultz, who had earlier been denied the Hillel rabbinical post at Ole Miss, was incensed. "My present congregation likes me," he told S. Andhil Fineberg at the American Jewish Com-mittee in New York City. And his "What America needs is more Mississippis" speech? It was, explained Schultz, "only to give a lift to the sorrowing citizens of Mississippi by saying they had certain good points. Was the timing bad? Perhaps. Were things read into it unjustly? Yes."

He closed with a plea and a threat. Can we, he asked, "all turn over a new leaf. . . . I value amity with my col-leagues." Failing that, he threatened to lay charges against some of the offending rabbis before the CCAR.

Nussbaum wasn't convinced of any mellowing on Schultz's part. "This is the time," he wrote Schultz soon after, "for the Mississippi rabbis to be extremely careful . . . not to cut the ground under the handful of Christians who are beginning to rebel against the fascistic atmosphere in the state." He warned Schultz: "You have become a fellow-traveler with those elements in the state to which I am absolutely opposed . . . because you refuse to see that your brand of political conservatism is meat and drink for the fascists who are in control of Mississippi."

Now in his seventies, Schultz is pleasant and responsive and proud indeed of his lifework.

In recent temple bulletins he has denounced anti-Semitism as well as assimilation. "Many of us flinch at the prospect of our children and grandchildren forsaking 'Shema Yisroel' and embracing the Cross," he wrote. The "Jewish religion is in danger," he also warned his members. When asked for material on Clarksdale's Jewish life he added a "column on my anti-Communism," still no doubt a central force in his life. The article was written by one of his old comrades, Morrie Ryskind, and had appeared in the *Memphis Commercial-Appeal*. Headlined "Early Evidence of Red Evil," the piece praised the rabbi as one who had pioneered in recognizing Soviet anti-Semitism, who had early on exposed "fellow travelers in church and synagogue," who had been a premature "anti-Red" and who had "the scars to prove it."

"I admired him for his guts," said one of his former congregants. "He took on the Jewish establishment virtually alone and knocked their heads together. Also, the civil rights thing was none of our business. But more than that, because what the hell is politics? I admired him because he was a damned good rabbi and an inspiration for all of us who were Jews but not leftists. That's epithet enough for any man."

In retirement now in San Diego, Rabbi Nussbaum thinks about the prospects for Jewish survival in Mississippi. The eroding influences, he believes, emanate mainly from the North. In the Deep South, with its fundamentalism, its insistence upon a Jewish church and Jewish spokesmen, the instinct for continuity will not easily diminish. Intermarriage will increase, but so will the tendency of the non-Jewish partner to convert. Congregations will go on struggling to avoid becoming the mausoleums they have become in the North. There is, he insists, Jewish learning in the South. And the problem of Israel is going to be with us for a long, long time. "That is bound to tie Jews to the local congregation, which is the only *physical* resource for secular Jewish causes as well as a refuge from the Klan-types, who will always be with us."

5. The World of the Orthodox

In the years after World War II, Orthodoxy reawakened. Seminaries such as Mesifta Torah Vodaath in Brooklyn started to expand, while in the upper reaches of Manhattan, Yeshiva University became more prestigious and academically respected. Its Rabbi Isaac Elchanan Theological Seminary has produced a steadily growing number of first-rate scholars and rabbis. Jewish day schools also mushroomed, up to 420 in 1976; according to an American Association for Jewish Education estimate, there were 15,000 students—predominantly Orthodox—in all-day Jewish high schools, an increase of nearly 76 percent since 1960. In addition, forty yeshiva seminaries were ordaining rabbis by 1977. There are innumerable youth, women's and senior citizens' groups, and a plethora of "cultural" agencies as well. Adherents to Orthodoxy—200,000, or 12.2 percent of all American Jewish heads of households, according to the NJPS study noted earlier—began soon after 1945 to include men and women in scientific and professional occupations, those who might normally pride themselves on nineteenth-century rationalism and its corollary, biblical (read, negative) criticism. Accepting Orthodoxy in any form meant meticulous observance of halakha as the binding authority, an obligatory tenet that every such Jew had to observe the mitzvot. But as one woman once said, Orthodoxy was also a guarantee that she would have Jewish grandchildren.

The different Orthodox groups also absorbed the practices of the sophisticated advertising and public relations industries. Well-edited periodicals emerged, written in English, increasing cohesiveness among the Orthodox but also appealing, subtly, to others. *Tradition, Jewish Life, Jewish Parent, Jewish Observer, Journal of Orthodox Thought* and others found a ready audience and an enthusiastic constituency. The Lubavitscher Hasidim especially, the best known of the smaller Orthodox sectarians, became marvelously adept at those publicity techniques, reaching out in seminars, summer encampments and various publications, most particularly to university students who had become discouraged with campus materialism and watered-down Judaism. Lubavitscher vans would park for the day along Manhattan or Philadelphia streets, or their loyalists would invade El Al's terminal at John F. Kennedy Airport, or hospital waiting rooms.

"Are you Jewish?" they asked men politely. "Are you wearing *tzitzit*?"* And to women: "Would you be interested in receiving a kit with a pair of candles and directions for the Sabbath lighting?"

Seen from the vantage point of sheer growth and organizational activity, Orthodoxy appears to have risen dramatically in acceptance and respectability, despite its claim to doctrinal "truth" and its general reluctance to compromise

---

* A fringed garment worn to obey God's command to Moses: "Speak to the children of Israel and bid them make fringes on the corners of their garments and that they put upon the fringe of each corner a cord of blue. . . ."

those doctrines. The religious history of this country, depicted earlier in this book, indicates why Orthodoxy was rejected in the nineteenth and early twentieth centuries. In 1905, David Philipson, a Reform rabbi and the American-born spiritual head of the ultra-Reformist Rockdale Temple in Cincinnati, a man with little sympathy for Orthodoxy, reflected in his journal entry the declining state of that movement. "Thousands are leaving the old paths," he wrote, accurately. "The religion of their fathers is repugnant to them. In many instances, it is hated because it is synonymous with the old life of the ghetto [and] oppression and of all things unprogressive, they consider the synagogue the most so. . . ."

The sociologist Charles Liebman has concluded that it was not until the 1920s, after the gates had been essentially shut to Eastern European immigration, that the Orthodox began slowly to reach out for new adherents. Until then, those who came were often the ones least likely to remain committed to shtetl traditions; these immigrants were willing to see America as a land of golden opportunity and thus were eager to assimilate.

"After all, who went to America?" asked the philosopher Milton Himmelfarb. "It was not the elite of learning, piety or money," he told the Rabbinical Assembly in 1962, "but the *shneiders* [tailors], the *shusters* [shoemakers] and the *ferd-ganovim* [horse thieves]."

The Rise of David Levinsky, Abraham Cahan's pioneering novel about one Jew's efforts to make it in the new land, is another familiar portrait of this widespread trend. Shopkeepers and factory owners remained open on Saturday, women scorned wigs after marriage or even refused to visit the mikveh. Increasingly, sons went off to college. When the rabbi of Slutsk visited New York City in the early 1900s and addressed a session of the Union of Orthodox Jewish Congregations, he took the opportunity to censure his listeners for having emigrated to so secular, so unbelieving or so pagan a country, a *treifa medina*.

Growth has to be measured qualitatively as well as quantitatively. Thus, there is a larger question, one that is virtually impossible to answer: To what extent is the renewal of commitment and interest in contemporary Orthodoxy genuine or merely cyclical? Are organizations such as Agudath Israel "really growing," as claimed by Rabbi Nisson Wolpin, editor of the *Jewish Observer*, or is it an illusion, a reflection perhaps of the turmoil and confusions of recent decades? Is it only an effort by beleaguered and frightened men and women seeking absolute answers?

Orthodoxy also has severe growing pains. For one thing, the movement is far from monolithic, in acceptance of authority as well as in its groupings and shadings. All the major branches of Orthodoxy uphold total obedience to halakha, laws that were codified in the *Shulhan Arukh* by Joseph Karo, in Maimonides' *Mishnah Torah*, in the Torah or Five Books of Moses and in the Talmud, the Mishnah and Gemara. But here the similarities abruptly end. Whereas the Conservatives, Reform and Reconstructionists each have a single seminar, a single rabbinic association and a single group for its congregational constituencies, there are at least three Orthodox rabbinic bodies and four congregational organizations, each of which reflects the distinguishing features and nuances of its religious ideology.

The Rabbinical Council of America, the rabbinic arm of the Union of Orthodox Jewish Congregations of America, the major national congregational organization, represents the largest bloc of Orthodox rabbis and clearly the most influential. Consisting mainly of pulpit rabbis, its more than 1,000 members reach from Portland, Maine, to Portland, Oregon. More than half of them are graduates of Yeshiva University's seminary, and like the "modern" Orthodox, RCA tries hard to stress the pertinence and viability of halakha as well as the common denominators binding all Jews.

The Rabbinical Alliance of America, RCA's chief competitor for allegiance, funds and power, was founded in 1944 to promulgate "Torah-true Judaism through an organized rabbinate that is consistently Orthodox." Together with several other ultra-Orthodox groups, it called in 1976 for an amendment to the Israeli Law of Return so that only those converted according to halakha (read, converted by an Orthodox rabbi) be recognized as Jews. Stricter than RCA, theologically more right-wing, RAA's 250 members include some members of RCA, together with about 100 active pulpit rabbis.

The oldest of the rabbinic groups is the Union of Orthodox Rabbis of the United States and Canada, or Agudat Ha-Rabbanim. Established in 1902, Agudat opened day schools and aided Jewish communities devastated by World War I in eastern and south-central Europe. Today however, it has little impact. The communal rabbi, Agudat's primary notion, was soon supplanted here by the congregational rabbi. Moreover, as Charles Liebman has written, "the issue which damaged the image of the Agudat Ha-Rabbanim type of rabbi was kashrut supervision. Rightly or wrongly, an image persisted of the communal rabbi, who pressured butchers, food processers and slaughterers to ease kashrut requirements [and] lowered the standards of supervision." And still another problem: "Members were required to have the qualification of *yadin yadin* [an additional, higher ordination] or at least be on the road to it, and this qualification demanded study beyond any offered by most [American] yeshivot. [It] close[d] the organization's ranks to American-trained rabbis. But it was the American-trained rabbis to whom the larger, more prosperous modern Orthodox congregations were attracted." These rabbis tended to join the RCA.

That these rabbinic groups do compete with one another

results in part from the absence in this country of a kehillah or official central communal authority, one that presumably speaks for all. Nor are there any chief rabbis here, although in 1888 an attempt was made to install one in New York City. Rabbi Jacob Joseph was recruited in his native Vilna, in Lithuania, and he arrived at the port of Hoboken on July 7, met by a vast crowd that had come to greet him and accompany him to his new home at Henry and Jefferson streets on the Lower East Side. His coming was sorely resented by the Anglo-Jewish press, then dominated by German Jews, and even by native American Orthodox leaders as Rabbis Henry P. Mendes and Sabato Morais. And, of course, by the Yiddish, often socialist, newspapers. The great wave of Jewish immigration had only recently begun, but even at that early stage many Jews had become too absorbed by the larger milieu—uninterested in, if not hostile to, organized religion, individualistic, on the move. Ultimately, the chief rabbi scheme collapsed, and like Avignon in the history of the medieval papacy, by 1889 there were two rival kehillahs with two chief rabbis, each battling the other to supervise kashrut. Four years later more chaos: from Moscow arrived Rabbi Y. Vidorowitz, who promptly declared himself chief rabbi of the United States and Canada. Now there were three, but actually each had only a small following.

Yet another aspect of this diversity among the Orthodox are the smaller groupings that tend to revolve about charismatic rabbis, each of whom offers his interpretation of "Torah-true Judaism." The Lubavitschers, with international headquarters in Brooklyn, are led by Menachem Mendel Schneerson, their seventh rebbe, who succeeded his father-in-law in 1951. Born in Mikolayev, Russia, in 1902, he received his degree in electrical engineering at the Sorbonne and then emigrated to this country. Schneerson now has an estimated following of 150,000 scattered throughout the world—in Rome, Rio de Janeiro, Copenhagen, London, Montreal, Melbourne, Paris, Caracas. They have fourteen yeshivot, the Beth Rivka School for girls, a rabbinical seminary, the Central Lubavitscher Yeshiva, and about 4,000 men pursuing advanced studies in Judaism, very few of whom become congregational rabbis because of the fear that doctrinal compromises could be forced upon them in the ordinary give-and-take of synagogue life. Nevertheless, their influence is felt far beyond their study halls. "When Lubavitscher sponsors an event," wrote Ruth Rovner in *Philadelphia Today*, "they manage to bring some Jewish luminary as the main attraction; Isaac Stern, Theodore Bikel and Herman Wouk have all come. When the [Lubavitscher] Center sponsored a Hassidic art exhibit, sculptor Jacques Lipchitz created a lithograph expressly for the Center." As Charles Liebman commented, the Lubavitschers do not recognize any differences within Judaism. They do recognize "only two types of Jew, the fully observant and devout Lubavitscher Jew and the potentially devout and observant Lubavitscher Jew."

There are other such groups. The Satmar rebbe, Yoel Teitelbaum (a few of whose followers hung the Lubavitscher rebbe in effigy from a Williamsburg streetlight during Purim, 1975), is undisputed leader of a highly disciplined group of 1,200 families in Williamsburg (the heart of Satmar Chassidus in America), Crown Heights and Borough Park, all in Brooklyn, and in Kew Gardens Hills in Queens. The Central Rabbinical Congress, *their* organization, speaks authoritatively for their own; their kehillha concerns itself with members' welfare, pensions, mikvaot and schools—there are 3,500 children enrolled. They are also aligned with the Naturei Karta in Israel, a fundamentalist sect living mainly in Jerusalem's Mea Shearim section in the Old City, who consider modern Zionism a blasphemous effort to alter the true character of Judaism. For unlike many of the ultra-Orthodox who do not condemn Israel, Naturei and its allies are deeply repelled by Israel's conscription of young women and by the fact that the state did not arise from the actions of the messiah. They are equally horrified by the practice of autopsy, by Israel's tacit approval of abortion and by the secular nature of that sovereign nation. In fact, the pages of Satmar's official weekly, *Der Yid*, makes no effort to conceal these beliefs. "Satmar's principled and zealous opposition to Zionism in every shape, form or vestige," comments Bernard Weinberger, an Orthodox, non-Hasidic rabbi in Williamsburg, "was beyond doubt the most difficult barrier in its relationship to an American Jewry that had been nurtured, reared and inculcated with an abiding faith in the importance of the State of Israel, if not in Messianic terms, then at least as the ingathering of exiles."

And still other forms of Orthodoxy abound. The Breuer Community in Washington Heights; the Mirrer Yeshiva community (many of whom were saved by the Japanese during World War II after their flight across Europe and Asia to refuge in wartime Shanghai and Kobe): the Klausenberger rebbe; the Skverer rebbe; the rebbes from Vishnitz, Bobov and other abandoned Eastern European towns and villages. Few of them are known to the typical Jew in America except under the general appellation of Hasidim. Yet few rabbis have such dedicated and fervent followers.

"It brings to mind the comic-tragic view of Jewry that the *New York Times* had," says rabbi-editor (of the Agudath's *Jewish Observer*) Nisson Wolpin. "It never knew of the dynamic and much revered leadership of Reb Aharon Kotler—even at the time of his passing, except as a 'dean in a small rabbinical college in southern New Jersey.' " Kotler had arrived in the United States in transit from Europe, on his way ultimately to Palestine. With the coming of war he remained here, started the Lakewood yeshiva and a *kollel*, or "graduate" level of study, organized day schools and laid the foundation for the revival of Orthodox education. When two of his *talmidim* (disciples) visited the office of the newspaper in 1963 to suggest that it cover his funeral, "the editor in charge checked his file and said, 'What for? We've got absolutely nothing here on him.' It was only when the streets of Manhattan were choked with 25,000 mourners that the *Times* realized that Reb Aharon had more than an eight-line constituency. So the *Times* wrote an expanded story."

Youngish and athletic in appearance, wearing modish clothing and stylish aviator glasses, the fringes of his *tzitzit* plainly evident hanging loosely over his belt, Wolpin belongs to the action-oriented Agudath Israel of America and is a graduate of Mesifta Torah Vodaath in Brooklyn. Founded in 1912 in Europe and transplanted to the United States ten years later, Agudath Israel was initially unable to expand beyond its limited circle of sympathizers. In recent years, however, it has attracted more followers and now claims 20,000 adult male members (75,000 if one includes entire families), with a growing influence among the Orthodox.

Critics charge that the Agudath lacks muscle in Jewish life and that the movement's inability to develop more strength stems from its disinterest in secular politics and from the intense sectarianism cultivated in its yeshivot. Their goal, critics say, is mastery of the Talmud and its innumerable nuances, and not the normal give-and-take of more worldly affairs.

But this judgment is not quite so. The Agudath is changing rapidly. Most of its members are American-born, and 40 percent of the leadership is under the age of forty. The Agudath's executive president, Rabbi Morris Sherer, testifies before legislative committees and practices quiet diplomacy with politicians.

"Rabbi Sherer can pick up his phone and get Beame,

Carey and nearly everyone else anytime he wants to," says a New York City politician. "He's the most politically powerful rabbi in the state." Indeed, his office walls seem to bear that out. Photographs of the powerful are framed: Lyndon Johnson, Teddy and Bobby Kennedy, Nelson Rockefeller, Hugh Carey, Abe Beame, Gerald Ford.

But whatever the true extent of his influence, Sherer and the Agudath speak publicly nowadays for what they perceive to be "the validity of Torah in establishing and enunciating Jewish policy." Consequently, Agudath has helped evolve state laws banning discrimination against observers of the Sabbath and forbidding restaurants and delicatessens from calling themselves "kosher-style." They have promoted a hospital patients' bill of rights. They favor government support for nonpublic schools.

In addition, the great issues that have seared all of world Jewry since 1933 receive a strong, if unique, response from the Agudath. Generally reluctant to join with other Jewish groups in public demonstrations, Agudath backed out of one "Save Soviet Jewry" rally, and members held their own public recitation of the Psalms as their manner of protest against Moscow. "We don't want to be just another yarmulke without any role in shaping policy," explains Sherer.

When all the major groups called a mass rally in late 1974 to protest the appearance of PLO chief Yasir Arafat at the United Nations, the Agudath charged that the rally sponsors were secular Jews—for the Agudath, almost a dirty word—"an anomaly . . . which we cannot accept." And since the Agudath views Israel as a religious rather than a lay political center, and that nation's conscription of women into the military and its approval of autopsies as anathema, "endangering the security and survival of our People," the Agudath prefers to act independently. It did finally agree to join the Arafat protest, but still managed to censure Moshe Dayan, one of the speakers. Dayan told the audience, "We have no one to depend upon but ourselves." Stunned, appalled, the Agudath replied: "He forgot the lessons of the Yom Kippur War; the delusion of might as the savior of Israel is bankrupt. . . . It is the Jewish people's unequivocal faith in G-d, who determines the fate of nations and men. . . ."

Further, when Jewish terrorists began attacking Soviet citizens and their property in this country, Agudath issued a "historic" document. "Violence and terror by Jews are contrary to Torah law," stated its Council of Torah Sages (comprised of six prominent rabbis and deans of yeshivot, in May 1976). "Whoever follows these ways will suffer extreme retribution. The general community should distance itself from them and their ways."

The Agudath also has a special approach toward pulpit rabbis who have a nonobservant constituency. There is always the apprehension mentioned earlier—that pulpit rabbis might have to compromise in halakhic matters.

"At Torah Vodaath," says Wolpin, "our Reb Feival Mendelowitz, whom we all honored and respected for his learning, always called himself *Mr.* Mendelowitz because he firmly believed that if anything was to be done for the future of American Jewry it would be in the classroom and not from the pulpit." Which is yet another way of saying that Agudath rarely concerns itself with the congregational and rabbinic considerations given so much time and energy by fellow Jews in other branches.

Wolpin adds: "The Agudath does believe in pulpit rabbis because we need mentors and guides in such questions. In fact, there is now a tendency among the young to designate their own rabbis. They call them 'teachers of the domain.' But despite this, yeshiva graduates who are congregational rabbis return again and again with their serious problems not to other pulpit rabbis but to their former teachers and yeshiva deans, who are totally immersed in Jewish law."

Those teachers serve in a wide network of yeshivas in such cities as Cleveland, Chicago, Baltimore, New York, Scranton, Denver, Philadelphia, Montreal and Toronto; their kollels are scattered throughout the eastern seaboard but have nothing to do with the organized rabbinate. Kollel graduates serve as pulpit rabbis in many sections of the country, but their essential responsibility remains mastery of Judaic scholarship. Rabbi Moshe Feinstein, one of the world's eminent talmudic authorities, revered by the Agudath for his personal piety, humility and knowledge, deals with religious law, not with the problems that occupy most rabbis.

There is a good deal of tension between some Orthodox rabbis and the Agudath. "While the Agudath rejects compromise in spiritual matters," says Sherer, "many pulpit rabbis, particularly in small communities, seem to believe compromise is the only way of keeping their congregants in the fold. This has led to a strained relationship with us." Sherer also insists that the Orthodox pulpit rabbis have lost their authority and have been supplanted by yeshiva deans. "In truth, the synagogue should take second place to the house of study. And the rabbi who counts most is the one who teaches you, not the one who preaches to you. Sermons and pastoral duties are hardly important by comparison with the rabbi's essential purpose—teaching."

The large Orthodox rabbinate rarely undergoes public scrutiny and self-criticism. Yet many of its dilemmas are the same as those of its counterparts in other branches of Judaism. Almost fifteen years ago, Theodore L. Adams, then rabbi of Congregation Ohab Zedek in New York City, published his findings. The goal of the Orthodox rabbi, he wrote, was quite at odds with what he actually did during the course of his working day. Ideally, the rabbi tried "through the acquisition of higher Jewish learning to prove himself an instrument of practical Jewish living." In practice, however, he wanted to get more influence on the way things worked in the larger world he encountered outside his synagogue. "Transmission and creation of Jewish knowledge" was one thing, but the Orthodox rabbi, concluded Adams, wanted a "share in the real management of the Jewish community from which he is excluded."

Apparently Orthodox rabbis have changed, moving away from the traditional scholar-sage image to more functional capacities long associated with non-Orthodox clergy. What did an Orthodox rabbi do as a pulpit rabbi? He was, said Adams, a spiritual leader, an authority on the law and its practice, a teacher of adults and children, a pastoral counselor, a developer of congregations, a school principal, a community worker, one who tried repeatedly to reach the "relatively informed with his interpretations of Judaism." He was also an envoy to non-Jews, an officiant at bar mitzvahs and services for young people, an attendee at congregational and community social functions and at ritual and educational committees, a lecturer, an invocation and benediction giver. The consequences, wrote Adams, were diversification and fragmentation. This conclusion was echoed in a *Tradition* poll of its Orthodox rabbinical readers in 1976; tentative results indicated their lack of time for Torah study, their desire for decision-making roles in general communal affairs and their deep concern over social and family problems in Jewish communities. This was a pace that deterred the idealistic young who might otherwise be attracted by the rabbinate. And then the major difficulty. How, in a workday that often ran twelve to eighteen hours daily, did an Orthodox rabbi—in fact, any rabbi who did his job well—find the time to study and reflect?

Sholom Rivkin relaxed in his simply furnished office on the ninth floor of a shabby building not far from Union Square in Manhattan. For decades orators and their critics had gathered in the tiny park below to argue politics rather than religion and its application to secular life, which is, after all, Rabbi Rivkin's central concern. He has an Orthodox congregation in Far Rockaway in the borough of Queens, but before that he worked in St. Louis and in Seattle, where, he said, he was especially happy. But his children were growing older, and life, even for the offspring of an Orthodox rabbi, was too open to the blandishments of a free Pacific Coast society, one which had few Jews and many temptations. Rivkin returned to New York City to be with his own, to raise his young in the communal womb of what many Orthodox Jews like to call "Torah Judaism."

Within that protective and symbiotic world, Rivkin also became the coordinator of a *bet din*, in whose offices he now sat. *Batei din* are religious courts which derive their authority from the Torah; their effectiveness emerges from the "willingness of Jews who are committed to the principles of Jewish law, to accept the court's jurisdiction." They deal with an extensive variety of personal and civil disputes. There are permanent *batei din* in Chicago, New York and Boston; when necessary, the courts are convened in other locations. In the Washington Heights neighborhood of northernmost Manhattan there is a bet din for business conflicts and divorce proceedings, where the disputants choose between *din* or strict law and *pesharah* or arbitration.

In 1968, in Boston, the Rabbinical Court of Justice of the Associated Synagogues of Massachusetts, an authorized bet din but one with a unique flavor under Rabbi Samuel I. Korff—the late brother of Nixon's passionate defender, Baruch Korff—heard an arbitration case between complaining Black and Puerto Rican tenants and Jewish landlords. Two members of each panel were approved by the tenants and landlords and one by the court. Their decision? To collect rentals but have them placed in an escrow account for emergency repairs.

The same bet din was also asked in 1970 to rule on the legality of American involvement in the Vietnam War to determine, said one of the petitioners, a professor, "if there existed a basis for conscientious objection among Jews." The answer was yes, a Jew could in good conscience be a C.O. But the larger purpose of the question, and of the court, was to uncover the moral guidance Judaism could offer on contemporary social issues.

Rivkin's court deals with many issues, but more often than not with the *get* or religious divorce. There are several stages in a get. The husband and wife meet initially with Rivkin and discuss their differences; if the situation is irreconcilable, as most cases are by the time they reach his ear, then divorce is permitted, although grudgingly, as a necessary evil to be avoided if possible.

There may be *too many* divorces among the Orthodox, Rabbi Moshe Bick of the bet din in Boro Park, Brooklyn, complained recently. There was, he said, an "epidemic" among yeshiva and Hasidic couples. He blamed the superior education females tended to receive. Virtually all the *gittin* that reached his court were begun by wives who "after the wedding" discovered that their husbands had "no manners" and did "not know how to talk to a girl." Rabbi Bick, the eldest son of the last rabbi of Medzhibozh, the shtetl of the Baal Shem Tov, founder of Hasidism, granted twenty-five divorces in 1974–1975.

"The reasons for divorce are common enough. Money, sex, in-laws, you name it," Rivkin says. "Once we had a husband who was indifferent to kashrut and Shabbat, and the wife and her family came to us. Another time the husband, an Israeli, had moved to the Far East, and we had to have a long-distance get with a surrogate named by the husband. Interestingly, I would say that 80 percent of those who come here aren't completely observant."

Batei din are composed of elderly, presumably learned

rabbis, trained in special texts. Rivkin says a vast number of volumes have been written merely to discuss how the names of the people involved are to be written. "We have four scribes who practice the same lettering as in the Torah." And when the special document of divorce is finally written, each witness reads it and the husband then states, in essence, in both Hebrew and English to his now ex-wife, "This is your get and receive this get to me, and with it you shall be permissible to any man." With these exceptions: The divorced woman cannot marry before ninety-two days have passed, so that if she is pregnant the baby's father will be known; no divorced woman can ever marry a Cohain (Leviticus 21:7); once divorced, the man may remarry the same woman if she has not remarried.

One afternoon on a cold spring day a couple in their early thirties sat next to one another on a two-seat plastic couch in Rivkin's outer office, waiting for the court to convene, never once talking with each other. Nearby sat another rabbi, with full black beard, oblivious to anyone else in that tiny anteroom as he wrote in the Hebrew script with quill and ink.

Out of hearing, Rivkin described their problem.

"Those two have refused to reconcile. They're about to be divorced. And we're obliged to grant their request. But still, the best time I've had recently was when two kids came in for a get. You know, I thought to myself, they still seem to like one another. They were so comfortable with one another. So I decided to try to bring them together again. They went home and gave up the divorce idea. Now that's my idea of being a good rabbi, too."

"I'll say this about the Rabbi Rivkins in America," said someone who has observed him in his Far Rockaway shul as well as at the bet din. "It's people like him who help make Orthodox Jewish life work. His life is dedicated to keeping people believing, practicing Jews and failing that, getting them to stay Jewish, even nominally. That kind of rabbi never makes the papers or TV, but they're saving us as Jews."

Meyer Meyerson, the spiritual leader of B'nai Israel in Middle Falls (near Los Angeles) and a member of RCA, was born in 1921 into an Orthodox family from the Fairfax section of Los Angeles.* At that time Los Angeles, according to Rabbi Meyerson, had a large Jewish population, many of whom were Orthodox. He left home in 1941, at the age of twenty, and traveled across the continent for four days by train to enter Yeshiva University.

"I was close to Rabbi Joseph Soloveitchik [acknowledged as the leading religious-intellectual figure in modern Orthodoxy], a great man. He has a tremendous mind, he knows profoundly talmudic literature as well as modern philosophy. His theme—which I have tried to live by—is that life is really philosophical struggle. I remember around 1948 there was a very popular book published by a Boston rabbi, *Peace of Mind*. Soloveitchik was bothered by its very premise. Peace of mind, he said, was for the dead. A person grows by struggle. Progress comes from it. So does poetry. And philosophy." "It was," Meyerson says, leaning back in his very small and modest office, "a very exciting time in my life."

Meyerson was ordained in 1945, "the year the camps were liberated," and he thought of himself as an ardent, idealistic Zionist. Today, he has four children. His twenty-nine-year-old son studies Talmud in a Chicago yeshiva. "He didn't want to waste time in secular learning," says Meyerson. More right-wing than his father, theologically speak-

* Meyer Meyerson, the synagogues mentioned and the towns in which he worked are pseudonyms created to preserve the privacy of a real-life rabbi and his congregations. The significant facts are otherwise authentic.

ing, the son wants to devote himself exclusively to Jewish thought, whereas the elder Meyerson is more concerned with development of a synthesis between study and the practicalities of everyday life he meets in his synagogue.

A second child, a twenty-six-year-old son, studied at UCLA and graduated Phi Beta Kappa in linguistics. He is presently at the University of Oregon studying for a master's in anthropology and works part-time at the university library. But, says Meyerson with pride, he is also involved in the *Midrash* (or the discovery of the nonliteral meanings of the Bible) and conducts Saturday afternoon classes for college and postcollege men and women. A younger son, twenty, attends a yeshiva in Los Angeles and takes classes part-time at nearby UCLA. "I think people need secular thought too, and I'm glad he's had some of it," says Meyerson. He and his wife also have a twelve-year-old daughter.

Before he arrived in Middle Falls, Meyerson worked for ten years near San Diego, in Locklear, amid 500 Jews. When he arrived, he says, there was an old shul near the abandoned Cook Road section of the town. There had been a very distinguished Orthodox rabbi in Locklear for a quarter of a century; he had been paid very little and subjected to a secession by a part of his congregation into the Conservative movement. Meyerson was hired after his death.

"I was very lucky, for we had a rebirth in Locklear. The shul blossomed. It attracted young couples, and I encouraged them to build a new Orthodox shul up the slope in town in a Jewish neighborhood. Over the years many became kosher. We built a day school from the kindergarten to the second grade. We started sending older kids to Los Angeles for special seminars. It was all so exciting. Imagine—we managed to build an Orthodox shul without an Orthodox population. In fact, the established Jews were upset by our new ways. I suppose they wanted us to remain quiet and out of sight lest the non-Jews confuse us with them. In the end, though, my little day school proved my

biggest disappointment. We had too small a town population to make up a third grade, and what with children of
my own, no day school meant—for Miriam, my wife, and
the children—no Locklear."

When he first came to Middle Falls, that onetime overwhelmingly non-Jewish community had begun to crack.
Nearby, Lake Middle Falls, a private development with
tree-lined streets and expensive ranch houses, began to allow
Jews to buy its homes. Its country club, which had long
refused to entertain the idea of anyone but white Christians
as members, also began to give way. Vast suburban developments were built, and the short freeway trip into the
city lured large numbers of Jews to Middle Falls' safe streets,
excellent shops, good schools and its abundance of synagogues and Jewish organizational life.

Today, he sees Middle Falls and its small but quite influential 5 percent Orthodox Jewish population as the
stronghold of Orthodoxy in Southern California. Dynamic
and well-organized, this Orthodox community has formed,
he believes, the nucleus of demonstrations for Israel and
for Soviet Jewry. Yet one issue that still pains him dearly
is the general deterioration of relations between Jews and
Blacks.

"I'm a religious and political liberal. In Locklear I was
active in many anti-discrimination movements. Here, I try
to stay out of politics, but when the focus is on the Jewish
community and especially on the Orthodox, I am *forced* to
take a stand."

To be sure, Orthodoxy has not really accepted the
prophetic tradition as a guide to social action, a term more
closely associated with Reform and Reconstructionist temples. When rabbis marched alongside Martin Luther King,
Jr., in Selma, Alabama, and in Cicero, Illinois, practically
no Orthodox rabbis or laymen were to be seen. Rather,
fears of Black anti-Semitism have consistently been voiced,
especially since large numbers of Orthodox Jews in New

York City and Philadelphia, for example, live in neighborhoods or have held jobs threatened by Black or Hispanic
aspirations. This explains, but only in part, Orthodoxy's
general reluctance to support the civil rights movement in
the 1960s, as it also explains, again only partially, why
Meir Kahane's Jewish Defense League has found so many
followers among the Orthodox young.

And although all the national Jewish religious bodies
sooner or later came to oppose the Vietnam War, official
Orthodoxy has, according to Conservative Rabbi Gilbert S.
Rosenthal, "either supported the war or [has] remained
neutral." Charles Liebman pointed out that while many
Orthodox blocs were openly pro-war, "no public Orthodox
leader denounced it."

On other, more national and secular issues, the organized
Orthodox are indifferent or silent, unless the issue im-
pinges directly on their religious lives. Federal aid to their
schools, abortion and divorce laws, the use of contraceptives,
Soviet Jewry, Israeli expansion into Arab lands on the West
Bank, efforts to resist "humane slaughter" groups who attack
Jewish animal slaughter as cruel and barbaric, the issue of
military chaplains—all these consume their time and interest. Obviously, though, individual Orthodox Jews are no
less concerned with general problems than anyone else.
Liebman discovered, for example, that RCA-member rabbis
were more against the Vietnam War than the council's
spokesmen. Responding to his questionnaire in 1967, 12.1
percent favored withdrawal and 53.2 percent were for
negotiations and deescalation.*

Meyer Meyerson's B'nai Israel congregation has 275
families, and the demands they make on their rabbi are

---

* In 1976 the Union of Orthodox Jewish Congregations of America publicly announced support for amnesty for draft resisters and
deserters. Pointing to Jewish traditions, it declared: "Those who refuse to serve, be it from conviction or cowardice, are to be granted
eventual re-entry into society."

much the same as on rabbis in non-Orthodox synagogues. Given this fact, the difference between Meyerson and many non-Orthodox rabbis centers to a large degree in the advice he seeks to offer and the help he tries to render. Essentially, he emphasizes the necessity of respecting halakha and kashrut and urging the few in his shul who do not to adhere to these rituals.

Some examples. Two sisters have not spoken to one another for years. Meyerson tries to arrange a reconciliation but fails. Then another chance arises when one of the women marries. Meyerson moves in quickly, affects a reestablishment of relations and then withdraws. Several years later he learns that once again the two have broken off in anger.

A couple come to him for help. They have adopted a non-Jewish infant and want Meyerson to see that he is properly circumcised. After, they draw closer to the synagogue and are accepted by the members. Meyerson is admittedly very fussy about conversions. Who shall he accept and who shall he not? Is it hypocrisy on his part to convert the child while his parents are not even *shomer Shabbat* (Sabbath observers)? As the child grows, however, he becomes very observant and is finally ready, at thirteen years of age, for his bar mitzvah. The parents then return to Meyerson. A cousin, they report, has married a non-Jew. Should they invite the couple to the ceremony? There would, said the father of the child, be non-Jewish guests in the shul, too. Meyerson ponders the question for a long time, and then opposes the invitation. (As liberal, as tolerant a man and rabbi as he thought of himself, Meyerson recalls, he felt one simply had to draw the line somewhere. The task of a rabbi was to try to help his people become more religious. To invite the couple, he told the parents, would be tantamount to approving religious intermarriage. And that, he believes, spells suicide for the Jewish people.)

Other cases abound. A graduate of a yeshiva is caught

selling drugs. Meyerson appears before the judge, pleads his case and has him released. One Monday morning (on Rosh Hodesh, he remembers) a wife waits for him on the bench outside his office. "Rabbi," she says quietly, "my husband beat me." On another day he learns of fake bankruptcies by local businessmen, which he privately derides as unethical and anti-Jewish. On yet another day, one of his loyal members tells Meyerson of his shock upon learning that his wife had been unfaithful. Then, too, there are newly arriving Russian Jewish immigrants to attend to— he tries to find them jobs during a recession, to locate furniture and clothing for their basic needs, to encourage them to send their young to yeshivot. His Rabbi Fund, for which he and his wife raise money, tutors them, hires a private nurse for those desperately ill, pays the $300 fee for a cemetery plot when one of them dies and finds a tutor for a sixteen-year-old from Odessa too old for yeshiva. All the while there are the inevitable bickerings among his congregants, the insistence by some on special favors, the appeal for particular honors, the pleas that bingo or "Las Vegas" gambling nights be instituted.

Nevertheless, it is his internal life that Meyerson finds most satisfying. In 1969 he received a master's from UCLA in American Jewish history. His thesis tried to evaluate the way leading Americans dealt with the Holocaust between 1941 and 1945. But his interests today are centered more on Jewish philosophy, Martin Buber and, of course, Joseph Soloveitchik.

"He comes to New York City every so often, and I try to fly there when I can. The rooms are jammed just to listen to him. His idea is to use talmudic texts and to try to make [them] relevant. For instance, my own interpretation is that when a person in *Shimona Esra* or the silent prayer says 'Blessed art thou our G-d,' in the Jewish tradition you bow down at the beginning saying, *ashem* (G-d). The question

is, should we prostrate ourselves when saying the name of
G-d? G-d makes people stand up. In sum, then, Judaism
wants to help individuals maintain dignity."

Or consider another example Soloveitchik gives. "There
is a kabbalistic concept of *tzimtzun* or withdrawal. The idea
being that when G-d created the world it was necessary for
G-d to withdraw. The moral is that parents have to allow
children independence so that they may find their own way.

"The role of the rabbi, as I see it then, is to try to study
talmudic texts and draw out [the] vital parts. Sometimes the
texts are very hard, so you have to struggle. But as I discovered early on, it is like a poem. Struggle gives to it
meaning. This aspect I have always enjoyed. I still like the
Talmud, but I find myself going back to the Bible, to simple
things. Now I even learn *siddur* [the prayer book].

"And yet, it's easy to become a hypocrite as a rabbi. It's
easy to preach and sermonize about others, say about going
on *Aliyah* (moving permanently to Israel) or about ethnics
or Blacks or war. For myself, I try to remember what the
Dubnar Maggid said to the Vilna Gaon in the Midrash:
You're sitting in the synagogue, studying. The real test is to
go into the marketplace and the street. You cannot be interested in just your own life. Job was generous until his
troubles. But on the other hand, Abraham went in search of
the poor and dispensed charity. This accounts in part for
the ordeal I have in writing sermons. I have a very intelligent, well-educated audience. So I ask myself: What's
meaningful to them? What clichés should I avoid? I'm not
like some rabbis who rely on books of sermons. So many
times I spend Friday struggling, trying to think up one
that's relevant but combined with halakhic texts."

In one sermon he extrapolated a commentary from
Nachmanides, a thirteenth-century Spanish talmudist, kab-
balist and biblical interpreter, the first leading rabbi to
declare the settlement of Israel a biblical "precept." Re-

reading Nachmanides, Meyerson realized that although Jews had never reached Israel, they did manage to reach Mount Sinai; there they built a sanctuary, thus redeeming themselves. His sermon pointed to the lesson. If, he said, one has a worthy model to follow in life, one finds it easier to cope. Defining "model" as a belief or tradition worth pursuing, he told his congregants on Saturday morning that even in their furiously paced worldly roles, so long as they held fast to that model they could survive and live with dignity and integrity. For Rabbi Meyerson the implication was crystal clear: the synagogue was a model, too.

And the rabbi?

The long-range tendency in Orthodoxy appears to be away from professional pulpit rabbis and toward religious scholarship. More young talmudic students want to teach in yeshivot, and the result has been a shortage of competent Orthodox pulpit rabbis. "The work is hard, it's full-time and we're not paid too well," says Meyerson. "I don't know if my own kids can take it." In fact, in his son's yeshiva virtually none of the students become pulpit rabbis. Meyerson thinks pulpit rabbis are looked down upon.

Not far from Rabbi Meyerson's office is a *shtiebl*. A one-time residence, it now serves as a gathering place for those interested in praying and studying one's own way, in one's own place. Founded originally in the eighteenth century by Hasidim, especially in Lithuania, as a revolt against rabbinic authority, it is still the typical Hasidic prayerhouse. It is also a concept now growing more popular among other Orthodox, especially those who resent building-fund donations, more formal group prayer and the petty rivalries that often develop among synagogue members. A visitor to a shtiebl in Middle Falls, a five-minute drive from Meyerson's synagogue, is welcomed and then left alone, as many of the worshipers sway to the rhythm of the chants. In what was once a living and dining room (and separated from the women by a wall), one man asks, "Why do I need a rabbi? Everyone here knows just as much, and we study more, too. We're small and manageable. Conservative and Reform rabbis are not worth anything. But a lot of Orthodox rabbis are no better. Here, I'm my own boss."

There is a sense of identity in the shtiebl, as well as an absence of authority, unlike—at least to many devotees— the more organized synagogue with its inevitable layer of officials. But others think the shtiebl a mixed blessing. The shtiebl-goers avoid shul membership and all that entails, yes, but—said another California rabbi, his voice rising in exasperation—"they forget we're a total community. Who but the synagogue worries about the mikveh, kashrut? Who has youth programs, forums, senior citizen activities? Not your shtiebl."

Meyerson shares these objections. But he also goes beyond them. The trends to him are reasonably evident. There will in the future be less need for pulpit rabbis; the shtiebl phenomenon will grow; the rabbis will increasingly have to turn to other authorities for the answers to serious questions. The result will be new types of Orthodox communities and organizational life.

"Don't get me wrong. The Orthodox rabbinate definitely has a future in America. In some very Orthodox communities there aren't too many rabbis. Many are ordained, but few practice. And yet many Jews, perhaps those who don't know as much or even those who do, need rabbis to teach and guide them.

"Orthodoxy is now on the go. The initiative is in our hands. The campuses are turning to us. Middle Falls is a creative place. Our day schools offer superior education. People everywhere are looking for genuine, more authentic roots. It took us fifty years to organize, establish schools and develop leadership. Now we're on the way.

"It's not simple-minded boosterism when I say this. But

we Orthodox are no longer defensive. We feel optimistic, even confident. We've got disunity, there's too much in-fighting, we often affect a good deal of lack of respect and tolerance for other, non-Orthodox Jews. The extremists among us have too much sway. But trends are trends."

The most obvious Orthodox forces are Soloveitchik, the moderate, his more than 1,000 students now teaching and writing; Moshe Feinstein, conservative sage of the yeshivot and Agudath Israel; and the two ultra sects, the Lubavit-scher and Satmar, with their circles of influence and authority. All four have in common the fact that none of the leaders are pulpit rabbis. Their power is exerted through their loyal followers.

"Practicing rabbis play second fiddle," says Meyerson. "We are bound by the authority of those authorities. So, it's fair to ask: If they're the authority, why bother with ordinary rabbis? My response is that we Orthodox need rabbis where the leadership and the laymen are weak, both organiza-tionally and religiously. And in terms of knowledge of Judaism. . . . Where people are highly educated in Jewish affairs they can manage their own services. But there will always be large numbers who need rabbis. Once the Ortho-dox rabbinate had to be like their peers among the Conservatives and Reform. Now in Orthodoxy, where scholarship is more vital, and sermons not crucial, and as many Jews become more knowledgeable and self-sufficient, the rabbinate will change. We will have different tasks in the next ten or twenty years. I think we'll be more the teacher, more the abitrator."

Two thousand miles to the east of Middle Falls, in the South Euclid suburb of the city of Cleveland—where virtually all the Jewish population has fled the city for the suburbs—Orthodox rabbi Shubert Spero ponders the chang-ing role of the rabbinate in the light of his experiences in

Cleveland and that community's history. What Arthur
Hertzberg wrote in 1966 about rabbis nationally may just
as well apply today to Cleveland's clergy. "The scholars
among the rabbis have no real power in Jewish communal
affairs," concluded Hertzberg. "There is hardly one rabbinic figure today who commands the attention of the entire
Jewish community." He is the "least powerful and least
effective" in influencing national Jewish life, declared Jacob
Neusner; he is the hired hand of an individual synagogue
rather than what he once was—a student of Torah, the
Hebrew Scriptures and the Oral Tradition, a leader and
sage who inspired and led an entire community.

But if, unlike the past, the contemporary rabbi serves one
congregation, it is at least his own. Despite the fact that most
of his members are far better educated—in worldly subjects
at least—than their parents were, they are no doubt less
knowledgeable in Judaic terms. Hence the possibility, certainly evident in Spero's Young Israel of Cleveland, that he
does teach people who eventually achieve positions of
wealth and power. It is a local and therefore a more restricted sort of influence, but influence nonetheless.

There are those who do not favor the "political-leader"
rabbis. "Power, national impact, the ability to make head-
lines in the *New York Times* and *Plain Dealer* and be consulted by the big boys. Imagine: 'Rabbi Spero called in for
Advice by President Ford' on Walter Cronkite's show. James
Reston and William Buckley debating the Spero Plan to
SAVE AMERICA. Who needs that?" asked an Orthodox doctor
in the Cleveland area, who prefers anonymity. "It's all so
pompous and sought only by the egotists for whom Jewish
life is only a marginal concern. The Orthodox *I know* want
our rabbi to be a first-class scholar, a guide through life's
problems, our main teacher, and accessible when we need
him. If any rabbi wants to dabble in outside politics, Jewish
or otherwise, okay. But his sole obligation to *us* is to attend

to *our* interests. Everything else is unimportant." Added his
wife: "I always ask rabbis who want to be nationally
heralded VIPs what relationship their views—which they're
so eager to air—have to halakha."

Shubert Spero, the rabbi, is not seeking national publicity.
He is, rather, a religious scholar and teacher. He has taught
philosophy at the Cleveland Institute of Arts, Case Western
Reserve University, Hiram College and the Cleveland College of Jewish Studies. More important to his members are
his customary functions, together with his writings on sickness, death, belief and faith. His many articles in the pages
of *Tradition*, published by the RCA, deal with such topics
as "Does the Science-Religion Conflict Rest on a Mistake?"
("It is not the conclusions of science that we fear but the
methods of science . . . before which religious beliefs must
either conform or show good reason why the logic of religious language justifies different criteria.") Other articles
include "Faith and Its Justification" and a variety of original
commentaries and derivative articles. When his congregation celebrated its fiftieth anniversary in 1972 and published
the usual ubiquitous and bland "souvenir journal" (a
euphemism for paid advertisements secured by twisting the
arms of local merchants), Spero couldn't resist the tempta-
tion to insert a sober discussion of the Book of Jonah "so
people wouldn't throw the journal away."

But power? And who indeed does run Jewish Cleveland?

"Let me tell you who runs what in this town," said a staff
member of a national Jewish organization in Cleveland.
"One day, the head of the Jewish Community Federation
discovered that unknown to him I had solicited his—and
Cleveland's—biggest contributor for my agency. Well, the
roof fell in. There were explosions from here to New York.
I had to lay off. And promise never ever to go that route
again. And believe me, I won't."

The same federation is the final authority, since it collects the money and decides on disbursement priorities. In Cleveland there is one annual fund-raising campaign. Anyone interested in giving to his pet cause, for example, must still make donations to the local federation. But then, part of the money ultimately goes to other worthy causes: to the Jewish poor, to day schools, to the elderly, to organizations publicizing anti-Semitism.

Still, there is endemic dissatisfaction with so forceful a display of muscle. In Rabbi Kenneth Roseman's pioneering study of power in Cincinnati he revealed, as mentioned earlier, that lay leaders, almost all wealthy and endowed more with a secular ethic than with any special insight into Judaism, did pretty well as they pleased, contacting rabbinical groups only as an afterthought. "I'm like that Miami Dolphin rabbi at their Orange Bowl games," said a Cleveland-area rabbi. "He roots them on, offers occasional invocations when his turn arises, and praises the game as the embodiment of progress and Americanism. But his influence *on the game* is zilch. Nobody asks him how to check off at the line or advise whether or not to play zone or man-to-man. He has nothing to say about profits. Those decisions are made by the bosses."

In Cleveland, some reach the same conclusions. Big Money is, as it is everywhere else, all-important. The Jewish Community Federation's self-perpetuating board of trustees does make most of the crucial decisions. But not all. And not always in utter isolation.

From the time he came to Cleveland, Spero says, there was a feeling in Cleveland that the rich should have the decisive voice because they gave most of the money. But despite this tradition, he argues, rabbis continue to maintain their influence, especially in areas that matter very much to them.

"There's room for everybody on the board of trustees. It's open. The federation cultivates younger people as leaders, getting them to understand Israel, Cleveland, Judaism. I myself am a delegate-at-large on the board, and while there's no accountability to the larger community, we all try our best. The federation especially is open-minded and they pursue Jewish interests. Once it was decided that a mausoleum in Mount Olive would be built, for Orthodox and non-Orthodox shuls. But, the Orthodox were opposed. It's against Jewish law, we said. They countered with a 'love it or leave it' attitude. So we went away angry and took out ads in protest, wrote news releases and got the federation people all excited. The upshot was that they tore down the mausoleum."

Does the pulpit rabbi then really matter in issues beyond the synagogue? To Spero, perhaps as a matter of self-defense and self-interest, he does, as do the other nineteen rabbis in Greater Cleveland. They have banded together loosely—five Conservative, five Reform, eight Orthodox—to press their "interests."

"We have power," insists Spero, "if we care to exercise it. For instance, the federation pays for kashrut supervision. All kosher butchers are certified by two inspectors. The halakhic committee is Orthodox. In 1960, ten years after I first arrived here, we had sixty butcher shops. Now there are sixteen. The federation's initial response was to let one inspector go to try to save money. We rabbis protested, in a bloc, to the board of trustees and reversed the federation's professionals. That's rabbinical power, even if it was negative. Moreover, the community needs the Orthodox if only for certifying kashrut. It's only in nonreligious matters that we are without influence."

But even there one wonders. When Blacks began moving into nearby Cleveland Heights in the mid-1960s, the estimated 15,000 Jews—out of a total population of 60,000—began to fear that their three synagogues and kosher butchers and their bakeries and falafel stores along Taylor

Road were endangered, together with their Jewish Family Service Association, the Bureau of Jewish Education, Cleveland College of Jewish Studies, Hadassah, indeed the entire structure that constitutes their communal life. They could point to the disappearance of Jewish Cleveland's 105th Street, Baltimore's North Gay Street, Boston's Mattapan-Dorchester and Brooklyn's Brownsville neighborhoods almost overnight. People panicked. But several factors ultimately helped to calm the situation. For one, the Jewish Community Federation, thoroughly experienced and highly professional, took the lead and sought to deal with day-to-day concerns such as getting more police on the beat, improved zoning and securing better street lighting. It also declared war against "blockbusters." Rabbi Louis Engelberg, for more than thirty-five years head of the Taylor Road Synagogue, said: "We won in getting streets paved and parks lighted. And we ensured, through zoning regulations, that only a reasonable number of people could move into a single house, to prevent slums from developing."

Then, in 1972, Rabbi Marvin Spiegelman came on the scene. He had been rabbi of the Orthodox Oer Chodosh Synagogue for nearly ten years and educational head of the Yeshiva Adath School for nearly four. Bearded, wearing glasses, and resembling Mitch Miller, he was soon nicknamed the "kosher stabilizer." With federation aid he instituted a mortgage-assistance program and interest-free loans to lure non-Jewish whites to the area, which is near Case Western Reserve University. He also backed open housing, saying, "You either have to live with integration or get off the globe." And he supported those words with his presence—he lives in Cleveland Heights—and his money. In 1974 several prominent Jews together with Oer Chodosh pledged $25,000 for mortgage aid. "Synagogues have capital funds," says Spiegelman, "so the leader of our synagogue, Herman Herskovic, said, 'Let's borrow from

them.' We developed a program where we have authoriza-
tion to borrow $100,000 from agencies and federation
guarantees against default. Oer Chodosh immediately produced a check for $20,000 with another $5,000 committed."

Shubert Spero's cousin, a thirty-five-year-old academician
at Cleveland State University, lives with his wife and three
children on Bendemeer, where a dozen Black families also
reside. The Spero family is spread throughout the Heights,
but according to one account, Abba Spero stayed on in
affirmation of his family. "We considered moving," he told a
visitor, "but only to another home in this general neighborhood. The dynamic Orthodox community is here, and this
is where we will stay."

After a quarter century of service, Shubert Spero's own
judgment now is a grudging acknowledgment that yes, perhaps rabbis can and do matter outside the synagogue, if
only because of their involvement in the personal lives of
people. Young Israel, he says, has an abundance of personally committed members who care passionately about
Judaism, and he offers to them, he believes, guidance and
the benefits of his knowledge. Like a good many other
rabbis who also serve subliminally as a father figure for the
erring and the lost, he says he receives his highest praise
from congregants when he denounces them for neglecting
the mikveh or the laws of kashrut. Again like his peers
elsewhere, he counsels, teaches and visits hospitals. He takes
pride in the fact that of the 280 families in his shul only
5 percent are nonobservant, while a second shul in the area,
with 800 families, has—or so he believes—a majority who
are not shomer Shabbat.

Above all he frets, most notably about the boys in his
shul who do not grow up Orthodox, who never wear *tfillin*
or enter a synagogue or who marry non-Jewish girls. They
and their families tend to be, in Marshall Sklare's phrase,
"nonobservant Orthodox," quite an anomaly. Most of his

members, despite their Orthodox pretensions and sympathies, have a sketchy Judaic education, yet they remain close to the shul. Which only forces him to admit yet another private concern. Those who were educated at his synagogue as youngsters and are now adults with their own young—are these adults "good" Jews?

At Hiram College, thirty-eight miles away from his modest, one-story synagogue, Spero teaches courses on American Jewish history, archaeology and the Bible and the phenomena of Jewish survival; he also teaches philosophy at the Cleveland Institute of Art and the Cleveland College of Jewish Studies. In a course on survival, with virtually no Jews among his students, Rabbi Spero asks on final examinations such questions as:

> What is the special relationship between Judaism and Christianity which impels Christianity to view Jewish survival as a religious mystery?

> To say *what* happened is to describe. To say *why* it happened is to explain. What is involved in the process of explanation? Wherein lies the explanatory force of a set of sentences that purports to explain?

> The Jews were not the only people to suffer the loss of millions during World War II. Russians, Japanese, Gypsies and others were also victimized in large numbers. Was there anything unique about the Holocaust?

One day, leaving a synagogue in South Euclid, I entered a cab. The driver, from Cleveland and a non-Jew, said he had once taken "Jewish" courses with Spero at Hiram. We chatted for a while, and then as I was ready to get out at my destination, the young driver turned to me. "Funny thing happened to me after those courses," he said. "I became so interested in Jews I married a Jewish girl. You know that Spero guy should have been a teacher, not a rabbi."

6. "Radical? No,
Only a Conservative."

Stephen Lerner's nondescript Manhattan synagogue, Tifereth Israel, the Town and Village Synagogue, dark, dank and uninviting from the street but warm and comforting inside, was, not too long ago, a Ukrainian Orthodox Church. It stands in a neighborhood of soaring housing developments and small businesses once described by the novelist Thomas Wolfe as awesomely ugly, devastated with its "slumlike streets of rickety tenements and shabby brick" which still abound. East Fourteenth Street, where Lerner serves as spiritual leader in a Conservative synagogue, is also one of the city's foremost centers for drugs and prostitution, near the home territory of an especially sullen and menacing breed of outcasts plying their trade in the sordid hotels and miserable bars dotting the adjoining streets and avenues.

Lerner today concentrates on his own Manhattan synagogue, but as a promising scholar and editor of Conservatism's official quarterly, his concerns go well beyond Tifereth

Israel. In a *Conservative Judaism* symposium he edited, he finished off by commenting that the conclusions indicated a "somewhat hopeful picture for Conservatism in America." Yet, unlike a few optimists among that movement's hierarchy, his long-range prognosis was somber, even pessimistic. "Conservative Jews are those who belong to Conservative synagogues; they don't believe in Conservative Judaism, nor do they practice it."

Having blossomed in the post–World War II decades, surpassing in sheer numbers the other branches of Judaism, Conservatism is showing signs of slipping badly. Many of its leaders are far from hopeful about the decades ahead. The problem lies in part in Orthodoxy's refusal to atrophy and die in this country, as early Conservatives believed it would. But there are other grave traps ahead. Conservatism's interpretations of halakha have backfired, Marshall Sklare insists. It has also suffered a steady decline in observance of the Sabbath and of *kashrut*, as well as falling synagogue attendance. But so has Reform; the *Yearbook of American and Canadian Churches, 1976*, published by the National Council of Churches, declared that although 40 percent of all American adults attend weekly religious services, only 16 percent of the Jews attend synagogue weekly, a drop of 3 percent from the 1975 *Yearbook* report. In contrast, the editors claimed that 55 percent of Roman Catholics and 37 percent of Protestants go to church regularly. For pulpit rabbis this is sobering news.

Moreover, the ideological underpinnings of Conservatism seem unclear. "Now to whom are you talking about ideology?" asked Rabbi Harry Halpern of Brooklyn of his peers gathered at a rabbinical convention. "Shall I talk about ideology to a congregant who feels that one of the great events of his existence is a breakfast with a sports hero? To such people you want me to talk ideology?"

Or ritual observance. Rabbi Gilbert Rosenthal of Oceanside, New York, calls it a "crazy-quilt pattern, ranging from full observance to virtual nonobservance." The result is an ominous state of drift. In the short run, one knows Conservatism will endure. But in the long run, will it be able to muster the vitality to avoid being swallowed by other branches of Judaism? Most grievous of all worries, however, is (as Sklare concluded in 1972) that the movement is "no longer confident that it can be attractive to its youth." And in the long run too, Steve and his wife, Anne Lapidus Lerner, both young and talented and thoroughly grounded in Judaism, sense quite rightly the larger "crisis" of Conservatism and America's Jews: Can the Jews as a people long endure in the freedom and materialism of American life? Can there be a genuine Jewish people without a genuine Jewish tradition and without faith?

Short and youthful (he is thirty-four years old), Lerner seems to flourish in this atmosphere. At first meeting he appears intense, often anxious and certainly impatient with fools, an impression that is reinforced in subsequent encounters. Sitting in his minuscule and inordinately cluttered office, surrounded everywhere with books, magazines, reprints of articles, mimeographed sheets and papers stashed haphazardly, he is repeatedly interrupted by the phone's ringing; sometimes he gnashes his teeth in utter exasperation after a clash with his secretary. Actually, Lerner seems the mind's-eye portrait of the city dweller, hurried, trenchant, abrupt, preoccupied and impatient, on the edge of being overwhelmed and inundated by the flood of work set before him and the incessant demands made on his time and life.

A rabbi's rabbi, said someone of him at the seminary. A comer, said someone else at a national Jewish agency. Still, he annoys some. A onetime congregant called him too ambitious as well as too innovative in the synagogue. Too Jewish, added the ex-member's wife. Too radical, said a visitor in their apartment—but, she added, the kind who carries as his stock-in-trade a degree of integrity absent in ordinary American Jewish life.

Diversity and intensity and passion were not mentioned by friends and critics, but they are qualities that apply to Lerner. In fact, he may well be all observers say he is, for he approaches life and his notions of Judaism with gusto. When, for example, he was moved to action by Jewish feminism he persuaded his wife—or so she believes—to support him in his convictions. With the support of his ritual committee and the males and females in the congregation (but not his board of trustees), he introduced a woman Torah reader at services as well as permitted one couple to be called to the Torah in sequence, so that both might be present when their infant daughter was given a Hebrew name. Hardly an insignificant feat, inasmuch as the Conservatives continue their sorry record in denying women full religious equality. In 1976 eighteen men were ordained as rabbis by the Jewish Theological Seminary; a short time earlier the seminary had refused to support admission of women candidates for the rabbinate, meaning that not until 1981 at the earliest will it be possible to ordain female rabbis. Is the drive for women's rights within Judaism motivated by "genuine deprivation, or [is it an expression of] a more superficial drive for equality and egalitarianism?" asked JTS Chancellor Gerson Cohen in the *JTS Bulletin* of January 1975. What impact might it have on "the meaning, cement and structure of the Torah"? But if Conservatism prefers to play it safe, Lerner and his wife do not.

"The last bastion of manhood is gone!" the journalist Roslyn Lacks once overheard the pilot of a small twin-engine plane at an airport in Maine say in surprise.

"A what?" he repeated to the slender and dark-haired young woman in blue jeans and white sweater seated beside her husband Dennis, a blond Panamanian-born rabbi. "You're going to be a WHAT?"

"A rabbi," said Sandra Eisenberg Sasso.

In her late twenties, Rabbi Sandy Sasso was ordained by the Reconstructionist seminary in Philadelphia. There are now women rabbis in New York City and London, and more are studying in Reform and Reconstructionist seminaries. Even a women's rabbinical alliance is being formed to represent their interests.

Lacks also uncovered little-known facts about Sasso's obscure predecessors, such as Martha Neumark, who, fifty years before Sally Priesand was ordained as its first woman rabbi in 1972, was refused ordination at Hebrew Union College.

Wrote Lacks: "When newspapers ran features on Martha Neumark in 1921, a sprinkling of other women began applying to rabbinical schools. Their applications received identical replies. Women might enter college and take all the work, but under no conditions would they be granted regular scholarships or the privilege of ordination." And Neumark herself added that "the admission of women as rabbis is merely another phase of the women question. Despite the fact that so many have achieved eminence in their chosen fields, a struggle ensues each time that a woman threatens to break up man's monopoly upon any industrial, political or social province."

Subtly, unknown to most Americans, Mordecai Kaplan's Reconstructionism had long pioneered in this field. His daughter was perhaps the first bat mitzvah back in 1922. In all thirty-six Reconstructionist congregations and havurot throughout this country, women are involved in every aspect of worship. In 1949 the Reconstructionists included women in the minyan. They honored them with aliyot. Women were permitted to read from the Torah and the *haftorah* and to act as a *gabbai*, or official of a congregation. Today, there are three Reconstructionist women rabbis; four are presently enrolled in the Philadelphia seminary, and eight were selected for the 1976–1977 academic year.

Lacks also wrote about the first woman rabbi, of whom very little is really known. Regina Jonas graduated Berlin's Reform Seminary just before World War II. "Her thesis question, 'Can a Woman Be a Rabbi?' received a flat No! from the Berlin Talmud professor who refused to sign her diploma," Lacks noted. "Dismayed but undaunted, Fräulein Jonas received ordination from a more receptive professor in Offenbach and served as a rabbi in a Home for the Aged until 1940, when she was taken to the concentration camp from which she never returned."

Women's lib led to Jewish women's lib and increasing restiveness and defensiveness. When Priesand applied for membership in the New York Board of Rabbis, an umbrella group which includes the Orthodox rabbinate, all the latter were incensed at her temerity. A columnist in the Orthodox and widely circulated *Jewish Press* promptly asked whether it was possible to be religious—that is, Orthodox—and a feminist. His answer was, of course, negative.

On the other hand, a Hillel study published in 1975 revealed that widespread changes were under way on the campus among women who wanted to be closely aligned to Judaism. Jewish females had adopted traditional male roles at college services, counted themselves in the minyan, served as cantors and read—as in Lerner's synagogue— from the Torah. A few even excluded males from services, but that move was faddish and extremist and proved ephemeral. In explanation, one young woman who had participated in such a service said it was less to keep out their male peers than to stress the distinctly female aspects of God. Nevertheless, true equality means no exclusivity.

A wide variety of experiments are being conducted, and it will prove difficult to limit or restrict them in the years ahead. At the University of Pennsylvania, the Haggadah has been revised to cite women in the Exodus. At Brown, an all-female service altered the prayer book, using a feminine pronoun for God and adding new verses and translations that "speak to us as women." The phrase "to bring forth" was edited to read "to give birth." At Chicago, Maryland, Miami, Texas, Michigan, Ohio State, Brandeis, Wisconsin, Oklahoma, Northwestern and many other schools—indeed wherever our daughters, sisters and wives study—feminist innovations have been accepted at Hillel-sponsored services, as well as in even more informal settings. At Harvard Hillel a woman hazzan has performed on Kol Nidre night. Friday night services are conducted without discrimination. At American University seminars, worship services and informal sessions have tried to raise a serious question: Has rabbinic tradition been correct in making women subservient to Adam, or does the Bible *as written* present a picture of equality not really understood?

Much attention has been focused in recent years on younger college women, but very little on the wives of rabbis. When a team of sociologists was asked in the early 1970s to study the Reform rabbinate, it spent comparatively little time on the rebbetzin, the rabbinical wife. The sociologists' conclusions were mixed. The wives, they found, were "ambivalent" about their roles. If they could relive their lives, 53 percent would want their mates to enter the rabbinate; 40 percent were fulfilled in their roles as rabbis' wives; but almost half the sample felt "the need for developing [their] potentialities outside the home and synagogue." A mere 6 percent would "prefer" their daughter to marry a rabbi.

To all this the senior rebbetzin of Atlanta's Hebrew Benevolent Congregation has much to say. She acknowledges that the traditional ideal portrayed the woman as wife and mother. (The *Zohar*: "The chief influence transforming a man's house into his home is his wife. The Sh'chinah will not foresake his house if his wife keeps it according to the ways of Israel.") But in the lost world of the East European shtetl, wives were compelled to work for economic reasons, to allow their husbands to study Torah. Their lives were consumed with holding the family together, raising the young, supporting and being supportive of their husbands. So there is a tradition of working wives.

And today? Until recently in this country the working rabbinical wife was the exception rather than the rule. Now the younger generation has begun to alter drastically that model.

"I see an entirely new ball game in young rebbetzinville from the one I entered," said Janice Rothschild, whose husband Jacob served in Atlanta for almost thirty years before his death. "Our generation formed relationships and habits before women's lib, traffic conditions, mobile society and the disappearance of domestic help radically changed almost everybody's way of life."

There is, indeed, a generational chasm between many wives (other than among fringe sects of right-wing Orthodoxy). "Marriage and children are part of my liberation," says Harriet, "but I want far more, too." Her husband is a rabbi near Pittsburgh, and they have been married fifteen years. "I rarely go to temple. I'd rather play tennis or sculpt. As far as I'm concerned, Al is a professional with his job. I've got my own interests."

Or Barbara, who has just earned her MBA and wants to pursue a career in management. It means traveling, often with male associates. She and her southern California husband have two children, five and eight, and she intends to leave them with a baby-sitter. "I went off to Chicago recently for a three-day conference. I was surrounded by attractive, bright men, men who would have taken me to bed the instant

I encouraged them. I didn't and I won't, but my husband is suffering. He's crazy jealous now. Once he searched my luggage to see if I had taken my diaphragm along on a trip. He wants me home. Wants me to go to those damned sisterhood meetings. I won't. We'll just have to work it out, or there'll be no marriage."

Phyllis, on the other hand, still studies psychology in the evening and cares for her three children. But she sees her task as primarily understanding and working with her husband. Her cousin Joanne just married a seminarian, and they live in Philadelphia, near the Reconstructionist school. There are tensions, Joanne and her husband admit, but these are more adjustment problems and economics than rabbinical. "Barry couldn't have chosen a better profession. My background is so-so in Jewish things, but through Barry and his studies I am discovering a whole new world, better than any I ever knew."

David Wolf Silverman and his wife Tziona, were rabbi-rebbetzin for nine years in Aurora, Illinois, and in the Riverdale section of the north Bronx before he left the pulpit for a professorship in medieval philosophy at the JTS. For them, at least, it was a good vantage point from which to observe the rabbinical wife—then and now. Both of them spoke to the 1976 seminary graduation class, and both came away feeling that while the feminist movement has no doubt left its mark and will continue to do so, there is too great an insecurity among the young wives. "I want my own life. . . . You can't buy me as part of a package deal" is coupled with confusion about the role they are expected to play. Obviously, the hoary tradition of the rebbetzin is dead, but what the years ahead will bring—or so the Silvermans believe—is increased tension for the confused women, tension with their husbands and consequently tension between rabbis and congregations.

And Anne Lerner?

"If someone asks me if I had a daughter, would I want her to marry a rabbi, I would answer I'd rather she became a rabbi herself."

Like many other wives of rabbis ("Don't call me rebbetzin," she says with some heat), Anne Lerner knows what is expected of her and her son. But she has many of the reservations shared by a growing number of younger, more worldly and certainly far better educated wives of rabbis. Increasingly one detects an air of professionalism in those intent on serving family, husband and self; an exceptionally large number of wives are advancing well beyond the limited and parasitic world of ladies' auxiliaries. Rabbinical wives and the females of the congregation have more than ever been descending from the balcony, winning access to male sanctuaries of authority and power. For many, it is an insurrection, even sacrilegious.

A friend and a colleague of many of the more active feminists, Anne is a professional in her own right—novel enough for most rabbinical wives. She is completing her Ph.D. dissertation in comparative literature at Harvard on "Gide's Saül and Its Biblical Background," and is an instructor in modern Hebrew literature at the JTS Teacher's Institute. She has also written for the *American Jewish Yearbook*.

Like Isaac Bashevis Singer's Yentl, who wanted desperately to become a yeshiva student, and like Martha Neumark and Regina Jonas, Anne Lerner has a knowledge of Judaism equal to, if not beyond, that of virtually all males who are entitled to religious prerogatives from which she is barred solely by virtue of her sex. Expressing her frustration, she asks, "If male Jews can use tfillin and other religious symbols, why can't I?"

Jewish feminists are quite different from feminists who happen to be Jewish. Many are against Zero Population Growth, for one thing, although they recognize that decent

Jewish schooling and not numbers alone will ensure Jewish continuity. Some also consider the traditional practice of the mikveh to be wise.

"The Jewish feminist is more tolerant of Jewish history than other Jewish women. Ours was a very progressive tradition until the *Shulhan Arukh*. After that, the regression began. It is this inequality I think that has to be revised. But we Jewish feminists have never said what the more superficially Jewish women have charged, namely that Judaism is 'bad' because of a traditional morning blessing thanking God that you're not a woman."

Sentiments which no doubt Stephen Lerner favors. On the other hand, as editor of *Conservative Judaism* he polled pulpit rabbis, and the results revealed yet another nuance. "Most of the rabbis," he reported to his readers, "seem cautiously in favor of granting religious rights to women, but are hesitant to push the issue because there is no groundswell of support from their women."

Still, much of this, while principled, is abstract. More concrete is Anne Lerner's role as wife and mother. Sometimes members are offended because she objects when they pick up the Lerners' small child. At other times she and her husband hear about the complaints familiar to all rabbinical families: "Rabbi, how come your kid doesn't wear a yarmulke?" "Rabbi, why doesn't your child sit still at services?" "Rabbi, why does your son have such long hair?" "Rabbi, do you think it proper to allow your daughter to wear such skimpy clothes?" "Rabbi, your wife comes so rarely to services."

The list is large and the effect immeasurable. In Lerner's symposium with other Conservative rabbis he raised the issue of pressures on their families. The replies varied, of course, but there were distinct traces of resentment blended with sometimes grudging acceptance of their unique roles:

A rabbi's schedule raises havoc with my home life.

(Nashville, Tennessee)

To be a rabbi's wife is not easy and to be a rabbi's child is also difficult. It is also difficult to be the husband of a rabbi's wife and the father of a rabbi's child. . . . We rabbis are husbands and fathers and in that respect we are like everybody else— only more so.

(Syracuse, New York)

As the son of a rabbi I knew that the life of a clergyman is not what one might call a sheltered existence. I try not to say or infer to my children that they must lead a super-good existence because of my position. . . . Nevertheless, it is difficult. . . . Plans are forever being interrupted because of congregational obligations.

(Howard Beach, New York)

The Lerners know their rabbinical peers must undergo these experiences. But their son is still quite young, and his mother part of a younger and newer generation that may affect future Judaism. The Lapiduses—her parents— were high school teachers, both with very strong ties to a Sabbath-observing Conservative Judaism. Anne's paternal grandfather lived in Palestine during the 1880s, a mark of pride no doubt among many Jews. Her maternal grandfather had been ordained, although he never had a pulpit. Anne, her sister and brother, and their spouses are all involved professionally in Jewish life. Her sister, the only recipient of a master of arts in teaching Jewish education at Harvard, is married to a Toronto rabbi; her younger brother worked for a philanthropic organization, and *his* wife taught at a Jewish Community Center before their emigration to Israel. "I attend Saturday morning services," she says, "but seldom on Friday nights. I don't like them and see no need for them." Nor will she attend a bat mitzvah, which, unless conducted on Saturday, she calls "made-up activity for young women," since no reading of the haftorah is required.

"But on Saturday I take David [their son] and I go to sisterhood meetings occasionally, mostly because I feel I should. But I don't like to be pressured. I remember one woman resented deeply our not stopping by and saying hello to her at a bazaar."

If there are problems in the rabbinical marriage, there are also rewards—of joy discovered, of lasting friendships, of mind renewed and refreshed, of help rendered, of loving partnerships—and, for a good many, there is an unbounded fealty to Jewish life. Anne Lerner deeply values her husband's life as a congregational rabbi. She sees him turning nominal Jews toward a more understanding faith, and thereby changing their lives; setting moral examples; and teaching the Torah and the warmth of a Sabbath shared with fellow Jews. She also admires his contentiousness and his principled stands. When he objected to certain Orthodox dietary practices, he did not hesitate to criticize them in print and be criticized severely in turn. Nor did he hesitate to institute, with his congregation's enthusiastic approval, what may have been the first draft-counseling service run by a synagogue during the Vietnam War years. He opened his doors to the pacifist Jewish Peace Fellowship. With equal fervor he has led his congregation of teachers, nurses, clerical workers, civil servants and self-employed professionals out onto East Fourteenth Street for Simchas Torah (commemorating the completion of the cycle of the Pentateuch reading and the onset of a new reading "in order that Satan," or so declared the fourteenth-century scholar Jacob ben Asher, "shall have no opportunity of accusing Jews of having finished with the Torah"), twice in the evening and once in the morning, where they danced and sang. Similar spontaneous demonstrations in Moscow and Leningrad (following the arrival in 1948 of the first Israeli ambassador to the U.S.S.R., Golda Meir) signaled a moving, if then poorly understood, recognition by thousands of young Soviet Jews of the universal tie between all world Jewry. If assimilated Soviet Jews could risk demonstrating in front of two shabby, barely attended old Russian shuls, why not free Americans?

But on East Fourteenth Street in Manhattan?

It's our holiday, it's important, it's our people, insists Lerner. Most of the participants were children naturally, but there were also large numbers of men and women. Immediately after one of the celebrations, Lerner led them back inside the synagogue, where the women received aliyot—the first time ever in his synagogue.

"I think I respect my husband most because he wants to live a 'Jewish' life," says Anne. "I remember a pediatrician friend of ours saying after he had watched Steve in action that he 'felt' for Steve. And why? 'Because,' he answered matter of factly, 'I have five dying child patients and I can't handle the parents. Could I send them to Steve?' "

It was, she surmises, a recognition of the role a rabbi might conceivably play in such tragic instances.

"I know rabbis who do little except give sermons, who don't step out in front of their congregations. Steve does. Because pulpit rabbis have a following, a constituency. A small power base, but a power base. They're close to people, and our people listen to Steve."

Steve Lerner was raised near Sheridan Avenue in the Bronx, which was overwhelmingly immigrant and Jewish in those years, but Lerner was far more open to the blandishments of secular America than to religious faith. To another ex-Sheridan Avenuer, the old neighborhood reminded him of his beloved Odessa. "All the young people were interested in assimilating. Yiddish was dying. The few Zionists cared about Hebrew, but almost nobody about *Yiddishkeit*." Reli-

gious observances, added one of his old friends, were
spiritless, superficial, sterile. It was a miracle, muses Lerner
looking back, that anyone learned anything in the Hebrew
school classes they attended after public school.

All the same, his father was religious, and Steve studied
Hebrew in junior high school. He recalls coming home from
school when he was twelve and being offered a Nabisco
cookie by his mother. "I always had this Jewish love in my
heart, mostly I guess from my father. So I said to my mother,
'either Nabisco leaves or I do.' She was astonished. But the
cookie, I explained to her, wasn't kosher."

At Columbia University he wrote editorials for the daily
Spectator. He also grew interested in ancient history because
of a non-Jewish instructor who specialized in the parallels
between the Gospels and the Talmud. "I know now that I
then needed a rebbe, a youth group, a movement, a Jewish
camp, *anything* that was entirely committed to Judaism. The
Bronx had been for me a vast Jewish wasteland, despite its
many Jews. I met two *Spectator* editors who were Orthodox,
the first peers who knew Judaism and took it seriously, I
saw immediately that a fusion of two worlds was possible."

But not quite yet, for he received a grant to study history
at the University of Iowa. He remembers stepping down
from the bus in the depot in Iowa City. "Where are the
Jews?" he asked himself, a little awed and frightened. Looking hard then for what is currently called "identity" and
what he prefers calling "authenticity," both efforts to define
the parameters of one's inner life, he found the local synagogue and began camping there Fridays and Saturdays. Soon
he was asked to teach in its religious school. "I loved that
shul and wanted so badly to be associated with something
Jewish. But I also wanted it to live and not just be a dead
remnant of history. Prayer, the synagogue, the rituals,
started to mean something special. Had I stayed in New
York City, it never would have happened."

Lerner was ordained at the Jewish Theological Seminary in 1967 and took his initial job in Riverhead, the county seat of Suffolk County on Long Island, one hundred miles from New York City and reached by sporadic and inefficient rail service or over badly designed and dimly lit roadways. It was the business center of what until recently was an agricultural community, dominated by Polish farmers, most of whom grew potatoes.

He had 125 families in his congregation, often more prosperous than his present temple membership. A few professionals, but mostly businessmen. Young, energetic, imaginative, single-minded in his determination to do things to keep Judaism alive and worth maintaining, Lerner worked hard to begin a thrice-weekly Hebrew school. "What do we need it for?" was a refrain he heard regularly. One weekly lesson was all that was needed to prepare the boys for bar mitzvah, many parents said. On Shabbat he formed a junior congregation and Bible discussion class. "What for?" some demanded to know, fearful lest their children become too Jewish or appear in any way markedly different from the majority of other youngsters in the town's schools and streets. It was as if they feared looking like Philip Roth's Eli the Fanatic, wearing caftan and sidelocks as he walked down a wealthy suburban street, scaring his more acculturated co-religionists. A similar—and true—example was demonstrated by the uproar created by some Jews in Teaneck, New Jersey, when an Orthodox group decided to build a mikveh in their suburb.

"I was a member of Lerner's temple when he was in Riverhead," said a retailer there. "Believe me, he was bad news. We want to be liked by people here and we are. I was in World War II for four years. I belong to the American Legion and VFW. We want our kids to be loyal Americans, not stand out the way those freaks on the campus did a few years ago. Like it or not, our kids have to be accepted so they can get a good education and decent jobs. We can't make waves. And then we got this guy telling us the way to act was like we were in a Bronx shtiebl. So, a lot of us said screw you, rabbi. There's plenty of potential anti-Semitism around here still, especially among the Poles and some of the old time WASPs. If you look too peculiar you can stir them up. For guys like us in business here that's the last thing we want to do."

Lerner persevered. He formed a United Synagogue Youth unit, affiliated with the Conservative movement. He tried to introduce new methods. Each innovation proved a Pyrrhic victory. Attendance on Friday nights was an utter failure, since all the stores had to remain open. On one such evening he remembers barely more than a dozen in the seats before him. Exasperated, deeply frustrated, even hurt, and smarting over a growing list of resentments, he finally went to the leaders of the synagogue with an ultimatum. Scream-ing, he says, he vented his fury in invective and sarcasm. Even earlier, during Yom Kippur, he let his members know what was bothering him.

"Why do you need a synagogue? he demanded of them. "You don't really call *this* a synagogue. It's a museum of Jewish antiquities."

"Why a synagogue, rabbi? It's all for the kids, rabbi, all for the kids," answered one of his allies, a clothing retailer who was ardently pro-Israel and also supported the Black and Puerto Rican migrant workers in the area who are ex-ploited by many local farmers. If there weren't any young, he suggested, most wouldn't need a synagogue.

Riverhead Jewry was really made up of two groups. The first group consisted of the older settlers. Many had been scarred by the hatreds endemic to the area. They could and did recite a litany of past biases by non-Jews, real or imagined, acts which tended to intimidate rather than steel them. One mother charged that a local school principal had not granted favorable recommendations to Jewish students for prestigious colleges. Another said when her kids had attended religious school she had wrapped their textbooks in plain brown paper. The result of all this was what is found among most smaller Jewish communities throughout the United States: timidity, anxieties about Jewish political activism and a hesitation to say or do anything that might be interpreted badly by the non-Jewish majority.

Lerner felt he could empathize with these sentiments but not condone them. These people were afraid, and perhaps with good reason. He was, however, more sympathetic with their reluctance to be practicing Jews, for they had, he says, no teachers of Judaism nor even anyone who could read a haftorah. And even more ominous for him as a beginning rabbi was the fact that the second group of Riverhead Jews, the newcomers from New York City, were even less interested in Judaism.

"My second year was the worst. *Four people* enrolled in my adult education course. One because he didn't want me to be alone. Another was an older woman, quite mad really, who had somehow 'discovered' a Jewish grandparent and who later wrote me a long, barely coherent letter urging me to accept Jesus as savior as we had crucified him. The other two were a Methodist minister and his wife.

"In the end, I offered the board three choices. (1) I'll quit. (2) I'll stay if you guarantee me a minyan. (3) Give me a day off on the Sabbath since I need to be with other Jews." The board chose the second and Lerner quit when his contract expired.

"How can Judaism be so good and yet so bad?" asked a Yiddish-accented, yarmulke-wearing questioner in the pews of the Touro synagogue in Newport, Rhode Island, during the Synagogue Council of America's bicentennial meeting. His son, he told the audience, attended the University of

Michigan with 12,000 other Jewish students, but only 30 showed up for Friday evening services. Martin Meyerson, president of the University of Pennsylvania, rose and agreed, saying that an overwhelming number of talented young American Jews were simply uninterested in Judaism.

The synagogue-as-a-wasteland is a hoary theme in American Jewish life, grown stale by repeated and documented tales of boredom, sparse attendance and pulpit gimmickry, indeed almost anything to draw a crowd. Most adults as well as the young have tended to view the synagogue as unnecessary, creating another fundamental problem for Lerner and his fellow rabbis. What should become of all that expensive real estate? What was Judaism without the synagogue? Was there still any life left in such an organized, centralized institution?

The high hopes of the Jewish counterculture of the 1960s and early 1970s—born of the civil rights movement and Black ethnicity, born of an unnecessary war in Southeast Asia, born of Israel's plight, born of the sudden *public* awareness of hundreds of thousands of poor, neglected Jews, born of personal rediscoveries (and, in many cases, merely discoveries) of certain elements of Judaism—gave rise to the so-called "New Jews," centered originally about Boston and ultimately organizing as a fellowship around rituals and ceremonies.

Havurat Shalom, probably the first of such recent youth groups, began in an unpretentious frame house in working-class College Road in Somerville, Massachusetts, in 1968. Whether many of the original founders were interested in Judaism or simply searching for other things is not clear, but certainly some were fascinated by the possibilities of fashioning a living Judaism. Many were associated with the Jewish Peace Fellowship, a group dedicated to nonviolence in the Jewish tradition; others were Orthodox; still more were Jewishly illiterate. But living together in their *batim* or houses, they struggled against the way Jewish education was transmitted, the ennui of the synagogues they knew in their childhoods, and most of all their exclusion from organized Jewish life. Synagogues, they asserted, resembled corporate life. The rich and mighty made all the key decisions. Women had no role of any importance. In 1969, at a Boston meeting of the very powerful Council of Jewish Federations and Welfare Funds, young pickets carried placards in Hebrew saying that those delegates who couldn't read them should not be distributing and spending Jewish money.

This inchoate rebellion of a tiny minority of young Jews and their equally fervent young rabbinical allies took shape in the formation of havurot, which Bernard Reisman and Kenneth Roseman defined as "groups without professional direction banded together on an adult and family basis for Jewish or social goals." In these cases, the rabbis were a "resource" rather than the central, dominating figure. Jacob Neusner rightly pointed out that the new communes were really patterned after very old ideas, especially the 2,000-year-old Dead Sea sect, the Yahad. But no matter, for as people came and went, stylistic and substantive changes evolved in the way they perceived their Jewishness. Studying Judaica, observing Shabbat, they tried—at least at first—to share problems mutually. When Elie Wiesel came to Somerville he pronounced it "the first sign of health" in American Jewry.

The writer Sylvia Rothchild has reported on this phenomenon and noted that six of the initial group were ordained rabbis, influenced by Abraham Heschel, Martin Buber and Franz Rosenzweig, along with a handful of Jewish professors in the heavily academic Boston area. Emulators soon sprang up on Manhattan's Upper West Side, in Washington, D.C., and in Denver. Shlomo Carlebach's House of Love and Prayer in San Francisco held daily private and group prayers, and members lived the communal life, taught one another Hebrew, Torah, Hasidic lore and Kabbalah. The Jewish Residence at the University of Pennsylvania had a cooperative. Jews for Urban Justice and Tsedek Tsedek, led by Arthur Waskow, settled down in the District of Columbia area and hoped to move American Jewry toward radical political and social change. Reconstructionists (who had pioneered the havurot in America in the early 1960s) and Hillel Foundations sponsored numerous variations.

The influence of the havurot even began to be felt in a few temples and synagogues. In Encino, California, Rabbi Harold Schulweis applied havurah principles to his Beth Shalom, dividing the synagogue into fifty havurot. Rothchild observed that a Conservative temple in Newton, Massachusetts, had a "sensitive rabbi wishing to be responsive to an excessively large congregation [who] persuaded a group of younger members to try a more personal way to belong." Nearly one hundred families have since been organized into small groups for study and prayer. "Most are under thirty-five. A few are trying to integrate three generations. There are groups willing to welcome single, divorced or widowed individuals who normally had difficulty finding their place in synagogue activities."

To all this Lerner is no stranger, for he observed the early havurot closely. An article he wrote remains the best comprehensive (and critical) treatment of the content and structure of those early groups thus far. "A real *havurah*," he wrote, "must remain small—forty to fifty members at the most—and thus its potential for influence is limited; too elitist; too uninterested in the religious survival of the mass of Jewish people." But, he continued, "If the *havurah* does nothing else it should remind [us] religious creativity, fervor and a sense of community have not passed. Business as usual at the *shul* is no longer acceptable. Rabbis will have to surmount their own inertia, the resistance of synagogue boards and ritual committees."

Lerner concluded: "If the crucial institution for genuine Jewish survival is the synagogue, then one wonders if it is the right place to concentrate these creative efforts? Can today's synagogue be changed into more personal settings through *havurot*? Or if not, can independent, few in number groups be 'strengthened and sanctioned?' Or, is it possible to create new *havurot* at the same time as synagogues are transformed?"

"Time may not be on our side," warns another young rabbi and havurah veteran, Ron Kronish.

But then again, it may be. For how long can the structured synagogue compete with the more open, questioning and areligious trends in American life?

Unlike many of those early comrades, Lerner is a congregation rabbi, and his own sense of worth and accomplishment is measured by what he deems important in *his* synagogue. Despite his support for women's rights, his refusal to wear a robe and other activities, he is no radical. He is, rather, a traditionalist trying to hold onto the best of the past but changing when necessary. One hundred people show up for one of his Saturday services when there is no bar mitzvah to lure them in. That one hundred New Yorkers will come voluntarily instead of for family obligations is for him a matter of pride and wonder. An equal number attended an evening talk by Rabbi Arthur Green, one of the Havurat Shalom pioneers. Fifty have registered for Lerner's adult education courses. "I may leave one day for a larger congregation," he said one morning, staring dreamily at an empty classroom, "yet have far less participation."

Trying to reach and affect people and quite naturally influence them in their transitional stages, he hears regularly from teenagers, college students, people passing through private crises. "Rabbi," they literally beseech him, "help me put my life in order." And yet he cannot. Life, at least a thoroughgoing Jewish life, cannot be refashioned easily. Yearning for personal stability, harmony and some sort of permanence, bewildered people find it difficult to concede, as I suspect Lerner does, that to live from crisis to readjustment and in disillusionment and renewal is the pride and penalty of being Jewish.

Lerner says, "Judaism is not going to live on in this country or anywhere else with Yiddish, secularism, the United Jewish Appeal, golf on Saturdays. It will only survive if Jews and their children live Jewish lives. A man came to me and said, 'I don't believe.' Fine. But when others say they want the Jewish people to survive as Jews but that they don't believe in the forms and rituals of belief, I'm upset. None of the nonreligious approaches work. Only religion does. And yet, one of the tragedies of modern Jewish life is that little is going on in the synagogues."

7. Small-Town Rabbi

Some years ago, outside a temple in Augusta, Georgia, I witnessed a curious sight. At the entrance stood two men and a woman with a small portable stand, an American flag and a cross. They were evangelists distributing religious tracts and New Testaments. None of the Jews who came and went refused their offering. Finally, the rabbi came to me, shrugged and said with a trace of apology, "They never leave us alone." Would the community protest, I asked? He smiled. "Down here we keep our noses clean, our mouths shut and we live well."

I remembered that scene while reading the sociologist Peter Rose's conclusions to his study of a small-town New York State Jewish community: "The isolated minority member rarely constitutes a threat to the established order, and community members are often willing to accept the individual outsider despite articulated expressions of prejudice."

Small-town Jews.

"Does the term refer to the 1,400 living in Baton Rouge? Or would it be the 800 in Waco, Texas? Or the three families in Anguilla, Mississippi?" asks Viola W. Weiss, director of community services for the Jewish Children's Regional Service in New Orleans. The definitions are unclear. The Union of American Hebrew Congregations defines small-town congregations as those with fewer than 150 families in towns served by only one temple. Others think of them as areas far from large concentrations of fellow Jews.

Whatever the precise meaning, it is clear that some isolated and smallish communities have atrophied and died or are perilously close to that state. Throughout the South and Southwest, for example, rural areas are being abandoned by Jews, the migrants moving to the larger cities of those regions. Temple Israel in Big Springs, Texas, has no more members. The Knesset Israel Congregation in Laurel, Mississippi, has been transformed into a trust fund. In Clinton, New Iberia and Opelousas in Louisiana, the early Jewish settlements have long since vanished. Jefferson, in Texas, has only a cemetery. Baytown and Rosenberg, other Texas towns, support only one congregation and a rabbi.

Ralph Marks recently reminisced about the eastern Texas he knew in the 1930s. From thirty miles around—from Longview, Gladewater, Kilgore, and other places in that lush farming country—young Jews and their fathers would come to Sunday morning meetings in a red-brick, Byzantine-styled synagogue in Marshall, Texas. There was a rabbi then, David Wittenberg, an elderly bachelor with a strong "Jewish" accent who led his flock of 200 people. "Growing up as a Hebrew in Marshall was unusual. We were about one-tenth of one percent of the 20,000 population." Marks and his wife returned not long ago and stopped at Louis Kariel's shoe store. Kariel's son had just graduated high school, and no Jewish youngsters were left in the local schools. With that, Marks noted, with a trace of sadness, a religion and culture had passed from the region. Death and emigration had taken all but six remaining aging adults. The synagogue was razed several years ago.

But there are small towns and small cities where Jews do survive and sometimes flourish. Hundreds and at times thousands of miles from their national agencies, far from kosher butchers and Jewish libraries and people whose daily talk is knowledgeably Jewish, living among people who know little of Jews and Judaism, they survive as Jews; often no better or worse off than their co-religionists elsewhere.

In all too many instances the small-town rabbi feels isolated and abandoned. The only one in town (or the entire region) who knows anything about Judaism, he may also resent the dead end in which he finds himself. Who can he talk to? Or study with? Or worse: Is anyone listening? The result among many is a deep estrangement.

Southern Texas has greater concentrations of feudal economic power than other sections of America. The huge ranches are there. The King spread, for instance, covers an area larger than Rhode Island and earns $25 million annually, mainly from oil. Not far away is Tobin and Anne Armstrong's ranch (she was appointed ambassador to Great Britain by Gerald Ford), almost as vast and profitable. Farther south, bordering Mexico, is the Lower Rio Grande Valley, with large farms prospering because of sophisticated irrigation techniques and a warm climate to nourish the cotton, vegetable and citrus crops. These crops are harvested by large numbers of Mexican-American farm workers, who comprise nearly 75 percent of the Fifteenth Congressional District (yet Cesar Chavez once failed in an attempt to organize the farmers there). They earn an average yearly income of $3,000. By contrast, in McAllen, the center of the valley, the Anglos lead comfortable lives and believe sincerely in the political and economic conservatism they preach.

Jews live in McAllen and its vicinity, at times mirroring the outlook of the land barons. Many came from the North to escape deteriorating neighborhoods and in search of greater economic opportunity. The farm operators, overwhelmingly non-Jewish, employ migrant Mexicans, the retailers are hostile to trade unionism and wetbacks are employed in homes and fields, underpaid and exploited.

The majority of Chicanos seem unaware of Jews as Jews. The fear—the big fear, really—among McAllen's Jews (as among the gentiles, too) is that their life of extraordinary ease might one day end. They are all upper-middle-class, with too much emphasis on the material and too little on the spiritual. Sometimes the rabbi wishes they were less materialistic. Then, too, being wealthy has tended to upset the priorities of a few. In 1975, when Mexico chose to support the United Nations resolution equating Zionism with racism, several McAllen retailers—of furniture, ready-to-wear clothing, appliances—anxious for the large Mexican trade across the river as well as in Texas, trembled over the possibility of a backlash. A few were "very sensitive" about the belligerent resolutions against Mexico emanating from northern Jewish groups. While the threat to their well-being touched a sensitive nerve, the community sided with Israel. The local B'nai B'rith supported its national organization's stand against the resolution. When one merchant criticized McAllen's rabbi for speaking on television against the U.N. action, he was told by his peers to hold his tongue.

One hundred and eight Jewish families live in McAllen—the closest substantial Jewish populations are in Brownsville (also in the valley, with fifty families), Corpus Christi, 150 miles away, and San Antonio, 220 miles distant. Almost all McAllen's Jewish families are affiliated with Rabbi Maynard Bell's temple. There are three kinds of local Jews. The transplanted Northerners came during the past twenty-five years. Latin American Jews have also arrived since 1965, from Mexico, Argentina, Bolivia, Colombia and Cuba. Originally refugees from the Nazis, they have adjusted easily, since they are familiar with the Spanish language and culture. Finally, there are the native Texans, or those who trace their parentage back forty or fifty years, when the valley began to be developed. Most Jews are involved in business, with a few in farming and a handful serving professionally—two lawyers, two doctors and a Department of Agriculture entomologist. None are in education.

Maynard Bell, who is twenty-seven and has lived in McAllen since 1974, served as a student rabbi in western Tennessee and Mississippi, and now considers those places, with their second- and third-generation Jews, as more assimilated, more classically Reform and more fearful in their isolation than McAllen, which has the advantage of a still-strong sense of Yiddishkeit stemming from its relatively recent newcomers. Bell finds an added advantage: McAllen's Jews, fairly secure *as Jews*, don't seem terribly anxious for Bell to serve as their ambassador to non-Jews. "Let him work among us," is the general sentiment. "We need the rabbi, not the goyim." Hadassah and B'nai B'rith have McAllen chapters. The yearly Hadassah fund-raising barbecue features 1,400 dinners in Texas. Bell's sisterhood also has an annual "tasting luncheon," which in 1975 drew more than 500 visitors to sample traditional Jewish foods.

"I feel a great sense of responsibility here," says Bell. "I'm supposed to develop their community. Intermarriage is very low: about 10 percent marry out, while another 15 percent have married non-Jews with their spouses converting to Judaism. Like most rabbis in isolated communities, Bell is frequently asked to solemnize mixed marriages, where one party is not Jewish. He refuses. "I'm not a justice of the peace but rather a purveyor of Jewish marriage." Nor does he ever co-officiate with Christian clergymen. "That demeans our religion, and I believe in maintaining a distinctive Jewish identification."

He also fills a vacuum, since—following a pattern repeated regularly in smaller communities—he is the only
Jewish "leader" in town. Elsewhere, the gap may be filled
by the federations, by Jewish community councils or by the
national secular and religious agency professionals. But
for the most part, these do not exist in McAllen, and the
rabbi wears many hats, even organizing the UJA campaign.
"When the Zionist organizations want data they call me.
The Israeli consulate uses me, and other rabbis in isolated
areas, as contact people to help on speakers and programs
for the Southwest, although Federation would normally do
the job. I want to do these things, and many of these are
worth my interest and participation. But at times I feel
uncomfortable because many of these Jewish groups are
disinterested in maintaining strong religious-value-oriented
approaches to Jewish education and stress instead ethnic
loyalties. Israel is no surrogate for a sound and creative
intellectual life among Jews in the Diaspora."

And his own life, so far from his peers?

"I miss Jewish cultural life, books, colleagues, anyone
with a strong interest in Jewish life and thought. There is
not enough anonymity in McAllen. I have to be friends
with everybody, but I can't be *intimate* friends with anyone.
Everybody looks at me *as rabbi*. I can't confide in others,
for my job—at least insofar as the congregation interprets
it—is for me to make myself available to them. And, I
have to be extremely careful never to divulge anything told
me in confidence."

The key to getting rabbis for smaller towns is not to look
for bargain rabbis—the peripatetics or the retirees. They
cannot give these isolated people the creativity and leadership they need. What small-town congregations must do is
seek out rabbis with ambition and promise, who, like Bell,
may not want to settle in permanently but are instead
willing to give the town a few good years. Otherwise it is

unrealistic to believe that good young rabbis will want to go to the McAllens at all.

Alexander Kline, who has spent most of his rabbinic life in southern and southwestern small-town congregations, once said that the young rabbi in a small town has a difficult adjustment period. Far better educated than his congregation, more worldly, tolerant and open-minded, he finds himself set down suddenly in provincial America. He serves Jews who rarely read serious literature. He goes into homes where Jewishness (let alone love of learning, the measure of a good rabbi) is unknown.

"More upsetting still, the young rabbi finds among his congregants a callous indifference toward any creative continuation of Judaism and even a lack of understanding about his role. 'We need you as our representative among the non-Jews, to mingle with them, to speak in their churches and clubs, to make a good impression. We do not need you for ourselves.' Well, for the old people, perhaps, and for the children, yes, once a week, but for the gentiles most of all!"

Controversy?

Small-town Jewry is mute, and that self-imposed censorship is applied to the rabbi. "Rabbi, you sound like a Communist!" Or, "Rabbi, we are sick of all this Zionist propaganda." Or, "Rabbi, you always talk about the suffering Jews abroad. We are Americans."

Soon, says Kline, the newcomer recognizes the anxieties and Jewish self-hatred of some of his members and senses how they are being shifted onto him. "Unhappy Jews are never his friends." In some cases there is a "viciousness" directed toward the rabbi.

More resentment builds. Meager income, for one, at least in comparison with his wealthy congregants. Frustrated, he starts to feel trapped. Once a small-town rabbi, always a small-town rabbi. He views with bitterness his classmates' apparent success in prestigious suburban and metropolitan pulpits. "If he were really good he would be in a big city" is an often-heard denigration of small-town rabbis.

Kline's autobiography? Perhaps. But one that is repeated endlessly. Still, there are nuances, not easily discernible to casual observers. Looking back now, Kline sees the small-town synagogue as a challenge. Jews, he feels, want some sort of religious symbolism, however much of a mishmash it may be. They want the comfort and inspiration they think Christian denominations offer their churchgoers. They also want "poetry, pageantry, ceremonial beauty. They want to be preached to and exhorted. They even want knowledge, interestingly presented, simplified, popularized. Like the Christians." They need the rabbi as a pastor, for the rabbi —and this to Kline is his greatest responsibility—"is the only one who knows anything about Judaism, the only dispenser of thousands of years of Jewish life for those who care to listen." Rabbis do indeed have a vested interest in preserving Judaism. But had Hillel lived today, says Kline, he might have said, "Where there is no Torah, strive thou to bring the Torah."

One summer evening Samuel Horowitz received a frantic phone call from Canada. Did he know if a certain young couple had arrived in Billings to be married? "The question of how those parents found me is simple: they asked the consulate. Ours is the only active synagogue in Montana and adjacent states."

Billings is Big Sky country, an area noted for its stunning natural vistas and its class wars involving Anaconda Copper, the public utilities, cattlemen, miners, environmentalists and unions. Billings has 40 Jewish families, about 100 Jews in all, living very far from Denver, Salt Lake City and Spokane. In all of Montana, of 710,000 people, there are only 300 Jews.

Horowitz, who arrived in 1954 by way of an army chaplaincy and the rabbinical post at the University of Washington Hillel, serves as the only rabbi for a vast area with a 500-mile circumference. The only other synagogue in the state is in Butte. Bar mitzvahs are prepared by "remote control." In 1969, for example, a University of Montana professor's son was bar mitzvah in Missoula, the family home. The Torah came from Helena, where there had once been a Reform temple at the turn of the century; the Holy Ark belonged to Horowitz, one he had used in India during World War II. Thirteen years earlier, Horowitz had visited a Jewish rancher 185 miles from Billings, 35 miles of which were dirt road, to prepare three youngsters for bar and bat mitzvahs. During the evening of his first call, a massive snowfall transformed the road into quicksand, known as "Montana Gumbo." It took half a day to push Horowitz's car toward the main road.

His synagogue, named Beth Aaron after Louis Harron, an early pioneer from Vilna and the Vilna Yeshiva who had gone west in the early 1900s, was built in 1940. Sporadic clusters of Jews arrived after that, singly or in family groups. By 1950, with the discovery of oil in the adjacent Williston Basin, the area's population soared, bringing fifty Jewish families to Billings. But the boom ended shortly thereafter, and today there are few Jews in the state.

Horowitz came originally for a one-year term but celebrated his twentieth anniversary in 1974. He finds this post deeply enriching and incredibly satisfying, hoping only for more Jewish families. "What we need," he pleads, is a "planned migration of 50 to 100 Jewish families from the congested, polluted and turbulent cities, to a healthy climate of Billings. While it still radiates Jewish life, there is hope for the future." But barring a larger community, all he can do is salvage work. "One-third to one-half fall away, lost as Jews. We started a religious summer camp in the middle

1950s in the Bear Tooth Mountains of the Custer National Forest, above Red Lodge. In 1955 we drew twenty-eight children, fifty the next year and thirty-seven the third. They were recruited from as far as South Dakota. But thereafter the child population began to decline, and we abandoned the project.

"Now I urge parents to send the kids to large universities with Jewish activities. When they go off to isolated colleges not much can be done."

Above all, says Horowitz, much could be accomplished if only the region had a circuit-riding rabbi, citing ten towns he visits occasionally in the state and in Wyoming with one or two Jewish families. "It would cost around $40,000 a year," he notes. The only circuit-rider at present in the country is in North Carolina, where Rabbi Reuben Kessner operates out of Whiteville. Fifty years old, unmarried, he wanders through small towns, using synagogues where they exist and living rooms where they do not. In Wallace, North Carolina, the ten Jewish families rent the American Legion hall for their seders and Israel programs. Born in Worcester, Massachusetts, and ordained at Tifereth Israel Rabbinical Seminary of America in Brooklyn, Kessner is a Whiteville police chaplain, the rescue unit chaplain, the chaplain captain in the Civil Air Patrol and the writer of a column in the weekly newspaper. Yet, most important of all, he is the only religious teacher for every Jewish child in his many congregations from first grade until high school graduation.

To all this, Horowitz is very sympathetic. As a military chaplain he traveled two weeks each month, serving GIs in dozens of military installations from the Himalayas to Ceylon (now Sri Lanka), some 7,000 miles logged monthly. If it could be done in India-Pakistan and Ceylon, he asks, why not Montana, Idaho and Wyoming?

In his seventh year as rabbi of the only Reform temple in Fort Wayne, Indiana, Brooklyn-born Richard Safran could

look back with pleasure to his eight previous years in Steubenville, Ohio. Still, Steubenville is a graceless and grimy
Ohio River factory town, one of the Midwest's many industrial slum towns, which (together with its sister city,
Wheeling, West Virginia, across the Ohio) has the distinction of having the dirtiest air in the United States.

For Safran then, one suspects, Fort Wayne may have
been heaven. Driving down Old Mill Road and into the
parking lot of Achduth Vesholom Temple, a Star of David
looming above its modern stone entrance, a neatly clipped
lawn surrounding the building, it is easy to see why. The
difference in attitudes and wealth between the two cities is
apparent.

When Isaac Mayer Wise visited Fort Wayne in 1848 the
temple was already in its twelfth year, the oldest in the state.
"Let me confess," admitted that intrepid rabbi-reformer-
editor in the pages of *The Israelite* in 1860, "I had a
prejudice against Fort Wayne." Wise was worried, need-
lessly it turned out, lest the local Orthodox resent his presence. He also guessed wrong in judging that the town was
not "much of a business place." Contemporary Fort Wayne
is the corporate headquarters of Magnavox, North American
Van Lines, International Harvester and Falstaff Beer. There
is a major General Electric plant and a branch of the state
university.

Fort Wayne's 1,250 Jews—there are 23,000 in all of
Indiana—live among 185,000 gentiles, mostly white
Lutherans and Catholics, a handful of Blacks and 4,000
Chicanos—"about three hours from everywhere," says
Safran.

"I can tell you this privately," said a onetime resident of
the town and member of the temple. "Not everyone cares
for Safran there. He's too Jewish for them." (Across town,
in the Orthodox synagogue, a rabbi with greater tenure
than Safran was being fired, in 1975, for much the same
reason.) Safran's Temple has an "old crowd" of German

Jews who think of themselves as an elite. The rabbi who preceded Safran served them for thirty years. This group worried when the press began to condemn the treatment accorded Jews in the Soviet Union. Did "Jewish" have to be displayed so prominently? And when Safran decided to place an Israeli flag on his pulpit, they were upset. What would non-Jews think? Wouldn't the specter of dual loyalty be raised anew? They agreed on a compromise. The American flag would be set behind the chaplaincy flag, with its Ten Commandments and Star of David.

One morning the rabbi walked slowly toward his study, stopping briefly to make small talk with several women who were unwrapping gifts to be sold in the temple shop. In his study the story about the older German Jews was related to him. Safran shrugged. Yes, it was true, he began, "but they're *shtadtlan* Jews, the kind that prefer working behind closed doors. It's one approach, their approach," he says. "And besides, they *do* have a vital sense of their Jewish identity."

There are two other groups among his 275 families. The first, from their mid-thirties to fifties, are the children and grandchildren of those earlier German arrivals. They are far from monolithic, ranging from assimilationist to classical reformers in the synagogue. The most active and brightest among them serve Fort Wayne's Democratic Party (especially in the party's reform wing), support the arts and participate in the city's cultural life. They actively opposed the war in Vietnam, unlike many smaller-community Jews who chose silence. Overall, Safran thinks, their involvement in the temple is greater than that of their elders but not as great as that of his other group, the "newcomers," those who have arrived since the 1950s. Most of these stem from Eastern European parentage and as a rule were raised in distinctly Jewish environments. They have now begun to exercise power in temple affairs.

While financial authority remains in the hands of a few

rich families, inside Jewish Fort Wayne there is no real power structure. Despite the city's German-American Bund and Ku Klux Klan past, the Jews are more secure than many of their counterparts in other parts of the country. There is less "What will the goyim think?" and more of a relaxed tone. Safran is an elected member of the Metropolitan Human Rights Commission, its only clergyman. He is left alone to say whatever he wishes, so long as he does not say anything under the aegis of the temple.

Can Jewish life continue in this way in Fort Wayne? Many say yes, with confidence and assurance. "We've been here since 1836" is a common refrain. "We want our kids to stay Jewish" is yet another. Unexamined is the meaning of that long and honorable history and any definition of what sort of Jewishness they hope to transmit to their young. Was there a Holocaust syndrome among his families? None. And the children? Surely they were aware of the nightmarish Nazi decades? Hardly. The tendency then is to rely heavily on the rabbi, too much of a burden for any one person.

But not everyone feels that way and those that do not are intensely, even passionately, aware that being Jewish requires an extra effort and added commitment. Forty percent of the temple's youngsters now attend the Union Camp Institute in Zionsville, near Indianapolis, where Hebrew studies are stressed. One of Safran's graduates has applied for matriculation as a rabbinical candidate at the Hebrew Union College. Several have recently left permanently for Israel. A number are very active in Jewish studies and activities at the University of Indiana in Bloomington. Safran has also succeeded in establishing an adult school that is highly thought of, and he has inaugurated a "Resident Scholar" program. Last year Martin Cohen, professor of modern Jewish history at HUC, spent four days in Fort Wayne. The year before Lawrence Hoffman, who teaches liturgy at the JIR, was the guest scholar and lecturer.

Nevertheless, the rabbi carries the largest burden. "Basically the ten grades in our school, the adult ed courses, the Hebrew, it's all a one-man operation. We have no Jewish resources, no Jewish institutions to call on for consistent help." Who will teach in Fort Wayne?

"Excuse me, rabbi," said a woman who opened the door to his study, "but the children want to say hello." Behind her a dozen youngsters gathered, all from a neighboring church. Safran rose, smiling warmly, and they quickly clustered about him, neither diffidently nor in awe. They were each trying hard to enunciate *Sha-lom*, as if for the first time. "Now try to remember and understand what I taught you," he reminded them. "Shalom means peace and good-bye. What does it mean?" he asked. "Peace and goodbye," they called back, in unison. Two small girls, about ten, giggled openly. "Shalom," called the rabbi, ushering them out. "Shalom, shalom, shalom," they cried in return.

He sat down and smiled, and then sighed.

"I have an M.A. in Hebrew literature. Whom can I talk to?"

The feeling of solitude is endemic.

"I feel the lack of close contact with my colleagues," says Michael Remson in Kenosha, Wisconsin.

"I'm the only rabbi here. We lack facilities. We need Jewish music, Jewish education. No one here knows anything about these. If only we had someone who knew Hebrew songs or even played a guitar."

Kenosha is a factory town along Lake Michigan between Chicago and Milwaukee. American Motors has a major plant here, but the town, like that automobile company, has experienced bad times in recent years; joblessness has been high on occasion. Most of the Jews—115 families belong to Remson's temple—are in commerce and exhibit considerable sensitivity to non-Jewish opinions. Also there is a Wisconsin ambivalence: In the past, isolationism among the large number of Germans and Scandinavians, plus widespread support for the demagogic Joe McCarthy, existed alongside the La Follette tradition of progressive reform. The result is, once more, Jewish silence, that consistent small-town fear of any contentiousness, whatever the issue. With one exception.

"The Elks Club is the most exclusive in Kenosha," says Remson. "During the sixties there were no Jewish members. A few were proposed but then blackballed, even two who eventually became temple presidents. So some of the Jews then said, 'Let's say nothing, the hell with them.' " Larry Mahrer, then rabbi, refused. For want of any other public issue, at least he had something with which he might embolden some fellow Jews. A small group of Jews began picketing the club. The public amazement was something to behold, fear and trembling mixed with anger and guilt. Today ten Jews belong to the club, although a few continue their boycott because of its past policy of exclusion.

Kenosha is a very Christian town. Christmas is celebrated everywhere, including the public schools. All the major school dances are held on Friday evenings. The young feel isolated, says Remson, and there is enormous pressure to conform. As a consequence, assimilation is widespread, he says. A prominent businessman, a Jew, rarely attends Friday night services. "It's his bowling night," notes Remson. He does come to "interfaith" services, because his gentile clients expect him there.

Above all, Remson's aloneness is magnified by his failure to attract sufficient numbers to his public events. They "never come" to his adult ed classes. And two recent forums, one on intermarriage (the rate is, of course, "very high") and the other on abortion, drew sparse crowds. The local B'nai B'rith chapter is floundering. Only forty people come on Fridays, a bit more than in the past but few nonetheless.

And Judaism?

"If it lives on in Kenosha it will be a kind of charity, in support of Israel and the poor. Nothing more."

Checkbook Judaism. Bagels and lox Judaism. The comic-with-Yiddish-jokes Judaism. Pro-Israel Judaism. For rabbis such as Remson the task at times seems insurmountable. Working with the kids, wearing a skullcap—the first Reform rabbi in the town's history to do so, in fact—keeping kosher, daring to put more Hebrew into the services, trying to define for his members (whose children and grandchildren may well cease to be Jewish) what his purpose really is. "I have to concentrate on being a Jew among Jews, especially in Kenosha," he says. Meaning, one imagines, that even a rabbi could slip in this no-man's-land of Americanism.

There are echoes of this young rabbi's predicament in other parts of the country. In Sioux City, Iowa, Conservative Ronald Garr is one of three rabbis for 1,230 Jews, the greatest number between Omaha (6,500) and Sioux Falls, South Dakota (280). A 1972 graduate of the JTS, Garr finds no intellectual stimulation in his small city (he did attend the University of South Dakota for his second master's) and is "very lonely indeed." Several years ago the local Jewish community advertised for new emigrants willing to settle in their city. Few came permanently, while the native young leave and rarely return. More than a quarter of the entire community consists of pensioners. The birthrate, like that of Jewish families everywhere, is drastically declining. "Small towns need great attention from the national Jewish agencies," says Garr, hoping no doubt that his next post will bring him closer to the larger centers of Jewish culture.

In Fond du Lac, Wisconsin, Morton Shalowitz, an Orthodox rabbi, attends to twenty-four families in addition to twenty-five single or widowed members. Shabbat services in his synagogue have ceased except when a bar mitzvah ceremony or yizkor service takes place. "It's a peaceful and quiet life. Low salary yes, and few Jewish activities, but at least I have time for study. As for the future of Judaism in Fond du Lac, the outlook is bleak."

Jeffrey Bearman served until 1976 (he has since transferred to a New Jersey temple) in Fargo, North Dakota, the only rabbi in the state. The story here is the same as elsewhere. Deeply assimilated children, merchant and business families, excellent relations with non-Jews. Bearman commuted to nearly abandoned synagogues in Grand Forks and Minot for special services, tried to fend off bitter clashes among his lay members and sought to create Jewish life in Fargo solely by virtue of his status. For one who attended both Conservative and Reform seminaries and lived for two years in Israel, it was a difficult and trying period.

In New York State's north country, Fred Davidow, who grew up in Greenville, Mississippi, serves a congregation founded in 1861 by German Jewish peddlers. Stark and almost hermetically sealed off from the more populous areas of the Northeast, Plattsburgh is part of the Adirondack Forest Preserve, "forever wild" by mandate of the state legislature. It is also a chronically impoverished region, badly hurt by the failure of the St. Lawrence Seaway to bring an economic boom in its wake. Plattsburgh has a branch of the State University of New York ("the Jewish profile on campus is very low," says Davidow) and an Air Force base and medical center.

When Beth Israel was opened in the first year of the Civil War, there were fewer than seventy-eight synagogues in the whole country. Today it is the sole Jewish institution in the north country, with a membership of eighty families. Davidow's isolation is "depressing and unrelieved."

"There are no rabbinic colleagues or Jewish professionals.

There will always be a Jewish community in Plattsburgh, but it will be weak and diluted in the quality of its Jewish life," he says.

Roughly 10 percent of his congregants are married to non-Jews. Others are antagonistic and belong only at the insistence of their spouses or "because of the kids." A few rear their young as non-Jews. Some wealthy supporters retire to Florida's warm climate. And for lack of response, Davidow, as so many other rabbis, holds no regular Saturday services.

Paradoxically, it makes him more intensely Jewish than he ever imagined possible. This is a phenomenon found among many small-town rabbis. Reacting to the indifferent attitudes of their co-religionists and shocked at the prevailing apathy, feeling abandoned and betrayed after the seminary and the high expectations of their student pulpit days, many rabbis such as Fred Davidow turn inward, back to the supportive tenets of the faith. "I see my life as a Jew," he says. "I am creating a great distance between the congregation and myself, wrapping myself continuously in Reform tradition. I'm not the ambassador to the goyim here. Instead, I am a teacher, a leader of services, devoting my time to compiling and constructing new services."

Some rabbis, like Stephen Marcu in Wichita, Kansas, are very optimistic and reasonably content. "A man converted to Judaism here. Did he want to put on tfillin, I asked? When he said he did, I went on to say that 90 percent always refused to do so. But he came back: 'I want to be 10 percent better.'"

The possibilities for a thriving Judaism in Wichita are very good indeed. Prosperous, benefiting from local airplane industries (Boeing and Cessna both have massive factories in Wichita), the Jewish community has been able to cope with the problem of the departing young. Because of the booming local economy, fifty new families arrived between 1972 and 1975, and community size has remained stable.

Marcu, who was ordained at the Orthodox Hebrew Theological College in Skokie, Illinois, explains the health of his community. "I surveyed my congregation after the Yom Kippur War. Almost 100 percent gave to the UJA. In larger cities many Jews escape and find identification elsewhere. Not in Wichita, where we stress education, build sukkot [the booths erected during the Festival of Sukkot], get packaged kosher meat from Denver sold by Safeway and find that more and more people are regularly coming to the synagogue."

When Leonard Helman served in Wheeling, West Virginia, he might have questioned Marcu's optimism. Now that he lives in Santa Fe, New Mexico, he might endorse it.

Wheeling, in the state's northern panhandle, is in steel and glassmaking country. With a population of 48,000, it is the hub for a large number of smaller communities in northern West Virginia and eastern Ohio. It shares the same problems of many old cities. It is dirty and polluted, and its municipal budget is shrinking as its population ages. The Jewish community is also declining.

In contrast, Santa Fe, although it also is an old city, is experiencing a renaissance. It has benefited enormously from the technological developments of the nuclear age. Los Alamos, some 40 miles northwest, is where the original research on the atomic bomb and systems of delivery was carried out. Elsewhere in the state—at the White Sands Missile Range, at Holloman Air Force Base and at various army installations, research of the tools of destruction and related activities continue under the aegis of the Energy Research and Development Administration (once the Atomic Energy Commission).

Santa Fe (and Los Alamos) has also acquired a reputation for being a particularly healthful location. The air is dry and pure, and even the winter cold does not penetrate the way it does in a humid climate. The hot, dry, sunny summer days alternate with cool nights. Hence the city and its environs, 7,000 feet above sea level, has attracted many retirees and various individuals and sects looking for physical and spiritual rejuvenation. Tourism is also big in Santa Fe, with skiing in the winter and the Santa Fe Opera in the summer the main attractions, along with the old churches, historic shrines, and even real cowboys and Indians.

German Jews started arriving in New Mexico territory in the 1840s. The first one was Solomon Jacob Spiegelberg, who came with the U.S. Army in 1846 on the way to fight the Mexican War and later, mustered out, was named sutler —or provider—to Fort Marcy in Santa Fe. Others followed. The first synagogue was Congregation Montefiore, established in Las Vegas (New Mexico, not Nevada) in 1884. Even so, the total Jewish population remains small, certainly when compared with neighboring Texas and Arizona. Albuquerque, a city of 300,000 and growing, has three rabbis (one is semi-retired) for its 2,000 Jews, three congregations, and 750 families; it even has a *havurah* of 40 families, most of whom are associated with the University of New Mexico. In Santa Fe, one hour's drive away, the state's fourth active rabbi serves 95 families, 60 more in Los Alamos, and "5 or 6" in Las Vegas, home of New Mexico Highlands University.

Leonard Helman, who was ordained at HUC, is a part-time rabbi. His synagogue, Temple Beth Shalom, could not afford a full rabbinical salary, and Helman accepted the pulpit with the understanding he could practice law. (Back in Wheeling, he commuted three evenings a week to Pittsburgh so he could attend Duquesne University Law School.) For the last several years he has worked for the New Mexico Public Service Commission as a staff counsel, picking his

way through the minefields of contention between the giant
private utility companies and the consumer and environ-
mental groups. One of his recent briefs ended up in the New
Mexico Supreme Court, where the prize was more than $20
million. In yet another case, two New Mexico-based utilities
wanted to participate in the building and operation of a
nuclear power plant in Arizona, the costs of which would
be borne eventually by New Mexico ratepayers, since the
additional electricity would serve the state's growing energy
needs. One billion dollars were at stake in this case.

"My congregation doesn't object to my work or my briefs.
In fact, I feel good as a lawyer and rabbi, believing as I do
that I'm fulfilling my sense of social justice." And New
Mexico Jews—there are 3,000 in all, less than 0.3 percent
of the population—seem secure. Henry Jaffe was Albuquerque's first mayor, and Nathan Jaffa was mayor of Roswell
and Santa Fe as well as lieutenant governor of the territory.
Today the mayor of Santa Fe and a judge of the court of
appeals are all unashamedly Jewish, as is the district
attorney of Bernalillo County, home of Albuquerque.

Pleased with Helman, Beth Shalom President Neil Weber
has spoken of the growing enthusiasm of the young in the
temple, "the greater feeling of belonging and of Jewish
identity. This is reflected in attendance at Friday night
services if nowhere else."

With so few Jews statewide, Helman's duties are rather
varied. He teaches a course in Judaism at the College of
Santa Fe. (In West Virginia he taught law and religion at
a Jesuit school, Wheeling College.) He also is called on
for comments on Jewish life. Once he was asked to do a
piece for a local paper on Christmas, while a priest con-
tributed an article on Hanukah. He is the first rabbi to serve
as chaplain of a Rotary Club in New Mexico. He was widely
quoted in the *Albuquerque Journal*, the only New Mexico
newspaper with a statewide circulation, when he spoke out

bitterly against the United Nations resolution condemning Zionism as a form of racism. And at the mass conducted the morning of the inauguration of the present New Mexico governor, Jerry Apodaca, Helman read a passage from the Hebrew Bible.

There is the ubiquitous question of intermarriage, where one partner is not Jewish and has no plans to convert to Judaism. The rate is high. Helman performs these marriages, as do some other rabbis, but with the condition that the couple rear their children as Jews. In Washington, D.C., for example, Rabbi Edwin Howard Friedman, a Reform rabbi in the 110-member Bethesda (Maryland) Jewish Congregation and also a family therapist at Georgetown Medical School and St. Elizabeth's Hospital, says that in the past sixteen years he has performed about 1,000 mixed marriages. He has complained of an "atmosphere of fear" that has transformed scholarly examinations of the subject into propagandistic exercises. Mixed marriages, insists Friedman, do *not* contribute to the extinction of the Jewish people. Denying that he is an advocate of intermarriage, Friedman says, "I'm trying to deal with it in a creative, healthy way." Helman's manner in New Mexico is not too different. "For several years I refused to officiate at mixed marriages. However, once the rabbi in Charles Town, West Virginia had committed himself to officiating at a mixed marriage, but his wife became ill and they had to go to the Mayo Clinic in Rochester, Minnesota. He asked me to help him, and I did reluctantly. Later, I developed a warm personal relationship with the couple with whom I'm still in close contact. And since then I have been officiating at mixed marriages, but never with a Christian clergyman. I don't insist on conversion and ask the couple to read certain books and promise to raise their kids as Jews." After the marriage, several of them have converted to Judaism.

There are other small communities that require the

services of rabbis—the military, for example. The record of the military and naval chaplains is a proud one, and many a veteran looks back in gratitude at the help and emotional sustenance provided during his stay in service.

Less well known are the rabbis who have become prison chaplains. Because the number of incarcerated Jews is small, most rabbis are part-time; nevertheless, each inmate can be counseled individually. Jerald Bobrow, spiritual leader of Congregation Adas Emuno in Leonia, New Jersey, is also the rabbi for twenty Jewish prisoners at the Wallkill (New York) Correctional Institute. However peripheral the connection many of these men have had with Judaism before their jailing, Jewishness becomes crucial while in prison. The religious experience can for many overcome the ennui of prison life.

"As their rabbi, I come less to preach and more to talk with my small Jewish congregation," Bobrow explains. "Our little synagogue is an island of refuge where men may be challenged as well as inspired. The synagogue is theirs, and they assume responsibility for its maintenance and upkeep. For many inmates, it is the first time in their lives they experience a bond with Jewishness and the Jewish people." One Sukkot the group gathered with their families to rejoice in their beautiful sukkah, and Rabbi Bobrow and the small band prayed: "Blessed art Thou our God, King of the universe, who hast kept us alive and sustained us that we might reach this happy time."

Eight hundred miles westward, the Moscow Symphony had arrived at Bloomington, Indiana, for an eagerly awaited concert. As the capacity crowd filed in, a small group of students stood outside the auditorium with lighted candles to protest the invitation. The demonstration, organized by Indiana University's Hillel Foundation, drew little attention, yet was part of the program—sometimes planned, sometimes spontaneous—of IU's Hillel.

Alfred Jospe, a Reform rabbi who was forced to leave Germany after Hitler's election, retired several years ago as Hillel's national director after thirty-five years as a campus rabbi. When he first came to B'nai B'rith's college program, Hillel existed on only nine campuses; today it has chapters at 326 schools.

"A Hillel rabbi is never sure who his 'congregants' will be, and each new freshman class can mean restructuring not only what he does but his notions of how to do it," Jospe once remarked. "The volatile ways of college youth, the congenial atmosphere of the academic community and your own freedom to experiment—much more so than what a congregation pulpit allows—these make things lively."

Which is what his successor, Rabbi Norman Frimer, first experienced. But he soon ran into serious dilemmas as others expressed their anxieties. Might not campus rabbis be too independent to handle? Were some of them calling for recognition of Palestinian rights? Or denouncing the lack of democracy in organized Jewish life? Whatever their pronouncements, the extent of dissent frightened some timid administrators.

The truth is that Hillel rabbis and chaplains differ as markedly from one another as they do from their administrators in Washington, D.C. They range from left to right, from passionate religionists to the relatively indifferent. There are, in addition, twenty-six full-time women "campus chaplains," including nonrabbis such as Brenda Gevertz at the University of Cincinnati and Edith Paller at Case Western Reserve University in Cleveland. All this is a far cry from the mid-1960s, when B'nai B'rith insisted that Naomi Bear of University of Arizona Hillel, "a lovely and maternal lady," could not serve as a Hillel director, inasmuch as the directors had to be ordained male rabbis. Few, if any, rabbis and chaplains now check with national headquarters before making public statements or organizing demonstrations. Frimer was therefore faced with a serious problem: To what extent could B'nai B'rith mandate a degree of conformity over so spirited a group? He would not even try, he told his anxious colleagues.

Indiana University is situated not far from the former bailiwick of the Ku Klux Klan in southern Indiana. The school had an enrollment of 30,000 students on its central Bloomington campus in 1976, 1,500 of whom were Jewish. There were, in addition, 200 Jewish faculty members.

This considerable community is a blessing for Rabbi Mark Shrager, who graduated from the JTS in 1969. IU Hillel is in an aging house, sparsely and cheaply furnished, but brimming with people and events. Kosher food is available. There are regular services. (The faculty members and their families have their own services through the University Jewish Community, which as yet has no rabbi; Shrager visits when he is free.) IU Hillel has invited Manes Friedman, a St. Paul Hasidic rabbi, to speak; held a Sephardic forum; asked Israelis to join with them in political discussions; listened to a Brazilian Jew living in Israel speak of his two lands. Ethnicity is "in" at Indiana, although there is a good deal of secularism as well. Even so, the vast majority spoke against campus Arabs during the 1973 war, and many wrote letters to *IDS*, the college daily. Said one young woman from Anderson, Indiana: "These years at Hillel are my first opportunity to get a really solid Jewish education. I'll never forget it."

Marvin Tokayer reached his study early. By 8:20 A.M. one morning in April his working day had already begun. One hour later, following some perfunctory attention to synagogue administrative details, he took time to open a book and study. It was, he thought, a marvelous time of the year, two months before he would complete a stimulating and memorable eight years in office. All the same, as he lovingly fingered the pages of the Midrash before him, he thought it might have been better if he had someone to study with. By 10:30 he had leafed through his correspondence. That week nearly one hundred letters, often queries for additional information on Judaica, had reached him, and he set about the laborious task of responding. At noon he taught a Bible class, and afterward one on the Mishnah. Three afternoons a week, Marvin Tokayer taught Hebrew school for the children. And there were the services, of course. Well attended, too. But equally pleasurable that morning were the people who would surely visit the synagogue that day. Someone wanted to write a master's essay or an analysis of a Jewish novelist, or perhaps there was a theater group interested in performing a play with a Jewish theme—whatever it was, they all came to him. The other day some visitors announced that Hebrew interested them and they wanted to begin study classes. How, they asked, did the rabbi propose they proceed?

All perfectly commonplace, except that since 1968 Tokayer has been the rabbi of the Jewish Community Center of Japan. The center occupies a stately mansion in the Shibuya ward of Tokyo, and has a largely American congregation. And by virtue of this role, plus the fact that he is the author of several best-selling books in Japan, Tokayer has become the "Jewish ambassador to Japan." Not the Israeli ambassador but the Jewish one, a distinction the Japanese prefer.

For Americans, Japan is exotic. For a practicing Jew, far from his New York home (he graduated Yeshiva University in 1958 and JTS four years later), terra incognita. Jewishness is an alien religion, and the Japanese, despite their fascination with some aspects of it, think no more about Judaism than the average Jew does of Shintoism. One Rosh

Hashanah, very early in his stay, Tokayer and several congregants were nearly arrested for allegedly trying to poison Tokyo's water supply. Police suspicions had been aroused when the strange-looking foreigners began throwing things into a stream. It had been the second day of the holiday and they were reciting *Tashlikh*, in effect casting away their sins. When the police arrived, Tokayer explained, "We have to cast away our sins." But *face*, not sin, is the Japanese concept, and a lengthy discussion ensued before the police recognized what had occurred.

"The hardest thing is for me to walk with my wife and children on, say, Yom Kippur, and look about the streets for some signs of the holiness of the day and its import. Naturally, there are none. We are, we had to remind ourselves at the beginning, in Japan. Still, I can honestly say I hardly had a bad day here."

There are 120 families in the Tokyo synagogue. It was founded in 1952 by Americans and Europeans living there and in nearby Yokahama, together with Russian Jews who had been born and reared in Harbin, Port Arthur and Dairen in Manchuria, and Shanghai, Tientsin and Nanking in China. Today the Russian founders have aged, died or moved away; their places have been taken by Israelis and, of course, Americans. The closest Jewish communities are Kobe to the south (with 19 families from Aleppo, Baghdad, Beirut and Damascus) and Hong Kong (with 250 families), four hours away by plane. Both, however, call on Tokyo for aid when necessary.

In this variant of a small-town setting, there are important nuances. For Tokayer is not only the rabbi of a synagogue, as in the United States, but the rabbi for an entire community. Within its walls the JCC has, in addition to a synagogue, a restaurant, a library (Jewish and general), a mikveh, a school, the Japan-Israel Friendship Association, the Japan-Israel Women's Welfare Organization, adult education classes, and Ikebana flower arranging and sumi-e classes.

Tokayer has also become a best-selling writer of Jewish books. In 1971 a book entitled *Japan and the Jews* was published anonymously in Japan. Allegedly written by a Jew born and reared in Japan, it dealt with both societies and viewed the Jew as clever and wise. One million copies were sold, and it won the coveted Oya Prize for Literature. It was, in fact, written by a non-Jewish Japanese, but the story had a dual fascination: first, in Jewish life (Jews were, after all, a curiosity, an ephemeral fad in a homogeneous and bland world); and second, in Marvin Tokayer, who everyone assumed was the author. He was not (although he insists he knows the real writer, whose pseudonym was Isaiah Ben Dasan), but the consequence was extensive media attention.

One publisher asked him for a manuscript on the Talmud, and he complied. Now in its twentieth edition, it has sold more than 100,000 copies. This was followed by five more volumes. The second book is a biblical exegesis, homiletic in style, offering gleanings from the Torah. Tokayer filled it with simple renditions of human-interest tales such as Cain and Abel, Isaac and Ishmael, Jacob and Esau, and Joseph and his brothers. Thirty thousand copies were sold. He followed this with a book on Jewish humor (50,000 sold), one on Yiddish and biblical proverbs (that one sold very well), a book on the so-called common-origin theory of Jews and Japanese, and another on concepts such as prayer and justice. Then another best-seller, this one on the contrast between Japanese schooling and traditional Jewish insights into education.

Even so, Tokayer remains the rabbi of an isolated community, one that has many American transients and which provides for its members "a home and a haven," he adds. "It offers identification as a Jew, a glimpse of our deeply shared roots. We are estranged from our homes and families, so people here draw together ever more intensely making the center warm, cooperative, *haimish*."

His wife has adjusted, as have their three youngsters. But many do not. Some of his congregants have serious marital problems he must cope with. Wives tend to get depressed because of the unique character of Tokyo. There are no street names and few numbers on houses. They cannot listen to radio or television or attend the theater or films. Newspapers and magazines arrive late. Not permitted their usual work in Japan, they lose a sense of purpose. There is a superabundance of maids and cooks, gardeners and chauffeurs. The Jewish wives are also challenged by the problems raised by the sexual infidelity of their husbands, since extramarital sex is easily available in Tokyo. And if these families stay long enough, their children lose all sense of who they are, becoming neither Japanese nor American.

Soon the community will be without a rabbi once again. Tokayer's predecessors were army chaplains or rabbis who did not please the center's board of directors. Tokayer did, and one Jew who recently visited Tokyo said his congregants were terribly sorry to see him leave.

"It's very hard to be Jewish there," he said. "After Tokayer, maybe they'll be lucky and get a sound replacement. If not, they'll drift along, occasionally getting a traveler who's a real *hazzan*. They'll have the Israelis send over a teacher for their kids. But it's kind of sad. With no rabbi, I think they will have a real struggle."

8. Sephardim in America

I long to go, mother
to Jerusalem;
to eat of her lands,
to eat and be sated.
—Judezmo ballad

It is not always easy to separate fact from fiction in any consideration of the Sephardim. There is the patrician antecedent, the tales of expulsion from Spain in 1492 and Portugal in 1497, encounters with Muslim empires and their arrival in 1654 in New Amsterdam. But walk into a Sephardic synagogue, such as the elegant Shearith Israel on New York's West Side, and the first impact is overwhelming. Even to the untutored ear, Sephardic services may seem to differ from the customary Ashkenazic rites, as the cantor chants aloud during the entire service. The Hebrew pronunciation differs from the Ashkenazic as well. The men and women use a Sephardic prayer book. The visitor also detects a special decorum in the synagogue (the oldest in North America), a propriety and quiet reserve and refined gracefulness that symbolize self-respect and a self-imposed aristocratic bearing.

Many of these presumed qualities are no doubt superficial, for there is much myth in the Sephardic American past. The historian Jacob Rader Marcus has criticized those early refugees and their heirs: "Colonial Sephardic

Jewry produced no great books, no great minds, no intellectual leaders, no literary creations of any lasting significance." Their descendants in some cases assimilated and became Christians, although other offspring continued as Jews. Still, they were few in number and to ask that they match the achievements of their European forebears may be too harsh a demand.

Nor are Sephardic Jews monolithic. The Sephardim in Western Europe are derived from Marranos who returned to Judaism after living through the Inquisition. They settled in Amsterdam, Bayonne, Bordeaux, Hamburg, London and Paris beginning in the fifteenth century. The patricians of Jewish civilization, they were the heirs to stunning Iberian Jewish achievements in philosophy, poetry and religion. It was from their numbers that Sephardim left for Curaçao, Surinam, St. Thomas, Jamaica and Recife, and later for North America.

Levantine Sephardim stemmed from the Spanish expulsion, and they went to Turkey, North Africa and the Balkans, eventually producing a Ladino and Hebraic literature largely unknown to the general Jewish world even today. Like their co-religionists elsewhere, they tended to suffer a gradual cultural erosion starting in the last part of the seventeenth century. The dismemberment of the Ottoman Empire in the second half of the nineteenth century, together with the Balkan wars on the eve of World War I, savaged Jewish life in such centers as Monastir (now called Bitola, in Yugoslavia), Castoria, Kavala, Janina and Adrianople. Refugees poured into such cities as Salonika. Two decades later, many of them were obliterated, together with other Jews throughout the Balkans, by the Nazis and their allies. Salonika, in northern Greece, had 56,000 Jews in 1940; today there are 1,200. The city's 500-year-old cemetery, which held the remains of the 1492 generation, was utterly destroyed, as were all other evidences of the 2,000-year Jewish presence in Salonika.

Confronted by centuries of man-made tragedies, some Sephardim drifted westward. The Levantine Jews (Ladino- or Judeo-Spanish speakers from Turkish and Balkan areas and from Salonika and Rhodes, Greek-speakers from Janina, French-speakers from North Africa, Arabic-speakers from Syria and elsewhere) began their trek to the United States at the start of the present century. Poorly schooled, lacking industrial skills, families fled the 1908 Young Turk rebellion and its institution of a compulsory military draft. By 1926, 60,000 had come to the United States. Fifty years later, more had arrived from Syria, Egypt, Lebanon, Iraq and other Muslim nations because of Arab persecutions. Jewish refugees from Cuba (some Ashkenazic) are now concentrated in Miami and Brooklyn. In all, 150,000 Sephardim live today in the United States, representing less than 3 percent of American Jewry.

For seven years Marc Angel has served as assistant minister at Shearith Israel (the minister, Reverend Louis Gerstein, is an Ashkenazi). Born in Seattle in 1945, Orthodox, he is the child of Seattle-born parents. His paternal grandparents came from the island of Rhodes, which was then Turkish. His mother's parents came from small villages near Istanbul.

"I was just finishing my second year at Yeshiva University when Shearith Israel had a vacancy. I was the first Sephardic student in YU's Sephardic Studies Program, and London's chief Sephardic rabbi was here at the time and recommended I serve under Rabbi Gerstein."

The term "Sephardi," he says, originally referred to Jews from the Iberian Peninsula, but the word has since come to embrace almost anyone without Ashkenazic background.

The congregation at Shearith Israel is composed of 425 families, half of whom are actually Sephardim and half Ashkenazim. The members pay a graduated scale of dues depending on their incomes. Rabbi Angel knows quite clearly what he may or may not do. He cannot introduce innovations into religious services; his congregants would have no part of such radical maneuvers. Nor would his senior rabbi. Nor, for that matter, would Angel. "This synagogue was founded on an ancient tradition, and we pride ourselves on continuing the music and prayer of the past. Even the building tends to awe people, to humble them, to make them feel alone in the presence of G-d," Angel explains.

Among other duties, Angel edits the synagogue's bulletin, and he is managing editor of the RCA's quarterly journal *Tradition*. In successive bulletin issues he informed readers of "the unique spiritual qualities of our *minhag* [certain well-established customs and liturgical rites that have developed the force of religious law], a ritual which has been part of our Congregation for centuries." Another issue featured an essay on Savannah's Congregation Mikve Israel, which traces its origins to a handful of Jews who reached that city on July 11, 1733, several months after Oglethorpe founded the colony of Georgia. In yet another bulletin, Angel published a letter from Gershom Mendes Seixas dated December 21, 1783. The past remains the valued guide for the present.

But in activities other than synagogue services he does try to effect change. He directs the adult education program, which has grown rapidly. He has also been involved in the problems of single Jews—widowed, unmarried and, increasingly, divorced. The problem of divorce is deeply troubling to all Jews, including the Orthodox; Rabbi Walter S. Wurzburger (the editor of *Tradition*) called it "catastrophic." Four in ten Jews are presently breaking up their marriages, Wurzburger told the 1976 convention of the Rabbinical Council of America. And, he went on, the rising tide of divorce also claims 10 percent of Orthodox Jewry.

Angel had been involved with early explorations of the problem under the aegis of the Federation of Jewish Philanthropies. "There are so many middle-aged singles, with no place to go," says a divorced woman in Manhattan. Moreover, many believe the cult of youth, the unbending family bias of synagogues and the general reluctance to accept such notions as people living together without marriage vows have led to a general refusal to deal with these people. "The local Universalist Church draws hundreds, mostly Jews, to their regular sessions," says Angel. "For me and those interested in these single Jews, the challenge was how to get synagogues aware of them, how to get the agencies to work for them. Above all, we wanted to house those meetings in a synagogue, to develop a sense of community."

One visitor recalled the session she attended. "People spoke about those of us living in Manhattan and the high cost of private as well as Jewish education for our kids. I thought no one would ever get around to that! Least of all in a synagogue." The Jewish Family Service sent a professional to several Shearith Israel seminars on single parenthood. And Angel? He pushes Judaism. Among the courses offered in the adult education program have been classes on Basic Judaism, Jews Under Islam, Modern Jewish Philosophy and Jewish Approaches to the Bible.

"Everything I do aims at infusing others with more understanding of Judaism," he says. "Rabbis have got to do it. Who else? To push people to Jewish consciousness. We need an Isaiah these days."

A few years ago Angel visited the island of Rhodes, off Greece, the city of his father's parents. Almost all the Jews of Rhodes had been murdered by the Nazis.

"After services, I walked alone through the old *juderia*. Along the stone-paved streets were the homes once inhabited by Jews. In their windows and at their doors, I saw the faces of Greek people. The *calle ancha*, the wide square at the hub of the old Jewish quarter, was filled with deeply tanned German and Scandinavian tourists. The name of the street running through the *juderia* is now called Martyron Evreon—the Street of the Hebrew Martyrs.

" 'Grandfather, grandmother,' I heard myself whisper, as I headed back to my hotel in the new city."

In Miami, Meir Matzliah Melamed's Cuban Sephardic congregation has 350 families, most of whom cannot yet speak English well, if at all. When Melamed grew up in Turkey his fellow Jews spoke Ladino (the historic tongue of Eastern Sephardic Jewry that was born in medieval Spain as a merger between Hispanic, Hebrew-Aramaic and Arabic elements) which only magnified their alienation from the Turks. But for the younger ones in his congregation this time it will be different, for English is and will continue to be their native language. Matzliah Melamed himself was born in Casaba-Izmir, Turkey, and was ordained there and in Israel. After World War II he began his journey as rabbi, first in Montevideo, then in Rio de Janeiro and finally in Mexico City. In 1971 he arrived in Miami to become spiritual leader of 2,000 Cuban Jews.

Like Angel, he speaks of Sephardic spiritual values, the contributions of Sephardim to science, art and letters, and of "our moment in the world, our splendid destiny." Still, America intrudes. As if in support of the Wurzburger thesis, 10 percent of his members' children have intermarried with non-Jews. Increasingly, too, the young are marrying Ashkenazim, which very much pleases Matzliah Melamed. "My dream," he says, "is that in America the old differences between Sephardim and Ashkenazim will disappear, and we will be one people, the Jewish people. We have the same hopes, the same Torah."

Arnold Marans is the rabbi of the Sephardic synagogue in Cedarhurst, New York, a parabola-roofed structure that also houses an interior chapel patterned after a fifteenth-century synagogue in Toledo, Spain. Marans, like Gerstein in Manhattan, is not Sephardic, but he has served a Sephardic congregation since 1954, following graduation from the JTS. Initially, he says, he was doubtful about the arrangement. Even many of the Sephardim were skeptical, afraid he might liberalize and innovate. But he decided to accept the job, thanks to the encouragement of Louis Finklestein and Wolfe Kelman at the Jewish Theological Seminary.

A good number of his members (there are 340 families in the congregation, 80 percent of whom are wholly or partially Sephardic, paying $300 and upward annually for membership) are from Monastir and Castoria, prominent Balkan Jewish settlements at the turn of the century. Next to Salonika, they were major spiritual centers for Ottoman Jewry. Grinding poverty, emigration and the Nazi murderers decimated the communities. "Today," says Uri Oren, an Israeli journalist, "there only remains in Monastir one lonely Jew."

Marans' members started arriving in the early twentieth century from Turkey, Greece and Yugoslavia. These are people whose families experienced the Holocaust directly— not like the Sephardic chief rabbi of Djerba (in Tunisia, off the North African coast) who, when asked in 1975 by a non-Jewish British professor about the possibility of faith after the *Shoah* or Holocaust, answered, "Shoah? Yes, I have heard of that—but I wasn't there and I really don't know. You must understand that these were not my people, and from what I hear they were all *mitbolelim* [assimilated] and therefore deserving of punishment."

Marans is a pastoral rabbi, a role he describes as "the fulfillment of every rabbinical student's dream." As rabbi he is the ecclesiastical authority, for the Sephardim, in his synagogue at least, take their rabbi very seriously. They need him less for prayers (led by the cantor or hazzan) than for the rites of passage. "The rabbi doesn't worship for the congregation," he says. "Everybody worships."

When a couple becomes engaged to marry, the family consults with Marans, seeking his counsel and blessings. In death he is crucial, as he consoles the grieving family and advises them on *shiva* (the period of mourning). He works with the *hevra kadisha*, those who do the ritual washing. He is called on for decisions and advice when the victim has died from an accident or by suicide.

While I was seated before the floor-to-ceiling window in Marans' elegant study, the wooden beamed ceiling lending a Hispanic touch to the room, a jet roared overhead. The temple is in the flight path of Kennedy Airport, and Marans has been involved in efforts to bar the Concorde SSTs from ever landing at the airfield.

"I'm extremely happy to be their rabbi," he says. "I have time to study and travel. I've been to Israel many, many times. As national vice-president of the American Sephardic Foundation—I'm the third-ranking officer—I recently visited Geneva and London for the World Sephardic Congress, where the agenda included helping poor Sephardim in Israel as well as their beleaguered brothers and sisters in Syria and Iraq. The lay leaders were invited, but my lay leaders don't go alone. They take their rabbi along."

9. A Final Word

Does the pulpit rabbi have a future? And if so, what role will he have?

The answer is that he does, but the evolving nature of the profession is largely out of the rabbi's hands. For rabbis the years ahead are marked by paradoxes. Questions of power and leadership remain constant. The older postwar leadership remains entrenched in rabbinic associations and seminaries. They continue to be baited by their legion of critics. There is, moreover, little evidence of any seminal religious scholarship under way. Synagogue innovations are rare. Backbiting and infighting remain the normal manner of combat, with the sides too often chosen on the basis of personalities rather than issues. And the more some speak of "identity," the less their fellow Jews attend synagogues or observe the religious rituals associated with Judaism.

Still, the rabbis and seminarians I met were, as a rule, reasonably well schooled in Judaism, serious and thorough-going professionals, and concerned about the course of American Jewish life. They tend to complain too much in their publications and at their conventions, but I suspect they are no more or less dissatisfied with their profession than are their peers in other fields. Indeed, on the whole, their spirit seems uncommonly high; amazingly, an incredibly large number of them have elected to remain in the rabbinate.

Then again, the future will depend to a large degree on Jews outside the rabbinate. With no unitary community, with rabbis—except for the right-wing sectarians—no longer called on to interpret the law or exact a measure of conformity, with Jews ranging from the religious to the nationalistic and from the emotional to the uncaring, rabbis are limited in shaping their future. Secularism and privatism have led to intense individualism, unheard of in the Central and Eastern European communities from which the modern rabbinate sprang.

The anguish of constant change has also affected every Western religious institution, Jews along with Christians, and the result is a society with little religious faith, despite what people tell touring pollsters. Stripped of that degree of belief—and in Judaism today that term must also embrace identification with the lot of fellow Jews throughout the world—what remains are diverse communities with shifting values and inexplicable standards by which society and its citizens may be judged. "How does a society without religion set standards of any kind?" asked one rabbi. "What is the source of ultimate meaning beyond time and place?"

The future depends also on the nature of American Jewry. How "Jewish" will they choose to be, and what precisely will that term mean?

Again, much of the definition will undoubtedly embrace a series of paradoxes. The evidence is clear that contemporary Jews are less and less interested in attending synagogues regularly, if at all. They do not eat kosher food, nor do they wear skullcaps. Large numbers of Orthodox Jews are not observant, their "Orthodoxy" stemming rather from

sentimental ties with the past. Jews rarely read Jewish publications. Politically and economically more secure than at
any time in this century, they marry out of the faith in
greater numbers and have fewer children. Too many Jews
have adopted Israel as a surrogate for Judaism. I believe
rabbis tend to know what Jewishness means. But the vast
majority of their fellow Jews do not, ending up, in Nathan
Glazer's keen words, "with a stubborn insistence on remaining a Jew, enhanced by no particular ennobling idea of
what that means."

Even so, alongside this indifference there exist the seeds
of stirring developments that have led some observers to
view this period as the "Golden Age" of American Jewish
life. Rabbis and others teach Judaica full-time or part-time
on more than 700 college campuses. The *Jewish Catalog*
shocked everyone by selling 200,000 copies with virtually
no advance publicity. Day schools continue to open. And
rabbis have even begun to infiltrate the federations and
national secular agencies. A rabbi serves as federation
director in Houston, and another in San Francisco. Rabbis
are staff members of the American Jewish Committee and
the Anti-Defamation League, among others. Growing numbers of congregations in Israel, Europe and Latin America
call for American-trained rabbis to lead their synagogues.

"Contrast all this with what went on in pre-Hitler Germany," says Trude Weiss-Rosmarin. "The Frankfurt Lehr-
haus, founded by Franz Rosenzweig, was highly praised
and held up as a model for other Jewish communities. But
it was a small learning house in comparison with the hundreds that now exist here. I see today and in the future a
great Jewish renaissance. Rabbis are an integral part of
that."

And in the future, will it be possible to return to the
model of a rabbi as saint and scholar? Or is a fusion of
scholarship and pastoral duties the best alternative? One

suggestion comes from a recent study of Christian and Jewish clergy. Seeking to isolate the qualities most desired in clergymen, the study found most congregants wanted a spiritual leader who was just that, one who would serve "without regard for acclaim," one who had "personal integrity." They were appalled by "self-serving" clergymen who avoided "intimacy and repel[led] people with a critical, demeaning and insensitive attitude."

Translated into specifically Jewish terms, several additional qualities would, I believe, have to be added. In one New York State synagogue, the search for a successor to a rabbi with a penchant for psychological emphases in the pulpit led the synagogue's selection committee to an insistence upon scholarship. The committee wanted above all a rabbi at ease with Torah texts, so that he might guide his congregants in the light of Jewish tradition. "What we want," said a member of the congregation, "is a rabbi who knows something about the Torah without slighting the prophetic tradition or his pastoral obligations." He was thinking of Torah study broadly, but in explanation he added that he wanted to hear sermons and engage in discussions that were not mindless repetitions of *Time* or *Newsweek*.

This is a search that will fail as often as it succeeds, for where will the rabbi find time for everything demanded of him? And how can he avoid the trap of becoming so ethnically self-centered that he ignores social injustices other than narrowly defined Jewish causes? But in the end, scholarship and learning are goals worth pursuing, for it is these traditions that tend to show the way, however ambiguous that path may be. Perry Nussbaum and Charles Mantinband walked in the steps of the prophets in Mississippi. Can anyone say the same of their detractors?

To be learned and still find time for the many tasks assumed by the rabbi—that is a heady responsibility—and

hard to fulfill. But, once again, worth pursuing. More congregations are employing assistant rabbis and religious
school teaching staffs. The result is that some rabbis can
concentrate more energies on their major job, teaching
Judaism. One rabbi spends most of his time stressing adult
Jewish education. In other large congregations many rabbis
have returned to the classroom. And in still others, growing
numbers of rabbis are trying to evolve, along with their
congregants, new ways of studying and discussing religious
texts. The list of these unheralded developments is quite
large.

The rabbi is part of the single greatest Jewishly educated
group in the country, the largest repository of what it means
to be Jewish and why. In Charles Liebman's apt phrase,
rabbis are the "most important figures in American Jewish
life today."

Someday, no doubt, their collective interests may compel
them to come together in labor unions. Or they may decide
to pressure their rabbinical associations to seek binding
arbitration with unyielding congregations. Or, as with the
American Association of University Professors, they may
one day have to declare certain congregations off-limits because of violations of ethical canons of behavior. They may
even become, once again, employees of unified communities
rather than of solitary synagogues. But whatever the years
ahead hold for rabbis and their congregational responsibilities, they will more than anything else have to seek a
dominant place for the Jewish religion and Jewish scholarship in an unbelieving synagogue and nonsynagogue population. Hardly an easy task. But the extent of their success will
determine the kind of American Jewish community that
will exist at the close of this century.

Soon after the end of the Holocaust, an American rabbi
attended the first *Yizkor* service in a displaced persons'
camp. "Instead of comforting the survivors over their losses,

a rabbi, himself bereaved, said: 'Observe the Sabbath.' I thought at first how unfeeling, and then I began to sense the wisdom of that ancient therapy."

Rabbi Philip Bernstein then drew his own conclusions.

"I am suggesting," he told his peers at a convention in 1969, "that we must bring to bear certain basic and essentially religious attitudes on the crucial problems of our times—the long view of history, the faith in the ultimate triumph of justice, the rejection of defeatism and the assertion of hope."

It remains sound advice for all Jews.

Glossary

aliyah (pl. aliyot): A "calling up" in synagogues to make the blessing at the reading of the Torah; the term also denotes immigration to Israel.

bet din (pl. batei din): Religious court.

bimah: The platform in the synagogue from which the rabbi preaches, the cantor or *hazzan* sings the liturgy and the biblical portion is read.

get: Religious writ of divorce.

hakham: Literally, a sage or wise man; among Sephardim the title is used by ordained rabbis.

halakha: The religious law which relies on Jewish legal interpretations, judgments, norms and codes.

havurah (pl. havurot): According to Professor Bernard Reisman and Rabbi Kenneth Roseman, a "group without professional direction banded together on an adult and family basis for Jewish or social goals."

hazzan: One specially trained in Jewish liturgical music who leads the congregation in prayer; also called cantor.

kashrut: Jewish dietary laws.

kehillah: Official central communal authority (e.g., the British Board of Deputies). In the United States today, voluntarism has supplanted the kehillah everywhere except among a few Orthodox sectarians.

kiddush hashem: From the Hebrew, "sanctification of the Name"; frequently used to include avoidance of actions likely to bring shame on Judaism; originally, however, the term denoted martyrdom to avoid idolatry, incest and murder, since the sacrifice of one's life for God's law was considered the ultimate sanctification of His name.

kollel: A "graduate" level of talmudic studies, more complex and sophisticated than the yeshiva.

maggid: Itinerant preacher.

mikveh (pl. mikvaot): Ritual baths for the wife following menstruation, used before the renewal of sexual relations; mikvaot are also used in Orthodox and Conservative conversions to Judaism as well as by some ultra-Orthodox for purification before the Sabbath and festivals.

minyan: Minimum quorum of ten adult males necessary for liturgical purposes; in many non-Orthodox synagogues, adult women are now included in the minyan.

mishnah: The oldest postbiblical compilation of oral interpretations, applications of the Torah and related decisions; the basis of the Talmud.

mitzvah (pl. mitzvot): Religious commandments traditionally believed to emanate from God; Jewish sages stated that the Torah contains 613 *mitzvot*, but many of them, limited to the sacrificial system and the land of Israel, can no longer be observed even by the most Orthodox.

mohel: Ritual circumciser.

rebbetzin: Rabbi's wife; the term is now in disfavor among many younger wives.

shohet: Ritual slaughterer.

shtetl: The hamlet, village and small-town Jewish communities of Eastern Europe, destroyed during World War II.

shtiebl: The Yiddish word for "little house"; a traditional room used for prayer rather than a regular synagogue.

shul: The Yiddish word for synagogue.

smicha: Rabbinical ordination.

tallith: Four-cornered prayer shawl with fringes at each corner worn during morning prayers.

tfillin: Phylacteries used in weekday morning worship; placed on the head and arm, they serve to direct the mind and actions to God.

tzitzit: Fringed garment worn under the shirt "as a reminder of God's presence."

yeshiva: Academy of Jewish learning.

A Note on Sources

In writing this book, I obviously relied heavily on interviews. In addition, the periodical literature was especially useful. For purposes of simplification I abbreviated those sources most often consulted.

AJA: American Jewish Archives (Cincinnati)
AJHQ: American Jewish Historical Quarterly (Waltham, Massachusetts)
AJYB: American Jewish Year Book (New York)
CCAR Journal: Central Conference of American Rabbis Journal (New York)
CJ: Conservative Judaism (New York)
JJS: Jewish Journal of Sociology (London)

Preface

Simon Greenberg's quote is from his article "The Rabbinate and the Jewish Community Structure," *CJ*, 23 (Spring 1969): 52–59.

Nathan Glazer's quote is from his book *American Judaism* (Chicago, 1957), p. 140; a revised edition, available in paperback, was published in 1972.

1. Master and Teacher

For information on the historical rabbinate I consulted Heinrich Graetz's *The History of the Jews*, 6 vols. (Philadelphia, 1898), and H. Shanks, "Origins of the title 'Rabbi,' " *Jewish Quarterly Review* 59 (October 1968): 152–157. I also read the relevant sections ("Rabbi," "Rabbinate") in the *Encyclopedia Judaica, Jewish Encyclopedia* and *Universal Jewish Encyclopedia.*

On colonial and postcolonial legislation see Jacob Rader Marcus, *The Colonial American Jew, 1492–1776* (Detroit, 1970), 3 vols., and more briefly, his "Jews and the American Revolution," *AJA* 27 (November 1975): 113–114. By far the best history of early Philadelphia is Edwin Wolf, 2nd, and Maxwell Whiteman, *The History of the Jews of Philadelphia* (Philadelphia, 1975). For information on Jacob Cohen and his "rabbinate," see especially pp. 114–145.

There is more on Jacob Cohen in Alan D. Corré and Malcolm H. Stern, eds., "The Record Book of the Rev. Jacob Raphael Cohen," *AJHQ* 59 (September 1969): 23–82. My information on the Clava case is from Wolf and Whitman, *Jews of Philadelphia*, pp. 129–130, as well as from "The Burial of Benjamin Moses Clava," *AJA* 27 (November 1975): 228–230. Nathan M. Kaganoff, "An Early American Synagogue Desecration," *AJHQ* 57 (September 1968): 136, offers a valuable footnote to colonial life. Kaganoff quotes the *New Haven Gazette and Connecticut Magazine* of November 22, 1787: "Charleston, S.C., September 18. Saturday night the Jewish synagogue was broke open. . . . The five books of Moses which contain the law and commandments of Almighty God, were wantonly thrown about the floor. The elders of the Society have appointed Wednesday next a day of fast and thanksgiving, for what has and has not been accomplished."

Also enlightening is Stanley F. Chyet, "A Synagogue in Newport," *AJA* 16 (April 1964): 41–49, yet another indication of the tendency of colonial Jewry to look abroad for advice and sustenance. Newport Jews, eager to acquire a synagogue, appealed for money to London's Bevis Marks Synagogue, to the Caribbean communities and to Shearith Israel in New York City. The Newport community bought the property in 1759 and then began to hunt feverishly for funds to erect a building. To pay off *that* debt required even more fund raising. Their first appeal was sent to Curaçao's Mikveh Israel, founded in 1656. Writes Chyet: "to what extent the Newport appeal was favorably received in Curaçao, we do not know." But we do know that Surinam agreed to send 600 guilders.

The most outstanding work on New York Jewry is Hyman B. Grinstein, *The Rise of the Jewish Community of New York, 1654–1860* (Philadelphia, 1945). The information about Leo Merzbacher comes mainly from its pages. On Abraham Rice, I relied on Isaac Fein, *The Making of an American Jewish Community: A History of Baltimore Jewry from 1773 to 1920* (Philadelphia, 1971), and Shmuel Singer, "From Germany to Baltimore: The First Rabbi in America," *Jewish Observer* 11 (January 1975): 16–19. Two helpful overviews of these and other years were Nathan Glazer, *American Judaism*, rev. ed. (Chicago, 1972), a valuable and thoughtful guide, and Leon A. Jick, *The Americanization of the Synagogue, 1820–1870* (Hanover, N.H., 1976). On Isaac Leeser, Jick was informative, as was Wolf and Whiteman, *Jews of Philadelphia.*

Cleveland's past is described in *The Temple (Congregation Tifereth Israel), 1850–1950* (Cleveland, 1950), and two articles in *Proceedings of the Conference on the Writing of Regional History* (Cleveland, 1956); Jack J. Herman, "Early Cleveland Jewry, 1840–1890: A Case Study," pp. 67–79, and Joseph Rappaport, "The Relation of Jewish and General Institutional Development," pp. 55–65.

For details about the life and times of Isaac Mayer Wise, I consulted his *Reminiscences* (Cincinnati, 1901); James G. Heller, *Isaac M. Wise: His Life, Work and Thought* (New York, 1965); and Israel Knox, *Rabbi in America* (New York, 1957). Wise's reflections on the Spanish Inquisition as he sat in a Philadelphia synagogue are from Jacob Rader Marcus, ed., *Memoirs of American Jews, 1775–1865* (Philadelphia, 1955), 3: 220. Joseph Blau's *Judaism in America* (Chicago, 1976), pp. 39–40, discusses Krauskopf. Leonard J. Mervis, "The Social Justice Movement and the Reform Rabbi," *AJA* 7 (June 1955): 171–230, and Kaufman Kohler, "A Call to Detroit," *AJA* 19 (April 1967): 34–40, explain other impulses in Reform.

The best exponent of Reconstructionism and Mordecai M. Kaplan is Mordecai M. Kaplan himself. *Judaism As a Civilization* (New York, 1957) and *Judaism Without Supernaturalism* (New York, 1958) are basic texts. Interpreters include Ira Eisenstein and Eugene Kohn, *Mordecai M. Kaplan: An Evaluation* (New York, 1952), and Milton Steinberg's *A Partisan Guide to the Jewish Problem* (New York, 1945). Two excellent studies are Gilbert S.

Rosenthal, *Four Paths to One God* (New York, 1973), and Charles
S. Liebman, "Reconstructionism in American Life," *AJYB* 71
(1970): 3–99. An acute appreciation of Kaplan and his contributions is in Trude Weiss-Rosmarin, "Mordecai M. Kaplan at Ninety-
Five," *Jewish Spectator* 41 (Summer 1976): 6–9.

Irving Howe's remarks about suburban Jews are in his *World of
Our Fathers* (New York, 1976), p. 621. The Eliezer Berkowitz
quotation is from "Conference Ponders Who's a Jew and Why,"
New York Times, May 26, 1976.

The best systematic study of Black Jewry is Howard M. Brotz,
The Black Jews of Harlem (New York, 1970). Also, Ruth Landis,
"Negro Jews in Harlem," *JJS* 9 (December 1967): 175–189. One
of the most recent is Murray Polner, "Being Black and Jewish,"
National Jewish Monthly 87 (October 1972): 38–43. The conver-
sation with Rabbi Aaron is from Elenore Lester, "Gays in the
Synagogue," *Present Tense* 2 (Autumn 1974): 12–15.

Andre Ungar's musings on his pulpits in Europe, South Africa and
New Jersey are in "Rabbi in Three Worlds," *Present Tense* 3
(Spring 1975): 15–18.

For background on Jewish organizational life and the question
of rabbinical and lay power, see Will Maslow, *The Structure and
Functioning of the American Jewish Community* (New York:
American Jewish Congress, 1974); Solomon Sutker, "The Jewish
Organizational Elite of Atlanta, Georgia," in *The Jews*, ed. Marshall
Sklare (New York, 1958), pp. 249–261; Simon Greenberg, "The
Rabbinate and the Jewish Community Structure," *CJ* 23 (Spring
1969): 52–59; Kenneth D. Roseman, "Power in a Midwestern
Jewish Community," *AJA* 21 (April 1969): 57–83; Daniel Elazar,
"The Decision Makers: Key Divisions in Jewish Communal Life,"
Dispersion and Unity 19/20 (1973): 21–30; Daniel Elazar, "Jewish
Survival and American Jewish Leadership," *CJ* 27 (September
1973): 44–51. Also, Allen S. Maller, "Rabbi Power," *Reconstruc-
tionist* 36 (December 25, 1970): 19–22; Bernard Weinberger,
"Confessions of an Orthodox Rabbi or a Tale of These Three
Bridges," *Jewish Life* 44 (Winter 1975): 15–27; Richard Ruben-
stein, *Power Struggle* (New York, 1974); Jacob Neusner, *American
Judaism* (Englewood Cliffs, N.J., 1972).

Arthur Hertzberg, "The Changing American Rabbinate," *Midstream* 12 (January 1966): 16–29, was a devastating criticism of
the men in the pulpit. Apparently he has since modified those views.
See Arthur Hertzberg, "The Changing Rabbinate," *Proceedings of*

the Rabbinical Assembly 38 (1975): 61–70. James Wax's travails are recounted in his unpublished memoirs in the American Jewish Archives. Trude Weiss-Rosmarin's defense of rabbis comes from her invaluable journal, *Jewish Spectator*: "The New American Rabbi" 31 (February 1966): 3–7 and "Rabbinic Self-Hatred" 34 (November 1969): 4–5. For a stimulating exchange of views on the subject of power or the absence of it, see in the same journal Gerald Bubis, "Brokha Brokers and Power Brokers" 40 (Spring 1975): 58–61; David Polish, "Rabbis and Federations" 40 (Fall 1975): 20–22; Gilbert Kollin, "Synagogues and Federations" 40 (Summer 1975): 18–21. Also, "Letters to the Editor," ibid., 73–76. The Cambridge, Massachusetts, student newspaper *Genesis II* regularly censures the federations and the manner in which they allocate money. For a recent defense of the federations see Sidney Z. Vincent, "Shaping a More Creative and Responsive Community" (New York, 1975), 8 pp., mimeographed.

2. The Seminarians

Concerning the Reform seminarian, I am indebted to Professor Norman Mirsky for the information contained in his doctoral dissertation, *The Making of a Reform Rabbi* (Ann Arbor, Mich.: University Microfilms, 1971). Even more critical than Mirsky's account is Theodore Lenn and Associates, *Rabbi and Synagogue in Reform Judaism* (West Hartford, Conn., 1972). The Lenn survey was commissioned by the CCAR. "This study," writes Lenn in a preface, "is not designed to *prove* anything. . . . All we have here is an inventory of findings." Those "findings" were shattering, perhaps none more so than pp. 319–342 on seminary students at HUC in Cincinnati. The survey also canvassed their wives, and the results were equally unsettling. Concluded Lenn: "So if some of our rabbis do not recall their seminarian days with too much glee, neither do some of their helpmates." As expected, the published reaction was largely hostile. See "Afterthoughts on Lenn," *CCAR Journal* 2 (Winter 1973): passim. The account of seminarian Lucas was written for the *RA* by Henry W. Levy, 1976, mimeographed.

On the training of rabbis I relied on Charles Sherman, "Factors Influencing the Selection of the Rabbinate as a Career," HUC dissertation, 1969. Marshall Sklare's authoritative *Conservative Judaism: An American Religious Movement* (New York, 1972) was essential, particularly pp. 166–174. Arthur Hertzberg's "The Conservative Rabbinate: A Sociological Study," in *Essays on Jewish Life and Thought* by Joseph L. Blau et al. (New York, 1959), pp. 309–332, was useful. See, too, Eliezer Berkowitz, "A Contemporary Rabbinical School for Orthodox Jewry," *Tradition* 13 (Fall 1971): 5–20; Charles Shulman, "How American Rabbis Are Trained," *Reconstructionist* 35 (July 4, 1969): 7–13, and "Preparing to be a Rabbi," *Reconstructionist* 37 (October 15, 1971): 29. Critical treatment is in "What's Wrong with Our Seminaries," *Response* 3 (Fall 1969): 2–20, dealing with three major schools. By far the best study on the subject thus far is Charles S. Liebman, "The Training of American Rabbis," *AJYB* 69 (1968): 3–115. At the Hebrew Teachers College in Skokie, Illinois, he noted that the number of Orthodox students who want a pulpit has declined. Rabbi Aaron Soloveitchik, the director, has extended the curriculum from two to three years and concentrates on Codes and Talmud, "for it is the primary responsibility of Orthodox rabbis" to resolve questions of Jewish law. The seminarians do study, however, "those portions of the law . . . thought particularly relevant to the contemporary Jewish community and the needs of the congregational rabbi." Classes are offered in Sabbath observance, marriage and divorce, funerals and mourning in order to encourage students who may want the pulpit as a career but feel "they could not adequately cope with some of the more complex questions of religious law that congregants might pose." The same is generally true for students at Yeshiva University's Rabbi Isaac Elchanan Theological Seminary. In reply to Liebman's questionnaire, 45 percent of the students judged their curriculum inadequate. Elsewhere, at the JTS, Liebman discovered that the "Scholar, not the rabbi, has the highest status," which does very little for rabbinic self-esteem. He also found the JTS with "probably the most discontented student body of any seminary" (cf. Lenn, *Rabbi and Synagogue*, pp. 319–342). At HUC, however, the stress was on the rabbinate as a profession, and the curriculum included human relations, speech and homiletics. *Their* problem, Liebman noted, was less the practical nature of course material than the school's academic inferiority complex. Its standards were perceived as low and its programs "easy." In conclusion, Liebman found that seminarians seek role models at their schools by which they tend to judge their own worth and that of their synagogues. At the seminary they live the "total way of life" Judaism demands of them; too often they don't find models to emulate. Liebman concluded: "There is no one person at any seminary whom most of the students regard as an exemplary religious figure," although 54 percent of the Reform seminarians did choose Eugene Borowitz, a theological existentialist and political liberal, as the rabbi "who best reflects their own religious-theological-philosophical position."

Conservative criticism of placement is from Martin Segal et al., "The Conservative Rabbi: An Economic and Professional Profile" (New York, 1971), mimeographed. Rabbi Panitz was interviewed by Henry W. Levy for the RA, 1976, mimeographed.

3. Suburban Activist

The story about Levittown is in Herbert J. Gans, *The Levittowners: Ways of Life and Politics in a New Suburban Community* (New York, 1969). Worthwhile books on Reform include Eugene Borowitz, *A New Jewish Theology in the Making* (Philadelphia, 1968); W. Gunther Plaut, *The Growth of Reform Judaism* (New York, 1967); Bernard Martin, *Contemporary Reform Jewish Thought* (Chicago, 1968). For new developments among Reform rabbis and the Association for a Progressive Reform Judaism, see Yisrael Ellman, "Reform Rabbis—New Directions" (Cincinnati, 1976), 9 pp., mimeographed, a translation of an *Al Ha Mishmar* (Tel Aviv) article.

4. Mississippi

The student rabbi's recollections are from Robert Alan Seigel, "Rosh Hashona: 5723," American Jewish Archives, Miscellaneous File, "Desegregation," October 25, 1962, 3 pp., unpublished. Mississippi Jewish history is from Charles Mantinband, "Mississippi, the Magnolia State," American Jewish Archives, Nearprint File, 1961, 9 pp., unpublished. Wilbur J. Cash's quotes are from *Mind of the South* (New York, 1941), pp. 305, 343. Note as well, Benjamin Kaplan, *The Eternal Stranger: A Study of Jewish Life in the Small Community* (New York, 1957), p. 156: "The Jews still find themselves far from constituting full-fledged members of the general community and their position remains one of ambivalence." See also Joshua Fishman, "Southern City," *Midstream* 7 (Summer 1961): 41—"When a town reaches a certain size . . . anti-Semitic forces begin to surface." The description of Delta Jews is by David Cohn, *Where I Was Born and Raised* (South Bend, Ind., 1967), pp. 20–21.

Perry Nussbaum's unpublished papers are on file at the American
Jewish Archives. His recollections of his early years in Jackson are
in his papers. I also used two letters he wrote me, dated November
20, 1975, and February 27, 1976, respectively; Perry Nussbaum,
"The Beth Israel of Jackson, Mississippi Story," 21 pp., unpublished; his "Oral History Memoir," August 5, 1965, unpublished;
and his "And Then There Was One—The Capital City of Mississippi," *CCAR Journal* 11 (October 1963): 15–19. Melissa Paisios,
"A Study of the Beth Israel Congregation, Jackson, Mississippi,"
American Jewish Archives, 31 pp., unpublished, offered background on his temple's history. Marvin Braiterman, "Mississippi
Marranos," in *Jews in the South*, ed. Leonard Dinnerstein and
Mary Dale Palsson (Baton Rouge, La., 1973), pp. 351–359, is
one example of the harsh criticisms leveled against Jackson's Jews.
Eli Evans, *The Provincials: A Personal History of the Jews of the
South* (New York, 1973), covers the two Mississippi bombings, pp.
255–259, and Mississippi and the civil rights crisis, pp. 310–326,
in effective fashion. For information on Charles Mantinband I relied
on his papers at the American Jewish Archives, along with his
Reminiscences, ibid., n.d. I also read his "Rabbi in the Deep South,"
ADL Bulletin, May 1962, p. 3; "The Horns of a Dilemma," *CCAR
Yearbook* 74 (1964): 242–249; and "In Dixieland I Take My
Stand," First Annual George Brussel Memorial Lecture, Stephen S.
Wise Free Synagogue, New York City, April 16, 1962. Allen
Krause's thesis, "Rabbis and Negro Rights in the South, 1954–
1967," appeared in abridged form in *AJA* 21 (April 1969): 20–47.
Krause discusses the role of rabbis during those stormy years.
Theodore Lowi's "Southern Jews: The Two Communities," *Jewish
Journal of Sociology* 6 (July 1964): 103–117, attempts to dis-
tinguish between old-timers and newcomers in their social and
political views. The sentiments expressed about Mantinband's fare-
well dinner in Hattiesburg were later delivered as a sermon by
Rabbi Leo Bergman, "Is There a Jewish Ku Klux Klan in Hattiesburg?" January 15, 1965, American Jewish Archives, 6 pp., unpublished.

On Vicksburg's history, I relied on Gertrude Philippsborn, *The
History of the Jewish Community of Vicksburg (From 1820 to
1968)*, (Vicksburg, Miss., 1969), mimeographed. Also, Philip
Sartorius, "Small-Town Southern Merchant," in *Memoirs*, ed. Jacob
Rader Marcus, 2: 21–46, and Stanley R. Brav, "Autobiography,"
American Jewish Archives, 1970, unpublished. On Vicksburg's de-

clining population, I leaned on interviews and Richard Marcus, "Congregational Makeup," *Memorandum*, February 14, 1976. The material on Rabbi Schwartzman is based on interviews and correspondence. Rabbi Moses M. Landau's comments are from his correspondence with Perry E. Nussbaum, September 25, 1964, and January 15, 1965, American Jewish Archives, Nussbaum Papers. The following books and articles, among others, provided contemporary perspective: Alfred O. Hero, Jr., *The Southerner and World Affairs* (Baton Rouge, La., 1965); Harry Golden, *Our Southern Landsman* (New York, 1974); Neal R. Peirce, *The Deep South States of America: People, Politics, and Power in the Seven States of the Deep South* (New York, 1974, especially pp. 226–234; Anthony Dunbar, *The Will to Survive: A Study of a Mississippi Plantation Community* (Atlanta: Southern Regional Council, 1969); Citizens Councils of Mississippi, "A Jewish View of Segregation," an anonymous pamphlet issued in 1954; Mark Pinsky, "South Toward Home," *Present Tense* 3 (Winter 1976): 70–73; Robert A. Polner, "A Great Neck Student Views the Jews of Mississippi," *Great Neck* [N.Y.] *Record*, March 4, 1976; Fred V. Davidow, "Growing Up Jewish in Mississippi," cassette recording, Plattsburgh, N.Y., August 1976; Harry Golden, "Hebrew-Christian Evangelist: Southern Style," *Commentary* 10 (December 1950): 577–581; Harry Golden, "A Pulpit in the South," *Commentary* 13 (December 1953): 574–579; David J .Goldberg, "In Dixie Land, I Take My Stand: A Study of Small-City Jewry in Five Southeastern States," 1974, American Jewish Archives, 69 pp., unpublished typescript.

On the Fuller Construction Company and Senator Stennis, see the *Delta Democrat-Times* [Greenville, Miss.,] February 15, 1976.

On Benjamin Schultz: "Rabbi Schultz Honored," *New York Times*, April 21, 1955; Victor Lasky, "Benjamin Schultz, the Rabbi the Reds Hate Most," *American Mercury* 81 (November 1955): 82–85; Benjamin Schultz, "Back to Patriotism," June 25, 1957, 4 pp., unpublished; Fern Marja Eckman et al., "The Strange Case of Rabbi Schultz," *New York Post*, December 6–7, 1954; Schultz to the author, March 15, 1976; *The Scribe*, publication of Temple Beth Israel, Clarksdale, Miss. For the six young northern Jews in Rabbi Schultz's temple, see "Jewish League Against Communism's Founder Turns Up in Mississippi Synagogue's Pulpit," *Connecticut Jewish Ledger*, August 27, 1964. Also, Perry E. Nussbaum *Correspondence*, American Jewish Archives, for letters to and from Sidney L. Regner, S. Andhil Fineberg and Benjamin Schultz. Also,

Morrie Ryskind, "Early Evidences of Red Evil," *Memphis Commercial-Appeal*, February 28, 1971.

On the South in general, I read Archibald T. Robertson, *That Old-Time Religion* (New York, 1950); C. Vann Woodward, *The Strange Career of Jim Crow* (New York, 1955); John Dollard, *Caste and Class in a Southern Town*, 2nd ed. (New York, 1949); Willie Morris, *Yazoo: Integration in a Deep Southern Town* (New York, 1971); Malcolm H. Stern, "The Integration of Norfolk, Va., 1958–1959," 1959, unpublished; James Lebeau, "Profile of a Southern Jewish Community, Waycross, Georgia," *AJHQ* 58 (June 1969): 429–442; Leonard Dinnerstein, "Jews and the Desegregation Crisis in the South, 1954–1970," *AJHQ* 62 (March 1973): 231–241; Jacob M. Rothschild, "A Rabbi in the South," talk given at the HUC-JIR in Cincinnati, January 9, 1970, American Jewish Archives, 7 pp., unpublished; Arnold Shankman, "A Temple Is Bombed—Atlanta 1958," *AJA* 13 (November 1971): 125–153; Alvin M. Sugarman, "Rabbi Jacob M. Rothschild's Sermons on Civil Rights, 1948 Through 1968," American Jewish Archives, 29 pp., unpublished; David Ritz's portrait of Rabbi Levi Olan, "Inside the Jewish Establishment," *D, The Magazine of Dallas*, November 1975, pp. 50–55, 108–116; Eli Evans, *The Provincials*, passim.

5. The World of the Orthodox

Charles S. Liebman's "Orthodoxy in American Life," *AJYB* 66 (1965): 21–97, like many of his other studies, is indispensable. On the chief rabbi I read Abraham J. Karp, "New York Chooses a Rabbi," *Publications of the American Jewish Historical Society* 44 (March 1955): 129–198, and Shmuel Singer, "A Chief Rabbi for New York City," *Jewish Observer* 10 (May 1974): 16–20. On the history of the gangsterism surrounding the kosher food business, see Harold P. Gastwirt, *Fraud, Corruption and Holiness: The Controversy over the Supervision of Jewish Dietary Practice in New York City, 1881–1940*. (Port Washington, N.Y., 1974). Other works about Orthodoxy include: Eliezer Berkovits, *God, Man and History* (New York, 1959); Norman Lamm, *Faith and Doubt* (New York, 1971); Emanuel Rackman, *One Man's Judaism* (New York, 1970); Leon D. Stitskin, *Studies in Torah Judaism* (New York, 1969); Israel Rubin, *Satmar: An Island in the City* (Chicago, 1972); George Kranzler, *Williamsburg: A Jewish Community in Transition* (New York, 1961); Solomon Poll, *Hasidic Community of Williamsburg* (New York, 1962); William Helmreich, *Wake Up, Wake Up to Do the Work of the Creator* (New York, 1976); Samuel C. Heilman, *Synagogue Life* (Chicago, 1976); David Singer, "Voices of Orthodoxy," *Commentary* 58 (July 1974): 54–60. The information about the Orthodox rabbinate and the war in Vietnam is from Charles S. Liebman, "The Orthodox Rabbi and Vietnam," *Tradition* 9 (Spring 1968): 28–32. The UOJC resolution on amnesty is in the *Jewish Telegraphic Agency Daily News Bulletin*, December 2, 1976, p. 4. The report on harried and overworked rabbis is from Theodore L. Adams, "The American Rabbi Today," *Jewish Life* 30 (February 1962): 18–24.

On contemporary Cleveland, Charley J. Levine, "Coping with the Changing Neighborhood: The Cleveland Heights Area Project, *The Times of Israel* 1 (April 1975): 48–51, deals with a racially integrated area that preserved its Jewish character.

A recent addition to Shubert Spero's bibliography is "The Religious Meaning of the State of Israel," *Forum* 1 [24] (1976): 69–82.

Also helpful in the development of this chapter were Egon Mayer, "Jewish Orthodoxy in America," *JJS* 15 (December 1973): 151–166, and his doctoral dissertation, *Modern Jewish Orthodoxy in Post-Modern America: A Case Study of the Jewish Community in Boro Park* (Ann Arbor, Mich.: University Microfilms, 1975). One conclusion: "Jewish Orthodox beliefs and practices can be safely sustained along with full participation in a universalistic and rational economy, educational system and political life. [Thus] acculturation without assimilation has become not merely a possibility but a high probability." I also profited from Howard W. Polsky, "A Study of Orthodoxy in Milwaukee," in *The Jews*, ed. Sklare, pp. 325–335; Nancy Schmidt, "An Orthodox Jewish Community in the United States: A Minority Within a Minority," *JJS* 7 (December 1965): 176–187; and Neal Kanfer and Zev Shanken, "An Interview with Shlomo Riskin," *Response* 10 (Spring 1976): 3–18.

The definition of a bet din is from Daniel Elazar and Stephen R. Goldstein, "The Legal Status of the American Jewish Community," *AJYB* 73 (1972): 3–89. The Massachusetts cases are in *Bet Din Zedek*, Rabbinical Court of Justice of the Associated Synagogues of Massachusetts (Boston, 1970). Rabbi Samuel Korff's account is in "A Responsum on Questions of Conscience," ibid. On divorce see Bernard Weinberger, "The Growing Rate of Divorce in Orthodox Jewish Life," *Jewish Life* 44 (Spring 1976): 9–14. On population statistics and the resulting interpretations I consulted the

National Jewish Population Study, issued by the Council of Jewish Federations and Welfare Funds (New York, 1973), and Fred Massarik and Alvin Chenkin, "United States National Jewish Population Study: A First Report," *AJYB* 73 (1972): 264–309.

6. *"Radical? No, Only a Conservative."*

Rabbi Sasso's and other rabbinical experiences are detailed in Roslyn Lacks, "Women and the Rabbinate," 1974, unpublished. Lenn's comments on rabbinical wives are in *Rabbi and Synagogue*, pp. 369–383. Janice Rothschild's response appears in "Afterthought on Lenn," *CCAR Journal* 2 (Winter 1973): 25–27. Another view is Joan Behrmann's "Rabbi's Wives: The Case of the Shrinking Pedestal," *Moment* 1 (December 1975): 49–53.

The literature on Jewish feminism is growing quickly. I read Paula Hyman, "The Other Half: Women in the Jewish Tradition," *Judaism* 23 (Summer 1972): 14–21; Chana K. Poupko and Devora L. Wohlgelernter, "Women's Liberation—An Orthodox Response," *Tradition* 18 (Spring 1976): 45–52; Sally Priesand, *Judaism and the New Woman* (New York, 1975); Leonard Swidler, *Women in Judaism: The Status of Women in Formative Judaism* (Metuchen, N.J., 1975). For Anne Lapidus Lerner's study, see " 'Who Has Not Made Me a Man': The Movement for Equal Rights for Women in American Jewry," *AJYB* 77 (1977): 3–38.

Martin Segal's *The Conservative Rabbi* was commissioned by the RA and issued privately. Among other findings, the Segal study revealed that the average age of the Conservative rabbi was 43 (in 1971); 95 percent were married and had children. Fifty-five percent were first-generation Americans, one of five was the son of a rabbi, two in five had attended Jewish day schools, and more than four in five had graduated from the JTS. Eighty-two percent held graduate degrees, nearly 11 percent of them doctorates. The rabbis' median income was $15,000, and the national salary range was from $2,750 part-time to $45,000 (for a handful). Forty-two percent received expense allowances, and 82 percent were granted housing or equivalent payments in lieu of extra salary. Almost all supplemented their incomes at weddings and funerals and by teaching and writing. Segal's conclusion: "Rabbis were not underpaid, despite the belief, widespread among rabbis." Segal did note, however, that contract negotiation vexes many rabbis. "It is one of the most troublesome areas. . . . The situation can be demeaning, embarrassing or destructive."

See, too, Jerome E. Carlin and Saul H. Mendlovitz, "The Rabbi: A Religious Specialist Responds to Loss of Authority," in *The Jews*, ed. Sklare, pp. 377–414. Vivian A. Zelizer and Gerald L. Zelizer, "The Conservative Rabbinate: In Quest of Professionalism," *CJ* 22 (Fall 1973): 490–496, urge stronger rabbinical associations and believe "with power will come autonomy." Stephen Lerner's symposium was published as "The Conservative Rabbi and the Conservative Synagogue," *CJ* 29 (Winter 1975): 3–96. Gilbert Rosenthal's description of Conservatism's "crazy-quilt pattern" is from his *Four Paths to One God*, p. 169. See also Lawrence J. Kaplan, "The Dilemma of Conservative Judaism," *Commentary* 60 (November 1976): 44–47.

On the havurot and the atmosphere in which they grew, I consulted James Sleeper and Alan L. Mintz, eds., *The New Jews* (New York, 1971), as well as the original *Havurat Shalom Community Seminary Prospectus* (Cambridge, Mass., 1969). Jacob Neusner's *Contemporary Judaic Fellowship in Theory and Practice* (New York, 1972) contains an introduction to both historical and modern havurot. Stephen Lerner's article was published as "The Havurot," *CJ* 24 (Spring 1970): 2–15. The "Time may not be on our side" quote is from Ron Kronish, "Restructuring the Contemporary Synagogue," *Genesis II*, December 1975, p. 3.

I also read with interest Sylvia Rothchild, "A Great Happening in Boston," *Present Tense* 3 (Spring 1976): 21–26; Bill Novak, "The Making of a Jewish Counter-Culture," *Response* 4 (Spring–Summer 1970): 5–10; Harold Schulweis, "Restructuring the Synagogue," *CJ* 27 (September 1973): 13–23. See also Lucy Y. Steinitz, "From Havurah to Havurot to What?" *Sh'ma*, May 16, 1975, and two responses to her piece: Avi Marcus, "A Personal View of Havurah Existence," and William Kavesh, "An Open Letter to Havera Lucy," ibid.

On Conservatism in general I read Sklare, *Conservative Judaism*; Jacob Agus, *Guideposts in Modern Judaism* (New York, 1954); and Robert Gordis, *Faith for Moderns* (New York, 1971).

7. Small-Town Rabbi

Systematic studies of small-town Jewish life are comparatively few. One of the best is Peter I. Rose, "Strangers in Their Midst: Small-Town Jews and Their Neighbors," in *The Ghetto and Beyond: Essays on Jewish Life in America*, ed. Peter I. Rose (New York, 1969), pp. 335–356. I also read the following in preparation for this segment: Joseph Greenblum and Marshall Sklare, "The Attitude of the Small-Town Jew Toward His Community," in *The Jews*, ed. Sklare, pp. 288–303; and Whitney H. Gordon, "Jews and Gentiles in Middletown, 1961," *AJA* 18 (April 1966): 41–72. Ralph Marks, "Eastex Exodus," *The Jewish Herald-Voice* [Houston], December 17, 1975, p. 28, recalls the lost world of eastern Texas. Alexander Kline's recollections and thoughts are in "The Rabbi in the Small Town," *CCAR Journal* 5 (April 1954): 10–15. For Montana, see Samuel Horowitz, *History of Billings Jewish Community, 1954–1975* (Billings, Mont., 1974). On Plattsburgh I consulted *Beth Israel Congregation* (Plattsburgh, N.Y., n.d.), mimeographed. Las Vegas, New Mexico, had a rabbi until 1931 and thereafter was served by laymen until Helman's arrival. For an early settler's recollections, consult the interview with Milton Tachiert (conducted by Louise Michaelson), July 30, 1975, William E. Wiener Oral History Library, American Jewish Committee.

See, too, the special issue "Small Town Jewry," *Jewish Heritage* 15 (Winter 1974), especially Eugene Schoenfeld, "Problems and Potentials," 14–18. His solutions include strengthening of home and family observances and developing a neo-havurot or what he prefers to call *mishpochah* or extended family group to reduce the isolation and alienation in small towns. Schoenfeld, a sociologist at Georgia State University in Atlanta, also believes that "a new attitude to intermarriage" is necessary. Since the rate of such unions will clearly continue to go up, Schoenfeld calls for an end to stigmatizing those marriages and urges, instead, a serious effort to bring the non-Jewish spouse into Judaism. "The motto should be cooptation instead of ostracism, conversion instead of exclusion. . . . Obviously this cannot be achieved without the help of rabbis and their willingness to reintrepret the *halakah*. One of the necessary changes should include the idea that marriage constitutes a legitimate reason for conversion. We cannot and should not indulge in a puristic value which specifies that only a true and deep commitment to Judaism can justify conversion and therefore all prospective converts must be discouraged three times before being accepted."

For circuit-riding rabbis I relied on a series of letters to the editor and reader responses in *Present Tense* 2 (Spring 1975): 2–5. For the rabbi who conducts mixed marriages, see Sheldon Kirshner, "Rabbi Performs Mixed Marriages," *Canadian Jewish News*, January 23, 1976, p. 9. For prison life I relied on my experience as a former teacher in a penitentiary, as well as on Jews who were or are incarcerated in prisons. Jerald Bobrow's "My Unique Congregation," *Jewish Spectator* 38 (January 1973): 21–22, is a faithful description of his unusual ministry. The material on Indiana University's Hillel comes from visits together with their *Hillel at IU, 1975–76, 5736* (Bloomington: B'nai B'rith Hillel Foundation, 1976). Alfred Jospe's views are in "Rabbi Discusses Campus Ministry," *New York Times,* February 16, 1975, and "The Jew on the College Campus," *Judaism* 25 (Summer 1976): 270–280. The latter discusses the impact, if any, of Jewish studies on the college generation, as does "The Long Range Significance of the New Jewish Consiousness on Campus," in *Analysis* (Washington, D.C.: Institute for Jewish Policy Planning and Research, 1972). "Programming Opportunities with Reform Students," by Purdue University Rabbi Gedalyah Engel (n.d., 4 pp., unpublished) reaches yet another conclusion. Purdue Jewish students from "committed Reform homes will continue to expect priestly service from their Hillel rabbis [but] are less likely to participate in group-oriented Jewish community activities." The debate over the extent of freedom to be granted Hillel chapters was based on interviews on the campus, in Washington, D.C., and in New York City. In early 1977 B'nai B'rith's Anti-Defamation League joined in an assault against Breira, a dovish group of critics of certain American Jewish and Israeli policies. The ADL demanded that Hillel directors who belonged to Breira be silenced. If the ADL was hysterical and overwrought, B'nai B'rith's President David Blumberg was not, naming instead a "blue ribbon" panel to study B'nai B'rith policy. Executive Director Daniel Thursz added that B'nai B'rith was "not seeking a McCarthyite witch hunt, nor do we challenge the principle of the right of dissent." Still, it remained to be seen whether the censors or the supporters of free speech would win. See David Friedman, "B'nai B'rith to Study Involvement of Hillel Directors in Breira," *Jewish Telegraphic Agency Daily News Bulletin,* March 4, 1977; "ADL for B'nai B'rith Breira Probe," *Jewish Week* [New York], February 27, 1977; and William Novak, "The Breira Story," *Genesis 2* [Boston], March–April 1977. Concerning women in the rabbinate, "26 Women Are Now Serving as 'Chaplains' at Hillel Centers" appeared in the *New York Times,* January 25, 1976. The Naomi Bear quotation is from Trude Weiss-Rosmarin, "Women 'Chaplains,' " *Jewish Spectator,* 41 (Spring 1976): 13. The segment on Japan was based on interviews in this country and in Japan.

8. *Sephardim in America*

Marc Angel is by now the foremost student of American Sephardic history. "The Sephardim of the United States: An Exploratory Study," *AJYB* 74 (1973): 77–138, is the first of its kind. I also consulted his *"Progress*—Seattle's Sephardic Monthly 1934–5," *American Sephardi* 5 (Autumn 1971): 91–95; "Roasted Pumpkin Seeds and Winding Roads of Memory," *National Jewish Monthly* 88 (October 1974): 41–45; "Notes on the Early History of Seattle's Sephardic Community," *Western States Jewish Historical Quarterly* (October 1974): 22–30; "The Sephardic Theater of Seattle," *AJA* 25 (November 1973): 156–160; "Sephardic Culture in America," *Jewish Life* 38 (March–April 1971): 7–11; and "Sephardim in America," *Present Tense* 4 (Autumn 1976): 12–14. The quotation by the Sephardic chief rabbi of Djerba is from Tudor Parfitt, "Passover in Djerba," *Present Tense* 3 (Spring 1976): 68–71. I am indebted to Jacob Rader Marcus, *The Colonial American Jew*; David and Tamar de Sola Pool, *An Old Faith in the New World* (New York, 1955); Stephen Birmingham, *The Grandees* (New York, 1967). The following articles were also helpful: Abraham D. Lavender, "The Sephardic Revival in the United States: A Case of Ethnic Revival in a Minority Within a Minority," *The Journal of Ethnic Studies* 3 (Fall 1975): 21–31, and Ben G. Frank, "Jews from Arab Lands: At Home in Brooklyn," *Congress Monthly* 43 (March 1976): 15–16. On recent events in the Sephardic world, see Vivian Gornick, "Sephardim of the East," *Present Tense* 1 (Summer 1974): 44–49. On the Holocaust and the southern European Sephardim, I used Edouard Roditi, "The Final Irony," *Present Tense* 2 (Winter 1975): 76–78, which discusses the fate of the Salonika community under the Nazis and their allies. On Monastir and Castoria, I read Uri Oren, *A Town Called Monastir* (Tel Aviv, 1971).

9. *A Final Word*

"How does a society without religion . . . beyond time and place" is from Martin Siegel, "The Rabbi as Vanishing Species," *Christian Century*, November 5, 1975, 988–989. The study on clergy is in David S. Schuler, Milo L. Brekhe and Merton P. Strommen, *Readiness for Ministry: Criteria* (Vandalia, Ohio: Association of Theological Schools, 1976), vol. 1. The quote by Philip Bernstein is from "The Role and Functions of the Modern Rabbi," *CCAR Yearbook* 79 (1969): 226–227.

Index

235

562